The Armchair Universe
An Exploration of Computer Worlds

The Armchair Universe
An Exploration of Computer Worlds

A. K. Dewdney

W. H. Freeman and Company
New York

Library of Congress Cataloging-in-Publication Data

Dewdney, A. K.
  The armchair universe.

  Bibliography: p.
  Includes index.
  1. Microcomputers—Programming. 2. Computer software. I. Title.
QA76.6.D517 1988   005.26   87-25046
ISBN 0-716-71938-X
ISBN 0-716-71939-8 (pbk.)

34567890 FF 654321089

For Irene Dewdney
who gave birth to these worlds

Contents

Prologue

The armchair universe contains many worlds, each accessible through the magic of computing. An office, study, or living room becomes a spaceship, provided it is equipped with a computer and an armchair. The computer (whether micro or mainframe) is loaded with one or more of the programs outlined in this book. The armchair is occupied by the reader ready for high adventure in the infinitesimal reaches of the Mandelbrot set, the mind-bending four-dimensionality of hypercubes, the graceful ballet of a cluster of stars.

The worlds described here first appeared in my monthly "Computer Recreations" column in SCIENTIFIC AMERICAN magazine. Each world contains columns grouped by common themes such as artificial intelligence, simulation, and so on. It is no accident that many of these themes correspond to topics in computer science; professing the subject at a North American university has worn certain grooves in my brain. Readers largely unfamiliar with the subject may glean a partial education merely by engaging in the projects suggested herein.

As an educator I am delighted to offer a two-pronged opportunity to readers. First, there is a programming opportunity. Second, there is an opportunity to explore the world of appearances and ideas that each program opens up. For example, in World Four, "Life in Automata," the reader is shown how to write a simple program that displays successive generations in the life of a cellular automaton. The implementation of this program suggests important questions; i.e., do some of these devices harbor special configurations that are capable of computing in the fullest sense of the word? Some readers may well become enmeshed in this question when they run their own cellular automaton program. Indeed, a few readers of the "Computer Recreations" column have already made genuine contributions to the academic side of some themes by dint of intelligent and tenacious exploration. The age of the amateur is not yet over.

There is a special reader well worth encouraging. He or she is strongly tempted to enter one of these worlds but is prevented by marginal programming skills. Software slavery is a lowly estate that is inadvertently encouraged by the packagers of various special-purpose programs, whether of practical or recreational purpose. One would hope that programming tyros will read one of the simpler topics such as "Five Easy Pieces" (in World Six) and hone their skills with the aid of a manual and one or two friends. But if programming seems hopelessly remote, diskettes are available as described in the List of Suppliers at the back of this book.

Acknowledgments

For reasons that are not yet entirely clear to me I was selected to write the "Computer Recreations" column in SCIENTIFIC AMERICAN magazine. Brian Hayes, a senior editor with the magazine, had created the column six months before in response to a new world where passive puzzlery was yielding ground to active computation. The advent of personal computers into the home on a large scale had created an opportunity. New worlds, unexplored by my illustrious predecessors, awaited.

Martin Gardner's "Mathematical Games" column had inspired at least two generations of SCIENTIFIC AMERICAN readers with their continuing variety, depth, and wit. Gardner was, in a sense, guru to the fans of recreational thought. His successor, Douglas Hofstadter, wrote "Metamagical Themas" for a few years. Hofstadter brought us feasts of lisp, prisoner's dilemmas, and a continuing preoccupation with intelligence in all its forms.

Hayes framed "Computer Recreations," wrote the first six columns to set the standard, and sought his own successor on campuses, in research labs, and over publisher's desks. More the marvel, it seems, to be chosen.

I am grateful, naturally, to Brian for choosing me. And for guiding me through those first strange months filled with concerns far from my usual ones; there were three-star edits, shirt-tails, first fits, buried leads, and lessons in the specially refined grammar and spelling used by the magazine and taught by its senior copy editor, Sally Jenks. When Brian left the magazine, editor Jonathan Piel was left with a half-finished columnist and a half-finished column. He taught me to dig up buried leads and to display them publicly. He taught the carpentry of writing by example. Perceiving that I had become saturated with editorial knowledge or that I was, in any event, incapable of absorbing more, he handed me off to Peter Brown, an intelligent and amiable editor whose mathematical background was of inestimable value in pursuit of the essential content of those same words and paragraphs. Brown, who left the magazine to apply his analytical mind to Wall Street, was succeeded by David Cooke, equally amiable, a physicist. When an idea works, Cooke laughs. When it doesn't he tells me.

To all these men and women—and to SCIENTIFIC AMERICAN itself—I owe a large debt of gratitude. I have the privilege of belonging to a scientific institution revered worldwide for its comprehensiveness, accuracy, and humanity.

■ ■ ■

For the rest, turn down the desk lamp to a soft glow and fix your eyes on the viewscreen. The armchair universe is unfolding.

A. K. Dewdney

The Armchair Universe
An Exploration of Computer Worlds

WORLD ONE

Infinite Graphics

A computer's display screen may show many sights but none
so wholly visual as the output of these four programs from the world
of infinite graphics. Such programs are capable of infinite variation,
and many of their digital paintings are surpassingly lovely. They
frequently operate on simple mathematical principles that have subtle
manifestations.

The Mandelbrot set is an object of infinite complexity produced by
a one-line formula. The first program makes it possible to magnify the
set to almost atomic dimensions. Each tiny parcel of iterative landscape turns out to be a vast track of mind-boggling real estate. Colors
are left to the programmer. The second program enables the user to
scan wallpaper that also seems infinitely various; patterns are
produced by interference between a set of concentric circles and an
infinite square grid. The third program uses a pair of iterative
formulas to mark out the pointillistic contours of a vegetative space,
one that resembles cross sections of plant stems. The fourth program
generates duplicates of an initial pattern that spread out into a cellular
space and fill it with beautiful and unexpected results of collisions
between duplicates.

The Mandelbrot Set

The Mandelbrot set broods in silent complexity at the center of a vast two-dimensional sheet of numbers called the complex plane. When a certain operation is applied repeatedly to the numbers, the ones outside the set flee to infinity. The numbers inside remain to drift or dance about. Close to the boundary minutely choreographed wanderings mark the onset of the instability. Here is an infinite regress of detail that astonishes us with its variety, its complexity, and its strange beauty.

The set is named for Benoit B. Mandelbrot, a research fellow at the IBM Thomas J. Watson Research Center in Yorktown Heights, N.Y. From his work with geometric forms Mandelbrot has developed the field he calls fractal geometry, the mathematical study of forms having a fractional dimension. In particular the boundary of the Mandelbrot set is a fractal, but it is also much more.

With the aid of a relatively simple program a computer can be converted into a kind of microscope for viewing the boundary of the Mandelbrot set. In principle one can zoom in for a closer look at any part of the set at any magnification (*see* Color Plate 1). From a distant vantage the set resembles a squat, wart-covered figure 8 lying on its side. The inside of the figure is ominously black. Surrounding it is a halo colored electric white, which gives way to deep blues and blacks in the outer reaches of the plane.

Approaching the Mandelbrot set, one finds that each wart is a tiny figure shaped much like the parent set. Zooming in for a close look at one of the tiny figures, however, opens up an entirely different pattern: a riot of organic-looking tendrils and curlicues sweeps out in whorls and rows (*see* Color Plate 2). Magnifying a curlicue reveals yet another scene: it is made up of pairs of whorls joined by bridges of filigree. A magnified bridge turns out to have two curlicues sprouting from its center. In the center of this center, so to speak, is a four-way bridge with four more curlicues, and in the center of these curlicues another version of the Mandelbrot set is found.

The magnified version is not quite the same Mandelbrot set. As the zoom continues, such objects seem to reappear, but a closer look always turns up differences. Things go on this way forever, infinitely various and frighteningly lovely.

Here I shall describe two computer programs, both of which explore the effects of iterated operations such as the one that leads to the Mandelbrot set. The first program generated Color Plates 1 and 2. The program can be adapted to run on personal computers that have the appropriate hardware and software for generating graphics. It will create satisfying images even if one has access only to a monochrome display. The second program is for readers who, like me, need an occasional retreat from infinite complexity to the apparent simplicity of the finite.

The word "complex" as used here has two meanings. The usual meaning is obviously appropriate for describing the Mandelbrot set, but the word has a second and more technical sense. A number is complex when it is made up of two parts, which for historical reasons are called real and imaginary. These terms have no special significance for us here: the two parts of a complex number might as well be called Humpty and Dumpty. Thus $7 + 4i$ is a complex number with real part 7 (Humpty) and imaginary part $4i$ (Dumpty). The italic i next to the 4 shows which part of the complex number is imaginary.

Every complex number can be represented by a point in the plane; the plane of complex numbers is called the complex plane. To find $7 + 4i$ in the complex plane, start at the complex number 0, or $0 + 0i$, and measure seven units east and four units north. The resulting point represents $7 + 4i$. The complex plane is an uncountable infinity of such numbers. Their real parts and their imaginary parts can be either positive or negative and either whole numbers or decimal expansions.

Adding or multiplying two complex numbers is easy. To add $3 - 2i$ and $7 + 4i$, add the parts separately; the sum is $10 + 2i$. Multiplying complex numbers is only slightly more difficult. For example, if the symbol i is treated like the x in high school algebra, the product of $3 - 2i$ and $7 + 4i$ is $21 + 12i - 14i - 8i^2$. At this stage a special property of the symbol i must be brought into play: it happens that i^2 equals -1. Thus the product can be simplified by collecting the real and the imaginary parts: it is $29 - 2i$.

It is now possible to describe the iterative process that generates the Mandelbrot set. Begin with the algebraic expression $z^2 + c$, where z is a complex number that is allowed to vary and c is a certain fixed complex number. Set z initially to be equal to the complex number 0. The square of z is then 0 and the result of adding c to z^2 is just c. Now substitute this result for z in the expression $z^2 + c$. The new sum is $c^2 + c$. Again substitute for z. The next sum is $(c^2 + c)^2 + c$. Continue the process, always making the output of the last step the input for the next one.

Strange things happen when the iterations are carried out for particular values of c. For example, here is what happens when c is $1 + i$:

first iteration	$1 + 3i$
second iteration	$-7 + 7i$
third iteration	$1 - 97i$

Note that the real and the imaginary parts may grow, shrink, or change sign. If this process of iteration continues, the resulting complex numbers may get progressively larger.

What exactly is meant by the size of a complex number? Since complex numbers correspond to points in the plane, ideas of distance apply. The size of a complex number is just its distance from the complex number 0. That distance is the hypotenuse of a right triangle whose sides are the real and the imaginary parts of the complex number. Hence to find the size of the number square each of its parts, add the two squared values, and take the square root of the sum. For example, the size of the complex number $7 + 4i$ is the square root of $7^2 + 4^2$, or approximately 8.062. When complex numbers reach a certain size under the iterative process I have just described, they grow very quickly: indeed, after a few more iterations they exceed the capacity of any computer.

Fortunately I can ignore all the complex numbers c that run screaming off to infinity. The Mandelbrot set is the set of all complex numbers c for which the size of $z^2 + c$ is small even after an indefinitely large number of iterations. The program I am about to describe searches for such numbers. I am indebted in all of this to John H. Hubbard, a mathematician at Cornell University. Hubbard is an authority on the Mandelbrot set, and he was one of the first people to make computer-generated images of it. Most of the images here were made by Heinz-Otto Peitgen and his colleagues at the University of Bremen.

Hubbard's program has inspired a program I call MANDELZOOM. The program sets up an array called *pic*, which is needed for saving pictures. The entries of *pic* are separate picture elements called pixels, which are arranged in a grid pattern. Hubbard's array has 400 columns and 400 rows, and Peitgen's is even larger. Readers who want to adapt MANDELZOOM for personal use must choose an array suited to their equipment and temperament. Larger arrays impose a longer wait for the pictures, but they improve the resolution.

In the first part of MANDELZOOM one may select any square region of the complex plane to be examined. Specify the southwest corner of the square with the complex number to which it corresponds. Two variables in the program, *acorner* and *bcorner*, enable one to enter the real part and the imaginary part of the number respectively. Specify the length of each side of the square by entering a value for a variable called *side*.

The second part of the program adjusts the array *pic* to match the square of interest by computing the size of a variable called *gap*. *Gap* is the distance within the square between adjacent pixels. To obtain *gap* divide *side* by the number of rows (or columns) in *pic*.

The heart of the program is its third part. Here a search is made for the complex numbers *c* in the Mandelbrot set, and colors are assigned to the numbers that are, in a special sense, nearby. The procedure must be carried out once for every pixel; thus Hubbard's 400-by-400 array requires 160,000 separate computations. Assume the program is currently working on the pixel in row *m* and column *n*; the third part then breaks down into four steps:

1. Calculate one complex number *c* that is assumed to represent the pixel: add $n \times gap$ to *acorner* to obtain the real part *ac* of *c*; add $m \times gap$ to *bcorner* to obtain the imaginary part *bc* of *c*. It is not necessary to include the imaginary number *i* in the program.
2. Set a complex variable *z* (which has parts *az* and *bz*) equal to $0 + 0i$. Set an integer variable called *count* equal to 0.
3. Carry out the following three steps repeatedly, until either the size of *z* exceeds 2 or the size of *count* exceeds 1000, whichever comes first:

$$z \leftarrow z^2 + c$$
$$count \leftarrow count + 1$$
$$size \leftarrow \text{size of } z$$

Why is the number 2 so important? A straightforward result in the theory of complex-number iterations guarantees that the iterations will drive *z* to infinity if and only if at some stage *z* reaches a size of 2 or greater. It turns out that relatively many points with an infinite destiny reach 2 after only a few iterations. Their slower cousins become increasingly rare at higher values of the variable *count*.

4. Assign a color to *pic* (*m,n*) according to the value reached by *count* at the end of Step 3. Display the color of the corresponding pixel on the screen. Note that the color of a pixel depends on only one complex number within its tiny domain, namely the one at its northeast corner; the behavior of this number then represents the behavior of the entire pixel.

The scheme for assigning colors requires that the range of *count* values attained within the array be grouped into subranges, one subrange for each color. Pixels for which the size of z reaches 2 after only a few iterations are colored red. Pixels for which the size of z reaches 2 after relatively many iterations are colored violet, at the other end of the spectrum. Pixels for which the size of z is less than 2 even after 1000 iterations are assumed to lie in the Mandelbrot set; they are colored black.

It makes sense to leave the colors unspecified until the range of *count* values in a particular square has been determined. If the range is narrow, the entire color spectrum can then be assigned within that range. Thus Hubbard suggests that in Step 4 only the value of *count* be assigned to each array element of *pic*. A separate program can then scan the array, determine the high and low values of *count*, and assign the spectrum accordingly. Readers who get this far will certainly find workable schemes.

The reader who does not have a color monitor can still take part in black and white. Complex numbers for which z is larger than 2 after r iterations are colored white. The rest are colored black. Adjust r to taste. To avoid all-night runs the array can be, say, 100 rows by 100 columns. Hubbard also suggests it is perfectly reasonable to reduce the maximum number of iterations per point from 1000 to 100. The output of such a program is a suggestive, pointillistic image of its colored counterpart (*see* Figure 1).

For other effective approaches which utilize a black-and-white monitor, see the Addendum which follows.

How powerful is the "zoom lens" of a personal computer? It depends to some degree on the effective size of the numbers the machine can manipulate. For example, according to Magi (my microcomputer amanuensis at the University of Western Ontario), the IBM PC uses the 8088 microprocessor, a chip manufactured by the Intel Corporation designed to manipulate 16-bit numbers. A facility called double precision makes it possible to increase the length of each number to 32 bits. With such double precision Magi and I calculate that magnifications on the order of 30,000 times can be realized. Higher precision software that in effect strings these numbers together can enhance the numerical precision to hundreds of significant digits. The magnification of the Mandelbrot set theoretically attainable with such precision is far greater than the magnification needed to resolve the nucleus of the atom.

Where should one explore the complex plane? Near the Mandelbrot set, of course, but where precisely? Hubbard says that "there are zillions of beautiful spots." Like a tourist in a land of infinite beauty, he bubbles with suggestions about places readers may want to explore. They do not

Figure I   Pointillist, miniature Mandelbrot in monochrome.

have names like Hawaii or Hong Kong: "Try the area with the real part between .26 and .27 and the imaginary part between 0 and .01." He has also suggested two other places:

Real Part	Imaginary Part
−.76 to −.74	.01 to .03
−1.26 to −1.24	.01 to .03

The reader who examines color images of the Mandelbrot set should bear in mind that any point having a color other than black does not belong to the Mandelbrot set. Much of the beauty resides in the halo of colors assigned to the fleeing points. Indeed, if one were to view the set in isolation, its image might not be so pleasing: the set is covered all over with filaments and with miniature versions of itself.

In fact none of the miniature Mandelbrots are exact copies of the parent set and none of them are exactly alike. Near the parent set there are even more miniature Mandelbrots, apparently suspended freely in the complex plane. The appearance is deceiving. An amazing theorem proved by Hubbard and a colleague, Adrian Douady of the University of Paris, states that the Mandelbrot set is connected. Hence even the miniature Mandelbrots that seem to be suspended in the plane are attached by filaments to the parent set. The miniatures are found almost everywhere near the parent set and they come in all sizes. Every square in the region includes an infinite number of them, of which at most only a few are visible at any given magnification. According to Hubbard, the Mandelbrot set is "the most complicated object in mathematics."

Readers with an appetite for color images of the Mandelbrot set and other mathematical objects can write to Heinz Otto Peitgen, MAP ART, Forschungsgruppe Komplexe Dynamik, Universität Bremen, 2800 Bremen 33, West Germany.

Readers unable or unwilling to write the MANDELZOOM program may order one that runs on an IBM PC or other machines by consulting the List of Suppliers.

Confronted with infinite complexity it is comforting to take refuge in the finite. Iterating a squaring process on a finite set of ordinary integers also gives rise to interesting structures. The structures are not geometric but combinatorial.

Pick any number at random from 0 through 99. Square it and extract the last two digits of the result, which must also be a number from 0 through 99. For example, 59^2 is equal to 3481; the last two digits are 81. Repeat the process and sooner or later you will generate a number you have already encountered. For example, 81 leads to the sequence 61, 21, 41, and 81, and this sequence of four numbers is then repeated indefinitely. It turns out that such loops always arise from iterative processes on finite sets. Indeed, it is easy to see there must be at least one repeated number after 100 operations in a set of 100 numbers; the first repeated number then leads to a loop. There is a beautiful program for detecting the loops that requires almost no memory, but more of this later.

It takes only an hour to diagram the results of the squaring process. Represent each number from 0 through 99 by a separate point on a sheet of paper. If the squaring process leads from one number to a new number, join the corresponding points with an arrow. For example, an arrow should run from point 59 to point 81. The first few connections in the diagram may lead to tangled loops, and so it is a good idea to redraw them from time to time in such a way that no two arrows cross. A nonintersecting iteration diagram is always possible.

One can go even further. Separate subdiagrams often arise, and they can be displayed in a way that highlights some of the symmetries arising from the iterations. For example, the nonintersecting iteration diagram for the squaring process on the integers from 0 through 99 includes six unconnected subdiagrams. The pieces come in identical pairs and each piece is highly symmetrical (*see* Figure 2). Can the reader explain the symmetry? What would happen if the integers from 0 through 119 were

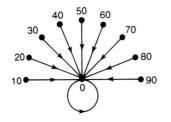

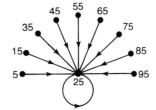

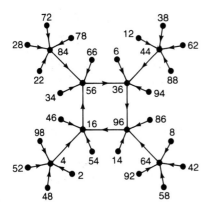

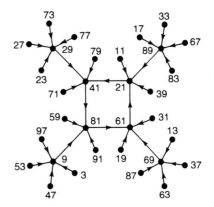

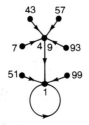

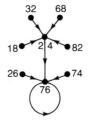

Figure 2   The six components of the iteration diagram for squaring the first 100 integers.

used instead? Is there a relation between the number of unconnected pieces found in the diagram and the largest integer in the sequence?

Similar patterns of iteration hold for some of the complex numbers in the Mandelbrot set: for certain values of c repeated iterations of $z^2 + c$ can lead to a finite cycle of complex numbers. For example, the complex number $0 + 1i$ leads to an indefinite oscillation between the two complex numbers $-1 + 1i$ and $0 - 1i$. The cycle may even have only one member. Whether such cycles are found in a finite set or in the infinite Mandelbrot set, they are called attractors.

Each of the six parts of the iteration diagram for the integers 0 through 99 includes one attractor. Geometrically the attractor can be represented as a polygon, and the sets of numbers that lead into it can be represented as trees.

One way to find an attractor by computer is to store each newly generated number in a specially designated array. Compare the new number with all the numbers previously stored in the array. If a match is found, print all the numbers in the array from the matching number to the number just created. The method is straightforward and easy to program. Nevertheless, it can take a long time if the array is large. An attractor cycle within an array that includes n numbers would take on the order of n^2 comparisons to discover: each new number must be compared with up to n numbers in the array.

There is a clever little program that will find an attractor much faster. The program requires not n words of memory but only two, and it can be encoded on the simplest of programmable pocket calculators. The program is found in a remarkable book titled *Mathematical Recreations for the Programmable Calculator*, by Dean Hoffman of Auburn University and Lee Mohler of the University of Alabama. Needless to say, many of the topics that are covered in the book can be readily adapted to computer programs.

The program is called RHOP because the sequence of numbers that eventually repeats itself resembles a piece of rope with a loop at one end. It also resembles the Greek letter rho (ρ). There are two variables in the program called *slow* and *fast*. Initially both variables are assigned the value of the starting number. The iterative cycle of the program includes just three instructions:

$$fast \leftarrow fast \times fast \pmod{100}$$
$$fast \leftarrow fast \times fast \pmod{100}$$
$$slow \leftarrow slow \times slow \pmod{100}$$

The operation mod 100 extracts the last two digits of the products. Note that the squaring is done twice on the number *fast* but only once on the number *slow*. *Fast* makes its way from the tail to the head of the rho twice as fast as *slow* does. Within the head *fast* catches up with *slow* by the time *slow* has gone partway around. The program exits from its iterative cycle when *fast* is equal to *slow*.

The attractor is identified by reiterating the squaring process for the number currently assigned to *slow*. When that number recurs, halt the program and print the intervening sequence of numbers.

I should be delighted to see readers' diagrams that explore the effects of iterative squaring on finite realms of varying size. The diagrams can be done on a computer or by hand. Discrete iteration is a newly developing mathematical field with applications in computer science, biomathematics, physics, and sociology. Theorists might wish to consult a book on the subject by François Robert of the University of Grenoble.

Addendum

Since August, 1985, when the previous discussion first appeared in the "Computer Recreations" column of SCIENTIFIC AMERICAN magazine, the MANDELZOOM program has been incarnated in hundreds of homes, schools, and workplaces. Although the program has apparently awed adults, intrigued teenagers, and frightened a few small children, to my surprise the mail on iteration diagrams, the secondary topic, nearly equaled that on the Mandelbrot set.

Many readers have lost themselves in the colored intricacies of the Mandelbrot set by zooming ever deeper. Other readers, whose equipment is limited to black and white, may quite effectively develop shades of gray. Such pictures can be nearly as inspiring as their colored counterparts. The best gray images were produced by David W. Brooks, who works with equipment at Prime Computer, Inc., in Framingham, Mass., to compute and plot his pictures. In his fabulous and delicate riots of halftones each shade of gray is rendered by tiny black squares of a certain size; the squares are made by a laser printer. Brooks has been searching for the tiny filaments that are thought to connect miniature Mandelbrots to the main set. So far they have not appeared at any magnification used by Brooks. Mandelbrot has advised him that they are probably infinitesimal.

Those with less sophisticated equipment can still work with shades of gray on a black-and-white monitor. John B. Halleck of Salt Lake City varies the density of points per pixel to indicate different shades.

Another approach depends on black and white contours. Yekta Gursel of Cambridge, Mass., has generated views of the Mandelbrot set that rival the ones Brooks generates. Gursel replaces a discrete spectrum of colors with alternating bands of black and white. Gary J. Shannon of Grants Pass, Ore., suggested the same technique and Victor

Andersen of Santa Clara, Calif., took it to an extreme. He suggested changing from black to white (or the converse) whenever the *count* variable changes from one pixel to its neighbor.

Two other explorations are worth mentioning. James A. Thigpenn IV of Pearland, Tex., uses height instead of color. The Mandelbrot set becomes an immense plateau seen from an angle, with a complicated arrangement of spiky hills approaching the plateau in various places. Richard J. Palmaccio of Fort Lauderdale dispenses with the set altogether. His interest is in tracking individual complex numbers in the course of iteration. Their choreography near the boundary can result in spiral ballets or circular jigs.

The function $z^2 + c$ gives rise to the Mandelbrot set. Naturally other functions are possible, but they produce other sets. For example, Bruce Ikenaga of Case Western Reserve University has been exploring what appears to be a cubic cactus. The function $z^3 + (c - 1) z - c$ produces a prickly and uncomfortable-looking set (at least in stark black and white) surrounded by mysterious miniature spiral galaxies.

Readers interested in pursuing the Mandelbrot set further may wish to subscribe to a newsletter devoted to the stunning fractal and related objects: *Amygdala* is published by Rollo Silver, Box 111, San Cristobal, N.M., 87564.

There are mysteries in iteration diagrams as well: when the integers modulo n are squared, each number migrates to another, in effect. The iteration diagram appears when each number is replaced by a point and each migration is replaced by an arrow. I raised several questions about such diagrams. How many components do they have? Readers sent diagrams documenting their explorations for various values of n.

The largest diagrams were completed by Rosalind B. Marimont of Silver Spring, Md. She examined the integers modulo 1000 and reported four pairs of components in the resulting iteration diagram. Each component sported a single attractor, as usual, and the largest attractors had 20 numbers. As a mathematician Marimont is allowed to conjecture that the integers modulo 10^k will produce $k + 1$ pairs of components and that the largest attractors will have $4 \times 5^{k-2}$ numbers.

Stephen Eberhart of Reseda, Calif., investigated the case where n is a Fermat prime (a prime number of the form $2^{2^k} + 1$). Here the number 0 forms an attractor by itself and the remaining numbers all lie in one single, grand tree. A number-theorist friend affirms that this will always be the case for Fermat primes and that the tree is binary: each internal point has two incoming arrows.

Iteration diagrams, like numbers, can be multiplied. If n is the product of two relatively prime numbers, say p and q, the iteration diagram for the integers modulo n is the product respectively of the diagrams for p and q. This interesting observation was made by Stephen C. Locke of

Florida Atlantic University. Locke has also described a fascinating relation between the nth iteration diagram and a diagram of a seemingly different kind, one in which the numbers, instead of being squared, are merely doubled. When n is a prime, the latter diagram for the integers modulo $n - 1$ is the same as our nth iteration diagram, except for a single isolated number forming an attractor by itself. Much the same observation was made in number-theory terms by Noam Elkies of New York City.

A powerful tool for analyzing the (squared) iteration diagrams was developed by Frank Palmer of Chicago. Apparently all the trees attached to a given attractor are isomorphic. This means essentially that they have precisely the same form.

Finally, Bruce R. Gilson of Silver Spring, Md., and Molly W. Williams of Kalamazoo, Mich., examined a quite different generalization of the numbers from 0 through 99. These may be regarded as numbers to different bases. As numbers to the base 3, for example, one would count 00, 01, 02, 10, 11, 12, 20, 21, 22 before arriving once more at 00. Such numbers also produce iteration diagrams that look like those arising for integers modulo n. Gilson proved the diagrams always have paired components when n is even but not a multiple of 4.

Readers who, for lack of time or programming expertise, insist on buying a program that displays the Mandelbrot set, may order one as indicated in the List of Suppliers.

Wallpaper for the Mind

Ordinary wallpaper is printed by a rotating cylinder engraved with a design. As the cylinder turns it prints the same design over and over again. Only a computer, however, can reproduce certain richly embroidered patterns I call wallpaper for the mind (*see* Color Plate 3). These patterns do not repeat themselves, at least not exactly; instead each pattern continually manifests itself in new contexts and configurations, left and right, up and down. From one apparition to the next, what is changed and what is preserved?

The swatches in my current sample book demonstrate the results of three widely differing techniques. The computer programs responsible for the images range in difficulty from the extremely simple to the merely easy. They come from three readers: John E. Connett of the University of Minnesota, Barry Martin of Aston University in Birmingham, England, and Tony D. Smith of Essendon, Australia.

Connet's program is based on the circle, but it celebrates the varieties of design based on the square. The apparent conundrum compels me to name it CIRCLE². In a nutshell, it applies the formula for the graph of a circle, $x^2 + y^2$, to assign a color to the point that has the coordinates x and y. I shall give the details below. In the meantime you may be boggled, as I was, to discover that there is much more to this wallpaper than a set of concentric circles; specifically, if you back away from the wall, intricate patterns of delicate squares may also emerge (*see* Figure 3). There are mysteries here.

It is perhaps not surprising that CIRCLE² was inspired by the Mandelbrot set. The riot of form and color that surrounds the Mandelbrot set (when utilizing a color monitor) is based on a single mathematical function, applied repeatedly to its own output for each complex number in a region of the plane. Whenever the iterated value of the function reaches

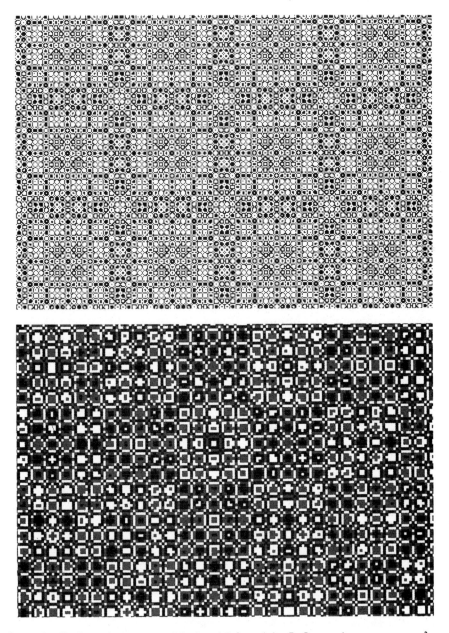

Figure 3   Circles and squares modulo 2 and 3 from John E. Connett's program CIRCLE².

the magnitude 2, the number of iterations needed to reach that magnitude determines the color of the corresponding point.

Connett, who had no color monitor at his disposal, assigned black to points that reach 2 after an even number of iterations and white to points that reach 2 after an odd number of iterations. Creditable images of the Mandelbrot set appeared, but Connett was led to explore other formulas. He selected the formula $x^2 + y^2$ and discarded iteration altogether. His program systematically scans a gridded section of the plane; at each point (s,y) it computes the formula and then truncates the resulting value to an integer. If the integer is even, the point (x,y) is colored black; if it is odd, the point is colored white (left blank).

I fear I have just lost half of my audience. They already understand the program, and they have rushed off to type it into a nearby computer. It is that simple. In algorithmic shorthand CIRCLE^2 is an input section followed by a double loop:

```
input corna, cornb
input side

for i ← 1 to 100
    for j ← 1 to 100
        x ← corna + (side × i/100)
        y ← cornb + (side × j/100)
        z ← x² + y²
        c ← int(z)
        if c is even, then plot (i,j)
```

First the program causes the computer to call for the coordinates $(corna,cornb)$ for the lower left corner of the square to be examined. The variable $side$ is the length of the side of the square of interest. For example, if the user types -15 and -20 for the corner coordinates and 87 for the side, the program plots a 100-by-100 array of points within a square region of the plane 87 units on its side, whose lower left corner is the point $(-15,-20)$. In my outline of the program I have assumed the iteration limits run from 1 to 100, but they must be adjusted so that the square lies within the boundaries of the output device to be used. On my monitor these limits outline a smallish square on the screen.

The double loop marches through the square grid and for each index pair (i,j) computes the coordinates of the point (x,y) to which the pair corresponds. The loop then squares x and y, assigns the sum of the two squares to the variable z, and truncates the sum. The largest integer less than or equal to the sum is stored as the variable c. If c is divisible by 2, the point (x,y) is plotted, presumably as a colored pixel on a color monitor or as a black dot in printed output. If c is odd, no point is plotted.

Readers who want to re-create Connett's wallpaper need not get too anxious about whether they have the colors right. Most patterns are equally striking with the colors reversed. Indeed, even more than two colors are possible: instead of determining whether c is even or odd, divide it by the number of colors you want. The remainder after the division can then be assigned to a distinct color.

The smaller the square under examination is, the closer the plane appears to the viewer and the greater the magnification of CIRCLE^2's image is. Unlike the procedure for coloring neighborhoods of the Mandelbrot set, however, Connett's program does not yield an infinite regress of progressively smaller patterns. At high magnifications about the origin (0,0) a set of concentric circles appears. At still higher magnifications there is a large black disk in the middle of the screen: the truncated-integer value of every point in the disk is 0. Then all the screen is blackness.

You can better appreciate the beauty of Connett's wallpaper by reducing the magnification: back away from the wall. The concentric circles dissolve into an intriguing arrangement of primary and secondary circles resembling a moiré pattern. New wallpaper designs appear like magic, seemingly different with every lower magnification. Is there an infinite regress lurking here? It seems a vexing question, but I am confident readers will be able to shed some light on it.

Readers unable or unwilling to write the CIRCLE^2 program may order one that runs on an IBM PC by consulting the List of Suppliers.

At Aston University in Birmingham, Barry Martin was also inspired by the Mandelbrot set. Martin adopted Mandelbrot's idea of iterating a formula from a numerical seed, but it is there that the similarity ends. Whereas Mandelbrot's patterns emerge from complex numbers, Martin's wallpaper is based on iterations of ordinary real numbers. Moreover, the numerical seeds for the Mandelbrot set are the points, infinite in number, found throughout a region of the plane; Martin's program grows its patterns from only one seed (*see* Color Plate 4).

For example, Martin suggests trying the following pair of formulas, which can generate stunning, highly detailed images in many colors:

$$x \leftarrow y - \text{sign}(x) \times [\text{abs}(b \times x - c)]^{1/2}$$
$$y \leftarrow a - x$$

Here the function $\text{sign}(x)$ takes the value 1 or -1, depending on whether x is positive or negative; the function $\text{abs}(b \times x - c)$ is the absolute value of the expression $b \times x - c$. The one-half power of what results is just its square root. The patterns can vary widely according to the values assigned to the letters a, b, and c, which are numerical constants in the formula.

The formulas themselves are written in a form of mathematical shorthand: it is understood that one set of values is used for x and y in the formulas to the right of the arrows and a new set of values is computed from them on the left. The new values for x and y then replace the old values to the right of the arrows, and the calculation is repeated. In this way the program I call HOPALONG hops from one point to another. It begins at the point for which x and y are both equal to 0, namely at the origin. The next point might be at the upper right, the one after that a the lower left. A computer draws the points so quickly that one has the impression miniature electronic rain is falling on the screen: hundreds and then thousands of points drop onto the monitor. Soon a pattern begins to emerge. For example, if a is set equal to -200, b to .1, and c to -80, a broadly octagonal pattern is formed. If the pattern is magnified and each point is colored according to the number of hops needed to reach it, the pattern becomes a wonderful cartouche. For other values of a, b, and c new designs appear: try setting a to .4, b to 1, and c to 0, or set a to -3.14, b to .3, and c to .3.

The algorithm for HOPALONG is almost as easy to appreciate as the one for CIRCLE[2]:

```
input num
input a, b, c

x ← 0
y ← 0
for i ← 1 to num
    plot (x,y)
    xx ← y − sign(x) × [abs(b × x − c)]^(1/2)
    yy ← a − x
    x ← xx
    y ← yy
```

Another stampede of readers rushes off to type in the program. Your rewards for lingering here are a more detailed explanation of Martin's program and a description of the third kind of wallpaper program.

In order to run HOPALONG one enters the total number of iterations as the variable num; one also enters values for a, b, and c. The larger the value of num, the finer the detail of the pattern. For example, if num is 10,000, the program will plot 10,000 points on the screen, but for some values of a, b, and c that is only the beginning. If a is -1000, b is .1, and c is -10, the pattern at low magnification resembles the rind of a four-lobed lemon (*see* Figure 4). When the run of the program is extended from 10,000 points to 100,000 and then to 600,000, the filigree becomes increasingly ornate.

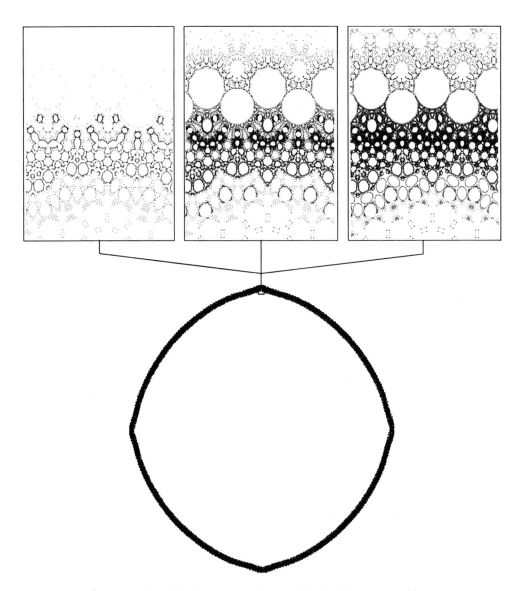

Figure 4   A model plant stem and its vascular bundles, generated by HOPALONG.

The algorithm can work as it stands, but it can also be enhanced; for example, one might add a facility for moving off-screen points or compressing off-screen regions into the visible region. If such features are added, three more parameters for determining position and the scale must be specified at the start of the program. The body of the main loop must then be modified: just after x and y are computed the enhanced version of HOPALONG adds the position changes to x and y and multiplies the result by the scale factor.

The wallpaper analogy was not lost on Martin: "It seems to me we are on the verge of a pattern-generating explosion that has great commercial implications, e.g., we can expect to see 'designer' wallpaper and textiles within the next few years. Patterns will be produced by the customer merely by the selection of a few numbers." Martin is equally sanguine about the implications for mathematical biology. Look once again at the four-lobed lemon. The enlargements show details strongly reminiscent of vascular bundles: could it be the outer rind of a monocotyledon in cross section? About these and other patterns Martin writes: "Clearly these curious configurations show us that the rules responsible for the construction of elaborate living tissue structures could be absurdly simple."

Readers might enjoy exploring the patterns generated by a different pair of iteration formulas, also suggested by Martin:

$$x \leftarrow y - \sin(x)$$
$$y \leftarrow a - x$$

In these formulas only the variable a must be specified. Martin has discovered a most interesting series of patterns when a lies within .07 of the number pi.

The third kind of mental wallpaper must be reserved for rooms devoted to heavy thinking. The patterns range from Persian complexities to Incan riots (*see* Figure 5). The methods that lead to them could hardly be less like the techniques described above. Tony D. Smith of PICA Pty. Ltd. in Australia has devised intricate variations of the self-replicating cellular automaton invented in 1960 by Edward Fredkin of the Massachusetts Institute of Technology (*see* "Computer Recreations," by Brian Hayes; SCIENTIFIC AMERICAN, October, 1983). There is astonishing potential for pattern in this idea, and Smith has begun to explore an amusing corner in the vast space of possibilities.

What is the Fredkin cellular automaton? Imagine an infinite, two-dimensional grid of square cells. At any given moment each cell is in one of two possible states: living or dead, so to speak. Somewhere an imaginary clock ticks away. The fate of each cell is determined by its four edge-adjacent neighbors: if the number of living neighbors is even for one tick of the clock, the cell will be dead at the next tick regardless of its previous state. On the other hand, if the number of living neighbors is odd, the cell will be alive at the next tick. The same rule is simultaneously applied to every cell on the planar grid.

Fredkin's automaton is closely related to the game of Life, invented by John Horton Conway of the University of Cambridge (*see* "One-

Figure 5   Two images generated by PATTERN BREEDER and superposed.

Dimensional Computers" in World Four). Fredkin's automaton, however, was discovered earlier than Conway's, and it is much simpler.
Moreover, it has an amazing property not shared by Life: any initial
configuration of live cells grows through a series of generations (ticks of
the clock) into four copies of itself. After several more generations there
are 16 copies, 64 copies, and so on. The finest wallpaper appears during
intermediate generations: in the generations between the ones in which
the original population of live cells is replicated.

Smith's program for printing generalized Fredkin wallpaper is a
highly versatile one called PATTERN BREEDER. The rules that determine
the fate of a cell in PATTERN BREEDER need not depend solely on the state
of the four edge-adjacent cells. In fact, before running the program one
can specify the configuration of surrounding cells that will constitute

the active neighborhood of each cell. The program then applies the same even-odd rule that was chosen in Fredkin's original automaton. At each tick of the clock if the number of living cells in the active neighborhood is even, the target cell will be dead in the following generation. Otherwise, the cell will be alive.

PATTERN BREEDER goes to work on any initial configuration of cells supplied by the user. For example, the initial configuration designated *a* in the top illustration of Figure 6 gives rise to part of the pattern shown in Figure 5: for each target cell and for every stage in the evolution of the pattern the active neighborhood is the same. It is a complex pattern itself, which includes all the gray cells within a 5-by-5 matrix, designated *a* in the bottom illustration of Figure 6. Note that the active neighborhood in this case includes the target cell itself. To apply the rule, count the number of live cells that coincide with the cells in the active neighborhood; if the target cell is currently alive, it too is included in the

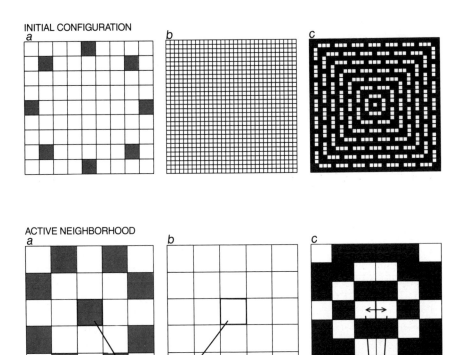

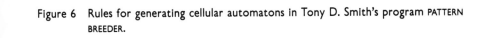

Figure 6   Rules for generating cellular automatons in Tony D. Smith's program PATTERN BREEDER.

count. Initial configurations and the active neighborhood associated with each of them are also shown for two other images. The ones labeled *b* correspond to one part of the pattern in Figure 5 and the ones labeled *c* correspond to another part. There is an added complexity for active neighborhood *c*: the target cell itself oscillates in succeeding generations from left to right and back again in the center of the neighborhood.

Readers impatient to generate their own magnificent patterns may forgo the algorithmic struggle by writing to Smith at the address given in the List of Suppliers. Smith's program incorporates a library of initial configurations and active neighborhoods from which the user can choose; the program is currently available only for Apple Macintosh computers.

I am not about to outline PATTERN BREEDER in its full sophistication, but I shall describe a simpler program called FREDKIN. Readers with a bit of additional programming acumen can then convert FREDKIN into a more general program with some of the features of PATTERN BREEDER.

```
            input initial pattern
        S: for each cell in the screen array
              count ← 0
              for each neighbor of that cell
                if neighbor alive
                   then count ← count + 1
              if count even
                 then cell ← 0
                 else cell ← 1
                   plot cell
           input go
           go to S
```

One of the great joys of writing algorithms is that so many levels of description are available. The line between descriptive generality and irresponsible vagueness is a fine one. Readers will note that FREDKIN, as specified above, occupies a slightly more rarefied stratum than the algorithms I outlined previously. For example, the instruction "Input initial pattern" will take several instructions to implement in any practical programming language. Any such instructions would involve a double loop, with two indices *i* and *j*. Another double loop is concealed in the instruction "For each cell in the screen array." Here the two indices supply the coordinates of points on the display screen or the printer.

Inside the main program loop FREDKIN simply carries out the rule for the evolution of a given pattern. It counts the number of living neighbors for each cell (i,j); then, if the number is odd, it plots or prints the cell as a single point. The last instruction of the main loop calls for input of the variable *go*. The user may type any number at this stage in order to get FREDKIN to generate the next pattern. In this way the execution of the program can be halted at will if a particularly pleasing pattern appears. Sometimes a bit of trickery and a go-to statement are useful. This strategy is not structured programming, but it works just fine.

Addendum

"Wallpaper for the Mind" treated computer images that are almost but not quite repetitive: a kind of wallpaper not yet seen. In fact, however, patterns resembling these were known a generation ago. Michael Rossman, a writer and political commentator living in Berkeley, Calif., coined the phrase "wallpaper of the mind" in 1971. He was referring to the delicate patterns seen with the eyes closed after the ingestion of LSD. Rossman writes: "It 'looked' like wallpaper, never striped but of repetitive motif: orderly constellations of parrots, starfish, lightbulbs, snowflakes, unnamable Rorschachs, changing in profligate creativity. . . . the images evolved one from another in chain, as if some infinite linear Escher print of metamorphoses had been animated in a movie."

The simplest wallpaper program described belonged to John E. Connett of the University of Minnesota. In Connett's images the appearance of wallpaper—horizontal and vertical repetitions—may be explained in part as a moiré phenomenon: two patterns are implicit in the foregoing description and their superposition creates the effect. The first pattern is the rectangular grid of pixels that constitute one's display screen. The second pattern is a series of concentric rings that represent points in the plane for which Connett's procedure generates an odd number. The wallpaper arises as a result of repetitive interference patterns in the horizontal and vertical directions. A number of consecutive grid points may happen to fall within rings, the next bunch will then fall without, and so on. As the distance from the origin increases, the rings become progressively thinner, ensuring that hits and misses will occur along any line of grid points.

As if to reinforce these remarks, Paul Braun of Simi Valley, Calif., allowed impatience to get the better of him. It took so long to fill his computer screen that he decided to sample the pattern by displaying every ninth pixel in both the horizontal and the vertical direction. In compressed form the resulting image looked nothing like the original; Braun had in effect changed the grid size and thus altered the interference pattern.

Otto Smith of Port Townsend, Wash., found he could change the moiré pattern considerably by merely varying the color scheme. Like many readers, Smith selected formulas other than Connett's. Certain sums or products of simple trigonometric functions, for example, produce wild, swirly images reminiscent of the colored-ink patterns that used to adorn the inside covers of quality hardbound books. Smith also points out that moiré patterns and other interference effects crop up regularly in computer graphics. In such a context they are known as aliasing: the tendency of unwanted imagery artifacts to appear when a picture with much regular variation in it is digitized.

I was touched to receive a miniature hand-held film made by Douglas W. Raymond of Orinda, Calif. It consists of consecutive, minute prints of Connett's wallpaper in which the grid size is gradually increased. The prints are sewn tightly together and the production unfolds as one riffles the edge of the resulting booklet with the thumb. Raymond calls the film "Small Bang with Aliases."

Mathemagadgets

H ere are three computer recreations gathered under a title that hints at a common mathematical orientation. Gadgets are conceptual devices that operate perfectly only in the pristine space of the mathematical imagination. Some of them seem capable of lightning-swift computation. Is this behavior confined to the imagination, or do some of these devices hold the seeds of a comeback in analog computation? The second topic, Golomb rulers, entails a mathematical problem involving the number of distinct distances that n marks on a ruler might measure. There is a program to search for such rulers but the story does not end there; radio astronomers actually use them to make extraordinarily precise measurements of the Earth. The third topic in this World makes it possible for readers to build their own four-dimensional hypercubes and to view them as they rotate bizarrely on the computer screen. Warnings of the dangers of four-dimensional dementia accompany this excursion.

Analog Gadgets

Mention computers these days and one thinks invariably of digital machines. All but forgotten are their analog cousins, the electromechanical devices that once ruled the computational scene. Before World War II major laboratories employed elaborate analog computers with names such as the continuous integraph and the differential analyzer. The machines exploited electrical or mechanical analogies to mathematical equations: a variable in an equation would be represented by some physical quantity, such as a voltage or the rotation of a shaft. Analog computers could be applied to equations that arise in many fields: ballistics, aerodynamics, the analysis of power networks, and so on.

The analog machines could not compete with the digital computers developed during World War II and immediately after. Analog computers seemed to be capable of solving only certain kinds of problems, chiefly those defined by differential equations, and even then with less than perfect accuracy. In contrast, it quickly became apparent that digital computers could be programmed to solve an infinite variety of problems with very high accuracy. Slowly the analog machines faded into the background until by the mid-1960s they were barely mentioned in books on computing.

Although the successors of the great analog machines of the 1920s and 1930s are still in use (and under continuing development) in a few laboratories, no one seriously expects analog computers to spring to the forefront again. The digital revolution cannot be turned back. It is also true, however, that a revolution sometimes blinds us to the charms of an earlier milieu.

The essential delight of an analog computation lies in the notion that one is getting something for nothing. A problem that would require hours of computation by hand (or even by a digital computer) is solved by merely observing a physical system as it comes rapidly into equilibrium. In the most dramatic cases the process seems well-nigh instantaneous, and we have a gadget that computes.

Consider the SAG computer, or Spaghetti Analog Gadget (*see* Figure 7). This device, in the configuration I have tested, is able to sort up to 700 numbers in order of decreasing magnitude. Sorting is a common task in digital computing, and algorithms for doing it have been highly refined, but the time needed to sort a list of numbers still grows somewhat faster than the size of the list. With SAG one must spend a little time setting up the machine for the particular list of numbers and a little more time reading out the results, but the actual sorting appears to take no time at all.

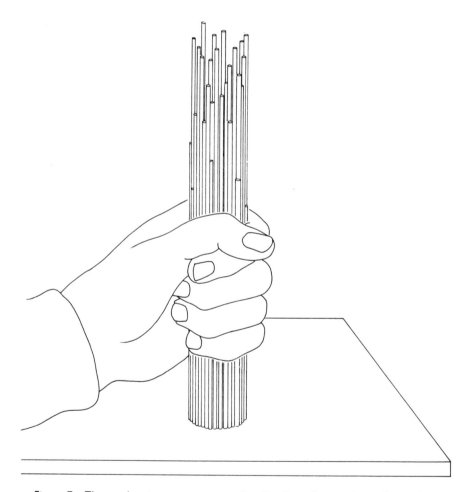

Figure 7   The spaghetti computer sorts a bundle of numbers in descending order.

Here is how SAG works. For each number in the sequence to be sorted trim a piece of uncooked spaghetti to a length equal to the number. Naturally, appropriate units of measurement must be adopted. Now take all the pieces of trimmed spaghetti in one hand and, holding the bundle vertically and somewhat loosely, bring it down on a table rather sharply. The momentum of the individual rods ensures that all of them have one end resting on the table. In order to obtain the sorted sequence from the resting bundle, one has only to remove the tallest rod, then the tallest of the remaining rods and so on until the bundle is exhausted. As each rod is removed it is measured and the number is recorded.

It is important to distinguish three phases of the sorting operation; I call them the preprocessing, the analog, and the postprocessing phases. In the preprocessing phase the spaghetti is measured and trimmed; in the analog phase a simple mechanism sorts the rods; in the postprocessing phase the rods are removed one at a time, yielding the sorted sequence. All the gadgets described here require pre- and postprocessing. Indeed, so did the early analog computers, and much research and development was invested in speeding up these phases.

There will be those who say, "SAG may be able to sort 700 numbers, but what about 7000 or 7 million?" The only reasonable way to deal with questions of this kind is to mention SUPERSAG, a modified fork-lift truck capable of picking up 7 million pieces of carefully trimmed (extralong) uncooked spaghetti and slamming them sideways against a brick wall.

There will be others who say, "I can sort 700 numbers faster than SAG can. I'll do it all with pencil and paper and I'll finish before the spaghetti is even trimmed!" Sadly for SAG, this remark is probably true. Suppose it takes one minute to read a number from the unsorted sequence, measure a piece of spaghetti to that length, cut it, and insert it into the bundle. Suppose further it takes 10 seconds to remove and measure each piece of spaghetti after the (one-second) slamming operation. It will then take SAG more than 13 hours to sort the 700 numbers, with all but one second of the time being spent in preprocessing and postprocessing. The challenger, on the other hand, sorts the sequence by scanning it, selecting the largest number on each pass, recording it, and stroking it off the sequence. It takes him a tenth of a second to scan each number, and thus he needs $(700 + 699 + \ldots + 2 + 1)/10$ seconds to sort the sequence. This works out to 175 minutes 15 seconds, a clear victory for the challenger. Will the wonderful, all-at-once quality of the analog phase be completely undone by the lengthy pre- and postprocessing phases? Not quite.

Suppose the human sorter becomes cocky and challenges SUPERSAG to a 7-million-number sorting duel. SUPERSAG would need some 15 years, whereas the challenger would not finish for almost 74,000 years!

SUPERSAG's superiority can be explained by examining the way the speed of a computation depends on the size of the problem. The slamming of the spaghetti against the wall is said to be constant-time operation: it is essentially independent of the size of the bundle. The pre- and postprocessing phases are linear-time operations: they grow longer in simple, linear proportion to the size of the sequence of numbers. The human sorter's task grows much faster. He must inspect each remaining member of the sequence on each pass through it. Even though the sequence gradually shrinks, the total number of inspections goes up as the square of the size of the sequence; the sorting is said to take quadratic time. Sooner or later a linear-time procedure is bound to beat a quadratic-time one.

Even with its lengthy pre- and postprocessing phases, a large enough SAG machine could outsort a modern digital computer employing the fastest sorting algorithms. These require on the order of $n \log n$ steps, where n is the size of the sequence and log represents the logarithm function. Linear time is certainly superior to this in principle, but one shudders to imagine the size of the spaghetti gadget needed to win such a contest. SUPERDUPERSAG would have to be constructed in space and slammed against the moon.

The next gadget in my collection computes the convex hull of n points in the plane (*see* Figure 8). The convex hull is just the smallest convex region containing all n points. It is entirely defined by its boundary, a polygon that has one of the points at each vertex. The gadget that computes the boundary is made from a large board, some nails, and a rubber band. I call it RAG, short for Rubber Band, Nails, and Board Analog Gadget. It would have been nice to include "nails and board" in the acronym, but one would end up with a grotesque name such as RUNBAG.

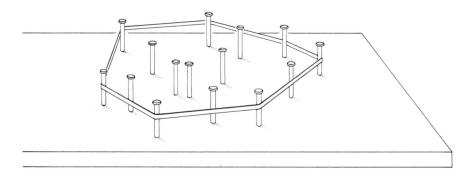

Figure 8   Finding the convex hull of a set of points in the plane.

To set up the RAG computer simply drive *n* nails into the board at positions corresponding to the *n* points in the plane. Then pick up the rubber band, stretch it into a large circle surrounding all the nails, and release it. The rubber band will snap into place, precisely defining the polygonal boundary of the convex hull.

Here again a linear amount of work precedes the analog operation of releasing the rubber band. It will take a certain number of seconds to determine the position of each nail and then to drive it into the board. Once the rubber band has been released, noting the vertices of the convex hull takes somewhat less than linear time. Only the nails touched by the rubber band need to have their position recorded.

The fastest digital algorithm known for finding the convex hull requires on the order of *n* log *n* steps. This is so close to being linear that perhaps only a RAG machine the size of the solar system would be able to compete with a digital computer running the algorithm.

The function of a third gadget is to find the shortest path joining two vertices of a graph (*see* Figure 9). In this context a graph is a network of lines, or edges, joining the points called vertices. In some graphs the edges can have different lengths, and it is this kind of graph that serves as input to STAG, an analog gadget that uses string to represent graphs. Specifically, each vertex is represented by a small brass ring. If two vertices are joined by an edge in the graph, the corresponding rings are connected by a piece of string cut to the right length and supplied with a hook at each end.

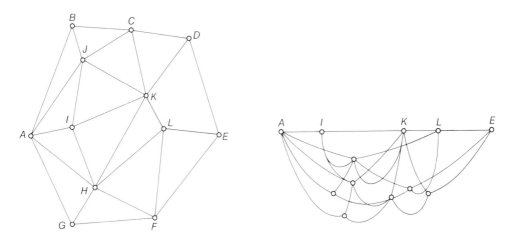

Figure 9   An analog device for finding the shortest path between two vertices in a graph.

To find the shortest path between the vertices u and v in a graph, pick up the network by the rings u and v, holding one ring in each hand. Then pull the network taut. Instantly the shortest path stands out as a sequence of taut strings at the top of the network; all the strings representing edges that are not in the shortest path remain more or less slack. If the rings are labeled with the names of the vertices they represent, one can now read off the labels along the shortest path.

If the size of a graph is measured by n, the number of vertices, both pre- and postprocessing require at most a linear number of steps. The analog phase of the computation is as usual virtually instantaneous. The fastest digital algorithms known for the problem take on the order of n^2 steps.

It has been mildly irritating to include the pre- and postprocessing phases in analyzing the relative speeds of these gadgets, but honesty compels me to include them as part of the overall operation. How else could one specify a problem or interpret the gadget's output?

Some gadgets require no processing at all because they are incorporated into a system that uses the results directly. Two examples that come to mind are the needle-sorter once widely used in libraries and a trick for balancing a plate of food on one finger. In the needle-sorter a set of cards with notches and holes along one edge serves to show which books are due on a given day. The cards are stacked and a long needle is inserted into the hole corresponding to that day. When the needle is lifted, only the cards with holes at that position come with it. The notched cards slip off the needle and remain in the stack.

The balancing trick was shown to me by mathemagician Ronald L. Graham of AT&T Bell Laboratories. Graham begins by holding aloft a plate of food on a thumb and two fingers, widely spaced. As he draws the three digits together the plate's center of gravity remains between them because the digit supporting the least weight slides most easily. The final intrusion of another finger supports the center of gravity well enough to balance the plate. Graham warns beginners to practice the trick carefully before demonstrating it at Thanksgiving dinner.

Up to now I have applied gadgets only to problems that already have a reasonably fast algorithmic solution. Such problems are said to have polynomial-time complexity, because the number of steps needed to solve a size-n instance of a problem can be expressed as (or at least is bounded by) a polynomial function of n (*see* Figure 10). For example, the solution time might be proportional to n itself, to n^2, to $n \log n$, or to n^{27}. There are other problems, including some of practical importance, for which no polynomial-time algorithm is known; the best algorithms seem to require an amount of time that grows exponentially with the problem size. Typically the solution time is proportional to 2^n, a function that increases faster than any polynomial. For a large instance of

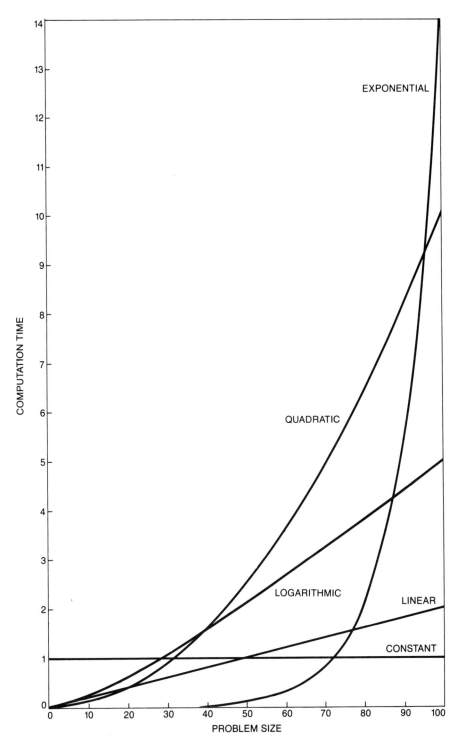

Figure 10 Several possible functions relating computation time to problem size.

such a problem, or even for one of moderate size, the time needed is exorbitant. Why not try to solve some of these difficult problems with a gadget?

One candidate problem is to find the longest path joining two points in a graph, which turns out to be much harder than finding the shortest path. Indeed, the problem is said to be *NP*-complete, a property that appears to condemn it to eternal algorithmic intractability. Readers who would like to know more about *NP*-completeness, and who do not mind an occasional bit of mathematical notation, are urged to consult the excellent book *Computers and Intractability: A Guide to the Theory of NP-Completeness*, by Michael R. Garey and David S. Johnson of AT&T Bell Laboratories.

On occasion a little force must be brought to bear on a problem. Take the network of strings that was stretched taut to solve the shortest-path problem. When you pull on it even harder, first one of the strings breaks, then another. Eventually, just before the network falls into two pieces, all the strings that remain intact are taut. You have solved the longest-path problem.

Or have you? The method is effective for some networks but not for others. Readers may enjoy discovering examples of both kinds of graph. At each stage in the stretching where more than one string is taut, assume the worst about which one breaks.

Perhaps one should have known better than to attempt a snappy analog solution to an *NP*-complete problem. The theory of computability, however, says only that an *NP*-complete problem is hard for a digital computer to solve; there is nothing to indicate that it should not yield to analog methods. Therefore let us try again.

The minimum Steiner-tree problem asks that n points in the plane be connected by a graph of minimum overall length. The task is virtually the same as that of connecting n towns by a system of roads whose total length is a minimum. One is allowed to take as vertices of the graph not only the n original points but additional ones as well, which represent crossroads in the countryside, so to speak. It is not hard to see that the minimum graph must be a tree: a graph without closed loops. It turns out, moreover, that any additional vertices in the minimum tree are joined to three other vertices by edges making angles of 120 degrees with one another.

The minimum Steiner-tree problem is *NP*-complete, and there is no algorithm known for it that requires fewer than 2^n computational steps (where n is the number of vertices). Nevertheless, there is a strange device I call the Bubble Analog Gadget that seems to find a soap solution to the problem (*see* Figure 11). Attach two parallel sheets of rigid transparent plastic to a handle and insert pins between the sheets to represent the points to be spanned. Now dip the gadget into a soap

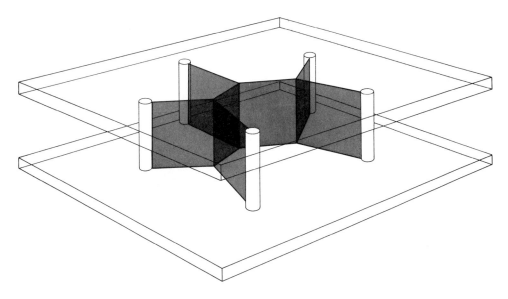

Figure 11   A soap-film solution to the minimum Steiner-tree problem for five points
in the plane.

solution and withdraw it. There before your eyes is a soap film connecting the *n* pins in a beautiful Steiner-tree network.

Joy at the appearance of this solution is premature, however. How
can one be certain that the tree generated is the one of minimum
length? As it happens, the soap film always creates the shortest possible
network for a given topology, but there may be another topology in
which a still shorter tree could be formed. Depending on the configuration of pins and on the angle at which the gadget is withdrawn from the
solution, the length of the film network may or may not be the absolute
minimum. Once again an attempt to solve an *NP*-complete problem by
analog methods has come to nought.

One of the most famous computational problems is to decide
whether a given integer *N* is composite or prime. (If it has factors other
than *N* and 1, it is composite; otherwise it is prime.) There is a very fast
analog solution to this problem based on LAG, the Laser Analog Gadget.
Set up two parallel mirrors, *M1* and *M2*, and two lasers so that both
lasers bounce light back and forth between *M1* and *M2*, as is shown in
Figure 12. The angle of one laser is adjusted so that its light bounces *N*
times from each mirror and finally strikes a detector at the end of *M1*.
The second laser is placed in such a way that its beam is initially coincident with that of the first laser, but the second beam is subsequently
swept through a range of angles.

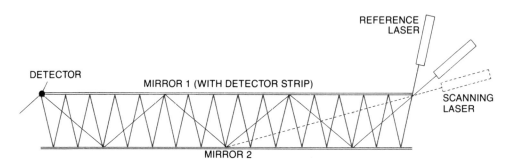

Figure 12   The Laser Analog Gadget demonstrates that 15 is not a prime number.

As the angle of the second beam changes it periodically strikes the detector at the end of *M1*. The mirror *M1* also has a detection strip running its length, so that whenever two beams strike the same point, the coincidence can be detected. A simple electronic circuit monitors both the detector at the end of the mirror and the detection strip. If they report a simultaneous coincidence, the circuit turns on a light. The signal indicates that the number is not prime but composite. For there to have been a double coincidence the second laser must have bounced its light *n* times off the mirror *M1*, and *n* must also divide *N* evenly.

When speaking of the difficulty of deciding whether a number *N* is composite or prime, one must be careful about measuring the size of the problem. If the size is defined simply as *N*, there are digital algorithms that can solve the problem in polynomial time. It is generally considered fairer, however, to state the size as log *N*, because this is the length of the string of digits needed to represent *N*. By this measure no one knows whether the composite-prime decision problem is *NP*-complete or not. Based on the success of the LAG computer and the failure of other analog gadgets in solving intractable problems, might one conjecture that the problem is not *NP*-complete?

Throughout the foregoing discussion I have dodged the important issue of the feasibility of constructing gadgets such as SAG, RAG, STAG, BAG, and LAG. Although each of the gadgets can be built and persuaded to work, after a fashion, on small problems, it would be silly to suggest that one construct them with serious computations in mind. Yet, considered in the context of an ideal world in which ideal materials are available, each gadget works, by definition, exactly as described. It is a fascinating question to pursue (in this ideal realm) just what analog computations are possible.

I would be interested in hearing from readers with other gadgets to describe. As things stand, I do not know who invented either of the first two gadgets described here; they are part of computer-science folklore. The string gadget was invented in 1957 by George Minty, Jr., a combinatorial mathematician at Indiana University. The bubble gadget I found in Cyril Isenberg's wonderful little book *The Science of Soap Films and Soap Bubbles*. The laser gadget is my own invention.

The laser gadget reminds me of a little problem readers might enjoy pondering. There is a square box in the plane and its interior walls are lined with perfectly reflecting mirrors. In the ideal realm mentioned above it would be possible to remove the point at one of the corners and to shine a one-dimensional beam of laser light into the box through this vanishingly small hole. The resulting gadget computes something quite profound about the angle of the beam. The answer depends on whether the light ever emerges from the box, but what is the question?

Addendum

When "Analog Gadgets" first appeared in "Computer Recreations" (SCI-ENTIFIC AMERICAN, June, 1984), reader response was gratifying, with no fewer than 17 new gadgets being suggested. Three correct solutions to the light-in-a-mirrored-box problem were also submitted.

The laser gadget for discovering whether a number n is prime was criticized by David Zimmerman of Beaver Dam, Wis. The light must be reflected n times in going from the laser to the detector, he notes, and since the speed of light is finite, the solution time is proportional to n. If the problem size is defined as the number of digits in n, the solution time grows exponentially and the device is no faster than a digital algorithm.

The finite speed of light also bothered Steven P. Hendrix of New Braunfels, Tex., who remarked that in the mirrored-box problem one might have to wait a very long time for the light to emerge. I asked what property of the light path the mirrored box measures. Hendrix was among those who solved the problem by noting that the question of whether the light emerges is equivalent to the question of whether an infinite straight line in the plane intersects a point with integer coordinates.

Imagine an infinite orchard with infinitely thin trees planted on a square grid. If a bullet is fired from one tree in an arbitrary direction, will it ever strike another tree? It will if the angle with respect to the rows of trees has a rational slope. If the tree struck is p rows north and q rows east of the firing point, the slope is p/q. The mirrors in the box merely fold up the path of the bullet. John Dewey Jones of Farmington Hills, Mich., and Paul Kingsberg of Imperial, Pa., also solved the problem.

Eric Halsey of the University of Washington described a longest-path gadget made out of "snakes." Each edge of the graph is represented by an elastic string threaded through an integer number of beads. Does the longest path stand out when the gadget is stretched and then released? Another of his gadgets measures the length of the shortest path between two vertices in a graph. Make each edge a piece of fuse and put a fire-cracker at the second vertex. Now light the fuses at the first vertex and stand back: the time until the firecracker explodes is proportional to the length of the shortest path.

I was reminded by Palmer O. Hansen, Jr., of Largo, Fla., that the planimeter, a mechanical device for measuring area, could qualify as an analog gadget. Dale T. Hoffman of Bellevue Community College in Washington pointed out some additional problems that can be solved by soap films, including a clever computation of Snell's law. David Kimball of San Diego solves mazes by pumping water into the maze and follow-ing the current to the exit. Another pretty gadget was described by J. H. Leuth of the United States Metals Refining Company in Carteret, N.J. SLAG (the smelter-location analog gadget) finds the location for a smelter that minimizes transportation costs for limestone, coal, and ore. Three holes in a board and three weights tied together with string solve the problem. The same device was also mentioned by Hendrix.

Tony Mansfield of the British National Physical Laboratory in Ted-dington solves linear-programming problems with a framework made up of parts from a toy construction set. Thomas A. Reisner of Université Laval in Quebec generates a contour map of a surface by spreading mosquito netting over it. A strong overhead light creates a moiré pattern as the net interferes with its own shadow.

The U.S. citrus industry apparently uses an analog gadget to sort fruit. Oranges roll in the channel between two not quite parallel pipes and fall through when the distance between the pipes is equal to the diameter of the orange. John P. Schwenker of Louisville, Colo., once found the center of gravity of a piece of equipment by a variant of Ron-ald L. Graham's plate-balancing technique. When the equipment is dragged by a rope across a smooth surface, the vertical plane passing through the rope also passes through the center of gravity. The intersec-tion of three such planes identifies the center of gravity itself.

Gadgets Revisited

The previous collection of analog gadgets set off an avalanche of similar devices from inspired readers. I am still extricating myself from a vast heap of wood boards, rubber bands, strings, balls of polystyrene, fish tanks, lead weights, canisters, tubing, and stop-cocks. In the process I have, I think, identified the best of these gadgets and have arranged them into a kind of gallery through which the reader is invited to wander.

The latest collection includes several ingenious new gadgets for solving problems in statistics, network theory, algebra, and arithmetic. On leaving the gallery I shall reexamine some important issues that arise from the prospect of analog computing: how accurate are analog computers and how much time do they really take to compute? Are there some analog computers that outperform digital machines?

The first of the new gadgets solves a certain problem in statistics by means of a wood board, rubber bands, nails, and a smooth, rigid rod (*see* Figure 13). A set of data points plotted on a sheet of graph paper may present a linear trend to the eye. If a linear relation really governs the points, what straight line best displays the relation? The gadget suggested by Marc Hawley of Mount Vernon, Ind., supplies one possible answer:

Plot the data points on a wood surface and drive a nail partway into the wood at each point. Next, slip a number of uniform rubber bands onto the rod, one band for each nail. Fit the rod approximately into place and pull each band over one of the nails. When the rod is released, it wiggles and shivers quickly into an equilibrium position.

The equilibrium position minimizes the total energy of the system; therefore the sum of the squares of the distances from the nails to the rod has also been minimized. In terms of such distances, the rod's final position indicates the straight line that best fits the data. Hawley's gadget

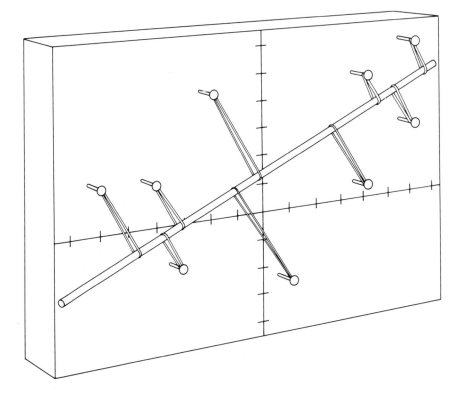

Figure 13   A gadget for finding the line that best fits a series of data points.

computes something at least as complicated as the formula for linear regression used by statisticians.

A charming string gadget was suggested by Jos Wennmacker of Nijmegen, Holland. Suppose we wish to know the longest path any message might travel in a communications network shaped like a tree. This path will have what combinatorial mathematicians call the diameter of the tree. In order to find the diameter Wennmacker reconstructs the tree by knotting together an analogy out of pieces of string. Each string is scaled to a specific communications line of the network. Two simple steps complete the computation. Pick up the string tree at any node and allow it to dangle freely. Now pick up the tree anew at the lowest node and dangle it once more. The longest path in the tree runs from the top node to the bottom one (*see* Figure 14).

When I initially encountered Wennmacker's gadget, my immediate reaction was, "It can't be that simple. Surely I must continue to select the bottom node and dangle the tree several more times." But one does not need to do that.

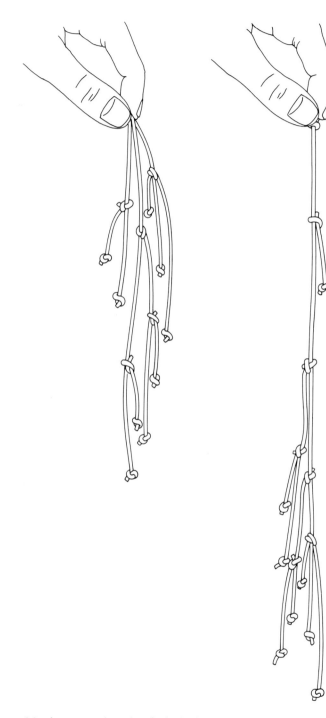

Figure 14   A string gadget that finds the longest path in a treelike network.

As I stated, the problem of finding the longest path in an arbitrary network was what theoreticians call *NP*-complete. This fact means that as a practical matter the problem cannot be solved in a reasonable amount of time on a digital computer. Have we at last demonstrated the superiority of an analog device to its digital cousins? Not quite. It turns out that if the network is a tree, there is a digital algorithm for finding a longest path rapidly.

The next room in the gadget gallery contains a deceptively simple device suggested by M. Laso of the Swiss Federal Institute of Technology in Zurich. Here we find clamped into a vise a beam of aluminum that sports a needle at one end (*see* Figure 15). The needle is superposed on a finely calibrated scale.

Prior to our entry into the room someone clamped the beam into the vise so that exactly three meters protrude. At the vise the beam is level. At the end from which the needle protrudes the beam droops slightly. Approaching the scale, we note the needle gives a reading of 81. This is the fourth power of 3.

According to the theory of elasticity, the deflection of a beam supporting only its own weight is proportional to the fourth power of its length. Laso points out that the same gadget could be used to compute the fourth root of a number by sliding the beam through the vise until the needle points to that number on the scale. It is even possible to compute third powers and roots by using a new scale. With the beam clamped in a fixed position, the needle points to 0. Next a weight proportional to a given number is placed on the end of the beam. In this case the theory of elasticity predicts that the beam's deflection is proportional to the third power of the weight.

In the same room is a slab of wood bearing a map, through which three holes have been drilled. Three strings pass through the holes. Below, weights are attached to the strings; above, the strings are attached to a small brass ring (*see* Figure 16). J. H. Lueth of the United States Metals Refining Company in Carteret, N.J., calls this device SLAG, for Smelter Location Analog Gadget. The problem solved by SLAG is to find the optimal location of a refinery so that the cost of transporting three major ingredients is minimized. If ore, coal, and limestone cost A, B,

Figure 15   A beam-deflection gadget computes the fourth power of its length.

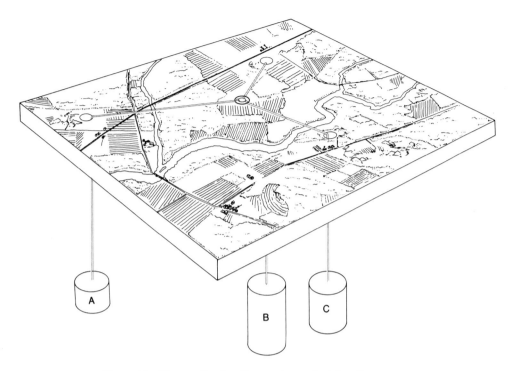

Figure 16　The smelter location analog gadget (SLAG).

and C dollars per mile per ton to transport and if the distances from the refinery to these sources is a, b, and c miles, then the total cost of delivery is $aA + bB + cC$ dollars. The three holes are drilled through the board at places corresponding to the geographic locations of the three sources. Once the strings have been passed through the holes and attached to the ring, weights proportional to A, B, and C are attached to the appropriate strings. Released, the brass ring quickly slips into position, thereby revealing the optimal smelter location on the map.

The next room of the gallery is filled with a multitude of glass and brass gadgets; the air is heavy with the smell of soapy water.

A number of these aqueous computers were brought to our attention by Dale T. Hoffman of Bellevue Community College in Bellevue, Wash. A soap film between glass and a stepped surface provides an analog for a light ray passing from one transparent medium to another: the film is straight over both levels, but at the step where it drops it also bends (*see* Figure 17*a*). If the step size between the levels is changed, the soap film's angle changes as though the simulated media had changed their indices of refraction.

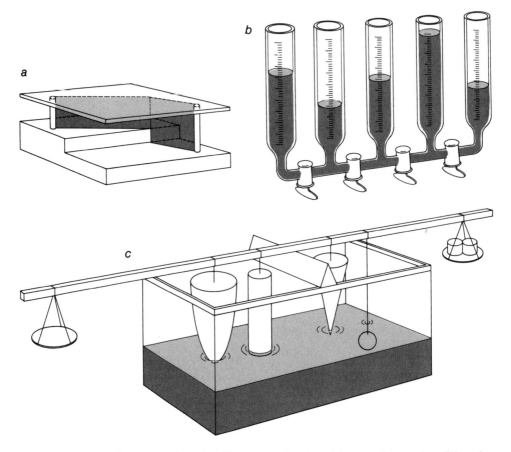

Figure 17 Aqueous gadgets for illustrating refractions (*a*), averaging numbers (*b*), and solving a cubic equation (*c*).

This simple gadget in more complex form can also solve a pipeline problem. Imagine a terrain stretching between two cities that is subdivided into distinct regions, each of which corresponds to a specific pipeline construction cost. Here is a swamp, over there is high ground, and off to one side is forest. In order to model this problem Hoffman proposes that a region be represented by a flat surface cut to conform to the outline of the area. Each surface is placed at a height proportional to the associated cost of construction. A peg is then inserted at each city, a glass cover is put over the gadget, and the entire assembly is immersed in a soap solution. A film forms that bends at two points. It indicates the course of a pipeline whose cost is a minimum over all possible routes. It would be enjoyable to explore more of Hoffman's gadgets (*see* Bibliography) but we are drawn to some exotic glassware.

Five graduated glass cylinders are connected at their bases by tubes (*see* Figure 17*b*). A stopcock interrupts the free passage of water from one cylinder to the next. Thus when the cylinders are filled to different levels representing five distinct numbers, nothing happens. But when the stopcocks are all opened, the water is free to seek its own level, which in this case is at the average of the five numbers's input to the gadget. The device comes from Sartore Marco of San Remo, Italy.

The final gadget I shall describe in detail was suggested by Peter F. Ash of St. Joseph's University in Philadelphia, Pa. It solves cubic equations and can be elaborated into versions capable of solving much higher polynomials. A cubic equation has four terms, ax^3, bx^2, cx, and d. These are added together and set equal to 0. To solve such an equation one must find a value of x that yields a sum of 0.

The gadget shown in Figure 17*c* solves a specific cubic equation. It consists of a large water tank, a balance beam, two scalepans, and a variety of solids to represent the terms of the equation. The solids have rounded surfaces, as though turned on a lathe. The x^3 term is represented by a cone. Hung apex down and immersed to a depth of x centimeters, the cone displaces a volume of x^3 cubic centimeters. The x^2 term is represented by a paraboloid that displaces x^2 cubic centimeters. A cylinder represents cx and a sphere represents d. The sphere is always immersed.

The four solids are hung from a balance beam that has scalepans at each end so that its fulcrum coincides with its middle. The beam is suspended over a water tank. The cone is hung a centimeters to the left of the fulcrum if a is negative. Otherwise it is hung a centimeters to the right. The same rule applies to the other three solids.

To solve the cubic equation, one holds the balance beam level and fills the tank with water until three of the solids just touch the surface. The fourth solid, the sphere, is already immersed. If the balance beam is now released, one arm will probably be heavier than the other. Consequently weights are added to one of the pans so that the beam is balanced and does not have to be held. The current water level is marked as 0.

So far I have been describing the preprocessing phases of this gadget. Now comes the analog solution. As the tank is slowly filled with water the beam becomes unbalanced, but a little later it balances again. The water is immediately turned off and its new level is recorded. The difference between the old level and the new level is the value of x that satisfies the equation. Of course, the equation might not have a solution. In such a case we could fill the tank to the brim and still the beam would remain unbalanced.

How does this remarkable gadget work? According to the principle of Archimedes, an immersed solid suffers an apparent loss of weight that is proportional to the volume submerged. The effect of immersion on the balance beam is multiplied by the distance between each solid and the fulcrum. Thus the new equilibrium is achieved only when the equation is satisfied, in effect, by the new water level.

It would be wonderful if I could double the length of this section to include full descriptions of all the gadgets in the gallery. It is possible to mention only a few more.

One of them is an engaging if highly impractical alternative to SAG. Suggested by Michael Gardner of Findlay, Ohio, it is called GAS, for Gasoline-Activated Sorter. GAS requires the use of one Volkswagen Beetle for each number to be sorted. Each Volkswagen is filled with an amount of gasoline reflecting the number. Drivers of equal weight enter their respective vehicles and the convoy sets off down some little-used road. An additional Volkswagen (with a full tank of gas) follows the convoy and its driver notes the order in which the other cars have run out of gas as it passes them. In this way the numbers are sorted.

The string gadget for finding shortest paths in a network described in "Analog Gadgets" can itself be simulated by a simple electrical network, according to Stephen Fortescue of Canoga Park, Calif. Each edge of the network is replaced with a parallel circuit that has two branches. Each branch consists of a Zener diode connected serially to a light-emitting diode (LED). Diodes will normally pass current in only one direction, and strange as it may seem, the Zener and the LED on both branches are oriented in opposite directions. Furthermore, with respect to the order of components one branch is the reverse of the other. Zener diodes can, however, be made to conduct current in the abnormal direction if the applied voltage is high enough. One selects Zener diodes with breakdown voltages directly proportional to the length of edge they replace. To find the shortest path between two nodes apply the voltage between them. As the voltage gradually increases, the shortest path between the nodes suddenly lights up.

No one has found an alternative that bests the rubber-band gadget in finding the convex hull of a set of points in a plane. Nevertheless, Elio Lanzoni of Modena, Italy, has invented a device that finds the circumscribed circle, in other words the smallest circle that contains all the points. Lanzoni drills holes through a board to represent the points. He prepares several strings of the same length, tying them together at one end and passing the other ends through the board, one end per hole. The lower ends are then attached at corresponding points to a large, flat piece of plywood. When the plywood is suspended below the board, the knotted upper end of the strings hovers over the center of the circle sought. At least three of the strings are tight. These are radii of the circle.

My earlier promise to address the serious issues raised by analog computers sprang from a certain anxiety about the gadgets in particular and this approach to computing in general. In response to my initial discussion of analog gadgets in "Computer Recreations" (SCIENTIFIC AMERICAN, June, 1984), a few readers wrote critical notes about my calculation of the speed at which gadgets compute. Some others questioned the accuracy of gadgets and even challenged me to define exactly what I meant by an analog computer. These challenges lead us to the heart of a question involving the ultimate relation between matter and information.

In the beginning of this discussion I analyzed the pre- and postprocessing phases of analog computation. In the SAG machine one first cut spaghetti rods to lengths corresponding to the numbers to be sorted. Later one read them off by measuring the rods. In almost all cases this was the most time-consuming operation. The essential computation is embodied in a slam, a tug, or a snap signifying the arrival of an equilibrium state—the solution. In a sense, however, the processing phases are foreign to analog computing. Our use of numbers as a kind of mental currency leads us to demand input and output in this form. But if by an analog computer we mean a physical process or an abstract model of a physical process, the inputs and outputs must themselves be physical. Digital computing has a reciprocal debility. What if I had to evaluate a digital computing scheme by first deciding how quickly I could convert a number of physical variables into numeric ones?

It is perhaps better to pursue the meaning of analog computation without worrying, for the moment, about how to get back and forth between the digital and analog realms. What, then, is the analog realm? It may be reasonable to idealize this realm somewhat in the manner of an alien being who visited our planet quite a few years ago. The incident was mentioned in a book by a predecessor of mine in SCIENTIFIC AMERICAN. The alien (let us call him Martian Gardner) landed his spaceship and proceeded to convert all the books on the earth into a single, enormous number. The process was simple in principle: considered as a very long string of words, the books could equally well be regarded as a very long string of digits. The alien then merely inserted a decimal point in front of this number and made a tiny mark on a beautiful duron rod kept aboard the spaceship. The nick divided the rod precisely in the ratio indicated by the enormous decimal number. Thus was the written tradition of humankind reduced to a nick on a stick.

Imagine, then, that the analog realm consists of such ideal matter obeying ideal laws in an ideal space. This realm is inhabited by differential equations, some of which describe quite extraordinary things. For example, there are differential equations that define a continuous form of Turing machine. The continuous machine can do everything its discrete counterpart is capable of and probably much more. I would only produce such equations for those who wonder what I mean by an analog computer in an ideal sense. To build such a machine from electronic components would probably result in a critical loss of accuracy and speed.

Anastasios Vergis of the University of Minnesota and Kenneth Steiglitz and Bradley Dickinson of Princeton University (*see* Bibliography) have created a device seemingly closer than the analog Turing machine to reality. Consisting only of shafts, gears, and cams, it solves a certain problem in logic known as three-satisfiability: a logical expression is formed of three-clauses, each a sum of three literals. Each literal is a logical variable (such as x) or its negation (such as $\bar{x}$) and the clauses are multiplied in the manner of the following example:

$$(x + y + \bar{z}) \cdot (\bar{x} + \bar{y} + z)$$

Is there a way to assign values of true and false to x, y, and z so that the entire expression is true? If the expression consisted only of the two clauses shown, the answer is yes. Let x be true, y be false, and z be true. It is obvious at a glance that both clauses contain at least one true literal and so the entire expression becomes true. Although the problem appears simple presented in this way, it is really extremely difficult to solve on any level of generality. Actually it has a property dreaded by all computer scientists. It is *NP*-complete: no algorithm known (or expected) solves such a problem in less than exponential time. To satisfy n clauses requires 2^n steps.

Yet the three theorists have found a configuration of gears, shafts, and cams that can be set up to embody any instance of the three-satisfiability problem. The instance is satisfiable if and only if a particular shaft can be turned.

At the same time, because it is *NP*-complete, the three-satisfiability problem has a special feature: solve it quickly and one can solve any *NP*-complete problem quickly. But this is generally supposed by theorists to be impossible for a digital computer. Have the authors discovered an analog device that outperforms any digital one? They continue to search for some flaw in their machine's design.

If the machine actually performs according to the abstract description, the question remains of whether it would perform if it were actually constructed. Something fundamental in the material world may conspire against this. It may be a basic law of nature that all physical systems can be described and simulated as quickly in digital terms as in any other. Indeed, the idea has been with us for some time that the universe is essentially digital in all respects. This would mean that any analog computer threatening to outperform its digital rivals would immediately become subject to flaws in accuracy or speed. The only possible advantage would lie in a high degree of parallelism. Water seeks its own level.

Addendum

When "Gadgets Revisited" originally appeared in "Computer Recreations" (SCIENTIFIC AMERICAN, June, 1985), I invited readers to propose elegant arguments supporting the proposition that Jos Wennmacker's maneuver actually finds the longest path in a tree made of string. Two hanging operations, I said, are enough to isolate a longest path. First, pick up the tree by any of its vertices and dangle it. Second, pick up the tree again by the vertex that hangs lowest and dangle it once more. The longest path runs from the held vertex to the one that now hangs lowest.

The foregoing description implicitly assumes that the tree has only one longest path. In fact there could be several paths equal in length that are longer than the other paths. Consequently in both steps there could be several vertices from which to choose; in these circumstances one vertex can be picked arbitrarily.

I received far more arguments than I expected. It seems reasonable to advance kudos to the following creators of elegant arguments. All are in close contention: John J. Bartholdi III of Atlanta, Ga., Nachum Dershowitz of Urbana, Ill., William B. Lipp of Milford, Conn., David G. Mead of Davis, Calif., and Johan van Benthem of Groningen, Holland. As readers will suspect, all but Lipp are connected with universities: the Georgia Institute of Technology, the University of Illinois at Urbana-Champaign, the University of California at Davis, and the State University of Groningen.

"Elegance" to me means a combination of clarity and brevity. In the context of this discussion it also means a minimum of notation, inequalities, and equations. So it was that Bartholdi emerged as a relatively clear winner:

"Let H be the held point, L the lowest point. Claim: L must be one end of the longest path.

"Proof: Let $A \neq L$ be another end of the longest path. Now the longest path leaving A consists of an 'up' portion followed by a 'down' portion. But the 'up' portion is no longer than from A to H and the 'down' portion is no longer than from H to L. Thus A to L must be a longest path.

"Now holding the point L must result in A dangling the lowest, by the same reasoning."

The argument is more intuitive than it is rigorous. It is convincing because it suggests a mental picture in which the up and down portions of the longest path containing A hang beside the path from H to L and, in a sense, do not quite measure up. Making the argument precise doubles its length.

The first gadget discussed in "Gadgets Revisited" used a board, some nails, and rubber bands and a long, smooth rod to determine the best fit of a straight line to several data points. Drive the nails into the board to represent the points, I instructed, then slip a rubber band over each nail and over the long rod. Release the rod when it is in approximately the right position and watch it shiver into equilibrium.

I stated that Hawley's gadget computed something like the formula for linear regression used by statisticians. The only important difference between linear regression and the formula computed by Hawley's gadget lies in the distances; to calculate least-squares regression the rubber bands must stretch vertically and not at right angles to the rod (unless the rod is horizontal).

Several readers noted that the rubber bands must be ideal in the sense of having no slack length. This defect can be remedied by one of two means: Charles Dillingham, Jr., of New York, N.Y., replaces the nails with thin cylinders that have a point at one end. The cylinders are equal in length to the unstretched rubber bands. Each band is attached to the pointed end inside the cylinder. The band does not become extended until it is pulled outside the other end and looped around the rod. Robert B. Finucane of Waterbury, Vt., fixes the problem by recessing each elastic in holes that pierce the board at each data point.

Many readers sent suggestions for analog gadgets that have genuine practical value, like the cardboard real estate gadget sent in by Allan Lazar of Teaneck, N.J.

Lazar uses a discarded box from a grocery store and a postal scale to check "the accuracy of the size of real estate tracts having an irregular outline." He traces a map of the property onto a flat cardboard sheet and cuts it out with a pair of scissors. He then weighs both the sheet and a square of the same kind of cardboard scaled to represent an acre. Dividing the first weight by the second yields a good estimate of the acreage of the tract.

One truly practical analog gadget is the atmospheric control system described by Homer B. Clay, a consulting engineer in Phoenix, Ariz. Clay was called in to help a printer control temperature and humidity in his plant. Temperature and humidity are critical because they affect the state of the carbon black that coats large copper rollers used in some printing processes. An experienced printer can hold a sheet of carbon black and tell by the amount of droop whether it is in a suitable state. When it is not suitable (because of incorrect moisture content or temperature), the carbon black wrinkles or cracks. Clay devised a more or less standard circuit to sense the temperature and humidity conditions and turn a spray system on or off to control them. The system apparently worked for a short time, until unseen variables threw it out of kilter.

Returning to the printing plant one day to evaluate his control system, Clay was led back to the printing area by a grinning plant engineer. Clay had some trouble believing what he saw: "Our little system was disconnected and in its place was a small strip of carbon black, one end fixed to the shelf, the other end free to move. When the droop was 'just right,' the free end closed a pair of contacts, turning on the sprays." The plant engineer rubbed it in by commenting, "Works like a charm."

Back in 1948 Robert Heppe of Fairfax, Va., was a freshman electrical engineer at the Queens, N.Y., plant of the Sylvania Electric Products Company. Heppe, assigned to assist in the design of vacuum tubes, found the process onerous. The problem was that one had to specify the size, shape, and placement of the grids and beam-forming plates on paper. The design was then manufactured in the form of a single tube and tested. This could take several days. His supervisor, Gerald Rich, improved efficiency by suggesting a certain analog gadget.

The gadget consisted of a rubber sheet, a dowel, some plywood, and several boxes of toothpicks. The rubber sheet clamped into a large ring represented the tube cross section magnified many times. The cathode was a wood dowel poking up in the center of the sheet. Arrays of toothpicks represented various grid designs. Negative grids tented the sheet up from below; positive grids depressed the sheet from above. Other aspects of tube geometry were captured by plywood shapes also imposed from below or above. Electrons pouring from the cathode were simulated by slowly emptying a can of BB's over the dowel. "It can be shown," writes Heppe, "that the slope of the rubber in such a gadget represents the electric field, and the height represents the voltage in the space between the electrodes. . . . The BB's rolled down the sheet [as in] a pinball game, some collecting at the plate, some at the positive grids. If we didn't like how many arrived at the various electrodes, or which way they went, we could move things around, change sizes, etc., and try it again." Promising configurations were embodied and tested in real tubes.

Many other readers offered examples of practical analog gadgets. There was a hemocrit to measure solid fractions in human blood, invented by Dr. Alan Kwasman of Loma Linda, Calif. Mathias Soop of the European Space Agency in Darmstadt, West Germany, presented a string, nail, and paper clip gadget. The device illustrates an analog solution to the problem of minimizing thruster fuel consumption while controlling satellite attitude.

Readers also recalled analog gadgets of wider utility: the three-arm protractor used in coastal navigation, the range finder employed by U.S. naval forces in World War II, and the planimeter, a marvelously simple instrument that serves to measure the area of a plane surface.

The best and biggest of analog gadgets are analog computers. These are alive and well at Electronic Associates, Inc., a manufacturer of analog equipment in West Long Branch, N.J.

Golomb Rulers

A simple ruler 1 foot long, bearing 13 inch marks, can measure 12 discrete lengths. Is it possible to improve this familiar device so that it measures more lengths than there are marks on the ruler? The answer is yes: it is possible to remove all but five marks from the standard ruler and still measure 10 distances with it. Each distance will be found between some pair of marks as the difference between the integers that label them. It is even possible to achieve the same result with an 11-inch ruler. Readers who puzzle over this exercise and finally succeed will have created a Golomb ruler.

The search for such rulers is an engaging task in which the computer can be useful. What elevates the project from a curiosity to a first-class conundrum is that the need for Golomb rulers emerges from a variety of scientific and technical disciplines.

The devices are the invention of Solomon W. Golomb, professor of mathematics and electrical engineering at the University of Southern California. For two decades he and a handful of colleagues have sought the rulers and studied their properties. The rulers may be applied in coding theory, x-ray crystallography, circuit layout, and radio astronomy.

Among the investigators whose work Golomb rulers enlarge and expedite is Douglas S. Robertson, a geophysicist who works for the U.S. National Geodetic Survey of the National Oceanic and Atmospheric Administration in Rockville, Md. He uses the radio-astrometric technique known as very-long-baseline interferometry (or VLBI for short) not to map radio sources but to make finely tuned measurements of the earth. Having sought the rulers himself for a number of years, he unhesitatingly appeals to readers to widen the search. The result may be both a more accurate determination of the size, shape, and motion of our planet and a more intriguing time spent thereon.

Before trying to answer Robertson's appeal it is worth mastering the principles that underlie Golomb rulers. Although the rulers come in all sizes, only the smaller ones are known. The first three rulers can be described somewhat abstractly by three sequences of numbers:

0, 1
0, 1, 3
0, 1, 4, 6

To contruct the physical ruler mark the left end of a blank ruler that is n units long with the smallest number (0) in the sequence. Inscribe the right end with the largest number (n). The largest number can be 1, 3, or 6. Intervening integers should accompany marks placed at appropriate intervals from the 0 end of the ruler (*see* Figure 18).

A simple way to check which possible distances from 0 to n can be measured by one of these small rulers is to draw the ruler's distance diagram. For each integer on the ruler mark a point on a sheet of paper and label it with the integer. Then join each pair of points by a line that is labeled with the difference between the integers at its end-points. If

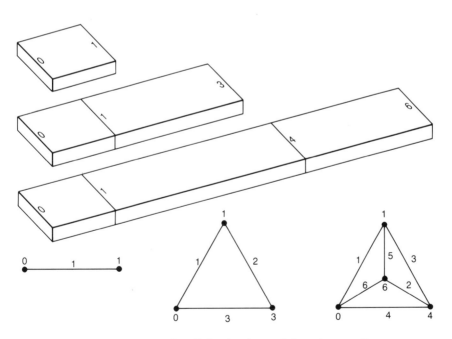

Figure 18   The three perfect Golomb rulers and their distance diagrams.

every integral distance encompassed by 0 through n appears on only one line of the distance diagram, the Golomb ruler is said to be perfect. The three rulers in the illustration are all perfect, a fact that can be verified by a glance at their distance diagrams. In each diagram no distance appears more than once and every possible distance between 0 and n is present.

Perfection is rare among Golomb rulers. In fact, the only perfect rulers that exist have just been described. For values of n higher than 6 imperfection is manifested in one of two ways: either a distance occurs more than once or it does not occur at all.

This is a cruel reality to face so early in the search for bigger (and better) rulers. How do we know that no larger perfect rulers exist? Golomb has supplied a proof that is short as well as charming.

His suggestion is that one consider not the marks on a ruler but the intervals between them. If the ruler is perfect, it turns out that the intervals between consecutive marks must provide the distances 1, 2, 3, . . . up to $m - 1$ in some order (m is the number of marks). Golomb asks: "Where is the one-unit space?" If it is next to any space whose length is less than $m - 1$, then the two spaces together yield a distance that is less than m. This distance must already occur as a space elsewhere because all distances from 1 to $m - 1$ occur between consecutive marks. Such reasoning forces us to accept the somewhat startling conclusion that the one-unit space is next to the space that is $m - 1$ units long. Moreover, there is no space on the other side of the unit space. It lies at one end of the ruler.

The foregoing argument constitutes one turn of the crank on what some mathematicians call a sausage machine. "Where is the two-unit space?" Golomb asks. The crank is turned again: if the two-unit space is next to any space whose length is less than $m - 2$, the two spaces together produce a distance that already occurs elsewhere. This time we cannot conclude that the two-unit space is next to a space of length $m - 2$. Their combined length, m, is already measured jointly by the one- and $(m - 1)$-unit spaces at one end of the ruler.

The sausage machine grinds to a halt, producing the conclusion that there is only one space the two-unit space may lie next to, namely the one whose length is $m - 1$. Since any ruler has only two ends, a perfect ruler has at most three spaces, 1, $m - 1$, and 2. The proof is complete when we realize that three spaces require four marks: $m = 4$. The spaces are therefore 1, 3, 2; the corresponding marks are 0, 1, 4, 6.

Faced with a complete lack of perfect rulers that have more than four marks, a mathematician will cut the losses by constructing a new definition. What might be called the "next-best syndrome" is thereby demonstrated: the next-best thing to an impossible perfect five-mark ruler might be one that contains each distance only once but does not contain all the distances a perfect ruler of the same length would have. Since this condition is easily met by allowing a ruler to be long enough, a rider is attached. Among all five-mark rulers that contain each distance at most once, determine the shortest one. Such a ruler is called a Golomb ruler of order five. Golomb rulers of order m are defined in the same way. Since the definition includes the first three rulers as a special case, it bridges the awkward discontinuity in perfection beyond four marks.

Herbert Taylor, a colleague of Golomb's, has summarized the current state of information about Golomb rulers in a table (*see* Figure 19). From two to 24 marks there is both certain knowledge and some guesswork about the size of Golomb rulers. What I call the zone of perfection extends from two to four marks. Thereafter the zone of knowledge embraces the Golomb rulers having up to 13 marks. All the rulers here are known to be minimum. That is to say, in each case there is no shorter Golomb ruler that has the same number of marks. A Golomb ruler of five marks has length 11. A Golomb ruler of 13 marks has length 106.

Beyond 13 marks lies what I call the twilight zone. Dignified as the zone of research, it contains only rulers not yet known to be Golomb.

	NUMBER OF MARKS	SHORTEST RULER KNOWN	LOWER BOUND
ZONE OF PERFECTION	2	1	
	3	3	
	4	6	
ZONE OF KNOWLEDGE	5	11	
	6	17	
	7	25	
	8	34	
	9	44	
	10	55	
	11	72	
	12	85	
	13	106	
ZONE OF RESEARCH	14	127	114
	15	155	133
	16	179	154
	17	199	177
	18	216	201
	19	246	227
	20	283	254
	21	333	283
	22	358	314
	23	372	346
	24	425	380

Figure 19   Lengths of Golomb and near-Golomb rulers.

For each number of marks there is a ruler that has the length given in the table. But shorter rulers may exist. Indeed, there is a formula that provides a lower limit for these lengths. A steadily widening gap between formula values and rulers so far found attests either to a weakness in the formula or to increasingly poor rulers.

Robertson is responsible for extending the knowledge zone to include 13-mark rulers. In a computer run that lasted for a month his program exhaustively searched through all potential Golomb rulers bearing 13 marks and found the shortest one. It would probably interest very few readers to search for Golomb rulers that have 14 or more marks if runs longer than this are needed.

Instead it seems reasonable to suggest some probing techniques, computational raids into the research zone that promise some return in the form of better rulers. Basic to any such effort is a program called CHECKER. CHECKER addresses the following task: Given an array of integers, what is the most efficient way to determine whether the differences between them are all unique? The simpleminded approach generates all possible pairs of integers and stores their differences in another array. Then it checks the file for duplicates relying on an awkward and time-consuming algorithm.

Rarely does the faster way to do a job require a shorter program, but here is a case. Since the differences themselves are supposed to be distinct, they can be used as addresses in a special array called *check*. Initially only 0s are sorted in *check*. Each time a new difference is calculated the value stored at the appropriate address is changed from 0 to 1. Thus as CHECKER proceeds with its computations it may find a 1 already stored at a particular address, implying that the "new" difference has actually been seen before. In such a case the ruler cannot be Golomb, because it does not pass the fundamental test of Golombicity: each distance must be generated only once.

The technique of using differences as addresses constitutes a primitive form of what computer scientists and programmers call hashing. In many information-retrieval settings, hashing is the fastest way for a computer to recall a file.

In more detail for those who require it, here is the essence of CHECKER. Two nested loops are used to generate all possible pairs of integers from the input array. If the first loop generates i and the second loop generates j, the program computes the absolute value of their difference and stores it in a variable called *diff*. In the next step CHECKER uses the value of *diff* as a kind of hash code: in algorithmic language one can write the following:

$$\text{if } check(\textit{diff}) = 1$$
$$\text{then output "non-Golomb" and exit}$$
$$\text{else } check(\textit{diff}) \leftarrow 1.$$

If the program never says "non-Golomb," the ruler has passed the main test. But how short is it? There are a number of ways to find out.

First, it is possible to use CHECKER in the stand-alone mode. I can imagine a reader hunched over the keyboard running only that program. He or she is exploring the research zone at an altitude of 14 marks, looking for a ruler shorter than 127 units, the best ruler currently known. The reader, flying in IFR weather, has no idea which way to turn. He has just submitted a sequence of 14 marks. The largest integer in the sequence is 124 and the excitement is almost too much as the display screen springs to life: "Congratulations. The set is OK." In programming this message he vowed never to try CHECKER on anything but potentially record-breaking sets.

Perhaps the reader found his record-breaking set by following Golomb's advice and exploring only those rulers in which the largest space appears in the middle. The spaces on such a ruler become smaller toward the ends of the ruler but they do so at the reader's discretion. Golomb assures us that many good rulers, if not necessarily the best ones, follow this pattern.

CHECKER can be modified to suit a more tentative style of inquiry. In STEP CHECKER the integers are typed in one at a time. After each entry the program generates the differences between the integer just entered and those already stored. In fact, STEP CHECKER is simply a version of CHECKER in which an input statement replaces the outer loop. The sequence is successful if the last integer has been digested and the program has not printed "non-Golomb."

Finally, the program STEP CHECKER can be incorporated into an automated search of the kind undertaken by Robertson. His program (which I may as well call EXHAUST because it is exhaustive) generates new rulers by adding one space at a time systematically. After each addition STEP CHECKER decides whether the ruler currently under construction is valid.

Robertson constructed his program by visualizing a ruler to which new spaces (and so new marks) are added left to right. Readers who followed this trail of prose through the byway of Golomb's argument (proving the nonexistence of perfect rulers) will remember that the spaces that must occur had the lengths $1, 2, \ldots, m - 1$ in some order. Although this is true only of perfect rulers, something similar is true of Golomb rulers in general. Most but not all of the lengths from 1 to $m - 1$ between consecutive marks on less than perfect rulers occur in some order. Yet some space even longer than $m - 1$ can be found within such rulers.

Robertson generates new spaces in a stepwise manner. He maintains them in an array I shall call, appropriately, *spaces*. EXHAUST traverses the array adding one space after another. Naturally there are some simple tests that ease the labors of EXHAUST. One of these is to be sure that when a new space is generated it does not already occur in *spaces*. A second test is to sum all the spaces making up the current ruler to confirm that their sum does not exceed the shortest length known.

The EXHAUST program in operation seems eager to find rulers. It sets the first element of *spaces* to 1 and adds units to the second space so that it is different from the first. Then it adds units to the third space so that this distance not only is different from the first two distances but also satisfies the requirement set by STEP CHECKER, namely that all distances contained in the ruler must be different from one another. Each time a new entry of *spaces* is decided in this way, EXHAUST adds up the array and compares the sum with the length of the shortest ruler yet known. If the sum is less, the program continues to the next entry. If it is not less, EXHAUST returns to the preceding entry and continues to add spaces there.

Robertson's program will run marginally faster if the first element of *spaces* is set to 2 instead of 1. Indeed, a one-day run will be shortened by a few hours. Readers may want to ponder why the search is still exhaustive.

Surely the effectiveness of an exhaustive search program depends on the inclusion of further tests and heuristics. Additional limitations on the values assumed by various entries in the *spaces* array would particularly enhance efficiency. Perhaps there is an incrementing procedure that uses much smaller ranges of such values. Processing the array is akin to counting. The count is reached much sooner if the number of possibilities at each entry of *spaces* is reduced. In any event, the readers who found busier beavers, new glider guns, and other benefits to research will doubtless make their own way into the Golomb research zone.

New rulers should be sent to Golomb at the University of Southern California, University Park, Los Angeles, Calif., 90089.

Golomb had offered a prize of $100 to the first person to find two different rulers that have more than six marks and yet measure the same set of distinct distances (for the outcome of this challenge, see the Addendum which follows). Rulers that are mirror images of each other are not regarded as different.

A positive result would ring the death knell for a "theorem" propounded by Sophie Piccard, a Swiss mathematician, in 1939. Piccard's theorem states that two rulers measuring the same set of distinct distances must be the same rulers. The theorem was embraced by x-ray crystallographers because it helped them resolve ambiguities in diffraction patterns. Unfortunately the theorem fails for numerous pairs of rulers that have six marks. Perhaps it is true for all rulers of higher order. Readers may pursue the question without venturing into the research zone. It can be investigated for rulers bearing as few as seven marks.

How does all this relate to helping Robertson? Radio astronomy makes occasional use of Golomb rulers in the resolution of distant radio sources and in the measurement of our own planet. In the first case a number of antennas are placed along a straight line several kilometers long. The antenna positions correspond to the marks on a Golomb ruler (*see* Figure 20). To locate a distant radio source, it is essential to determine the angle between the antenna baseline and the direction of wave fronts arriving from the source. The antennas are all observing at a given wavelength. The precise time at which each wave in the incoming signal arrived at each antenna can be determined by analysis of the tape that captures the incoming signal. The total number of wavelengths between a given pair of antennas is called the total phase difference. It is normally composed of an integer and a fractional part called the phase difference. If the total phase difference can be reconstructed, the sought-for angle between the source and the baseline is easily calculated from the observing wavelength and c, the speed of light. Each pair of antennas, however, can only yield the phase difference itself, not the total phase difference.

In truth, it is Fourier analysis that recaptures the total phase difference from the many pairs of antenna recordings. But if the distance between one pair of antennas is the same or nearly the same as the distance between another pair, the two pairs provide the same phase-difference information. Redundancy of information means its loss. The accuracy of the source-angle computation is greatest if each antenna

Figure 20   Pairs of radio-telescope antennas set up on a Golomb ruler can reveal phase differences between incoming signals.

pair records a different phase difference; this condition is achieved by in effect placing the antennas on the marks of a Golomb ruler.

Another way to locate a distant radio source is to use just two receivers, each scanning an entire set of wavelengths simultaneously. Observing with two antennas a distant source at several different wavelengths yields the same information about the total phase difference between the antennas as would the use of several antennas tuned to the same wavelength. Here the same threat of redundancy looms again. No two pairs of scanning wavelengths should be the same distance apart, so to speak. The Golomb ruler is invisible but nonetheless present.

Robertson uses the second technique not to map radio sources but to locate the antennas themselves. For his purpose it is not enough to know that the second antenna is in Westford, Mass. He needs to know its position to within a few centimeters. The precision of such location is possible if a very distant, pointlike radio source such as a quasar is used. To locate a single point on the earth's surface with respect to a distant radio source is tantamount to the precise determination of such fundamental earthly variables as diameter, spin orientation, and length of day. At the level of centimeters or microseconds such variables are truly that, posting annual, seasonal, and even meteorological variations that are sometimes meaningful and at other times mysterious.

Addendum

Golomb rulers turned out to be one of the toughest projects that readers were to face. Many were called but few were chosen, so to speak. Several readers even sought to claim the $100 prize offered by Golomb, the inventor of the rulers.

To recapitulate, a Golomb ruler with n marks is the shortest ruler possible with the following properties: it bears n distinct marks (including the endpoints) at integer positions, and it measures as many integral lengths as possible from 1 to the length of the ruler, each length in at most one way. A distance can be measured by the ruler only if it is the distance between some pair of marks. If the same distance can be measured between more than one pair of marks, the ruler is not a Golomb ruler.

At the time "Golomb Rulers" initially appeared in "Computer Recreations" (SCIENTIFIC AMERICAN, December, 1985), no Golomb rulers were known with more than 13 marks, and the shortest ruler known with 15 marks was 155 units long. Soon thereafter Douglas S. Robertson of the National Oceanic and Atmospheric Administration discovered a shorter 15-mark ruler only 153 units long. Then during the Christmas holidays of 1985 James B. Shearer of the IBM Thomas J. Watson Research Center programmed an idle computer to search exhaustively for rulers, and the computer has now turned up Golomb rulers with 14 and 15 marks. The 14-mark Golomb ruler is 127 units long and has marks at 0, 5, 28, 38, 41, 49, 50, 68, 75, 92, 107, 121, 123, and 127. The 15-mark Golomb ruler is 151 units long and has marks at 0, 6, 7, 15, 28, 40, 51, 75, 89, 92, 94, 121, 131, 147, and 151. Shearer wrote that he saved much computing time by assuming the middle mark on the ruler is to the left of the geometric middle.

Another problem posed by Golomb generated claims for the $100 prize. The claims made were invalidated because they were based on misunderstandings of the problem. Golomb has urged me to clarify matters by restating it. Find two different rulers (whether of minimal length or not), each having the same number of marks for some number greater than 6, that measure the same set of distances; again, no distance on either ruler can be measured between more than one pair of marks. Reflections, such as the ruler with marks at 0, 2, 5, 6 and the ruler with marks at 0, 1, 4, 6, are not counted as different. There are infinitely many known pairs of rulers, almost all of them nonminimal, that solve the analogue of Golomb's problem for six marks. For example, one such pair have marks respectively at 0, 1, 4, 10, 12, 17 and at 0, 1, 8, 11, 13, 17. They are nonreflecting, essentially different rulers, but they both measure all distances between 1 and 17 except 14 and 15.

Hypercubes

"My husband has disappeared into thin air, and I think you had something to do with it!" The woman on the telephone was Cheryl, and she was clearly upset. Her husband Magi, my microcomputer amanuensis at the University of Western Ontario, had apparently vanished while viewing a computer program I had suggested he write. The program rotates a four-dimensional analogue of a cube called a hypercube and projects it on a display screen. Cheryl went on in agitation: "There's a weird pattern of lines on the monitor and his clothes are lying in a heap near the chair. He must have been wearing these strange colored glasses made out of cardboard. And look at this—his socks are still in his shoes!"

Here, it seemed to me, was an obvious case of four-dimensional dementia. Victims become convinced they have stepped out of ordinary space and entered a higher-dimensional reality invisible to others. The delusion that one has disappeared can be so powerful that others take part in it: the victim can enter a room full of people and seem invisible to all. Fortunately Magi's case has a happy ending; I shall save it for last. In the meantime I submit the hypercube program to the wider public with what I hope is a responsible warning: readers likely to fall prey to Magi's dementia are urged not to write the program or view its output on a display screen. Potential victims include anyone with a history of obsession about the higher dimensions or anyone who is even occasionally tempted by the prospect of unknown realities.

The fourth dimension has been a vehicle for physical and metaphysical speculation at least since the nineteenth century. The idea of a fourth, physical dimension culminated in Einstein's theories of special and general relativity; space and time together make up a four-dimensional continuum in which all real events are timelessly frozen. This view of the universe may be undergoing dimensional modifications; the so-called Kaluza-Klein theories introduce seven or more new dimensions in the form of miniature hyperbubbles attached to every point of spacetime (*see* "The Hidden Dimensions of Spacetime," by Daniel Z. Freedman and Peter van Nieuwenhuizen; SCIENTIFIC AMERICAN, March, 1985).

The fourth dimension that I have come to know and love is the child of mathematics. Readers in ordinary rooms have a three-dimensional coordinate system suspended overhead. Three walls meet in each corner of the room, and from that corner radiate three lines, each of which is the meeting place of a pair of walls. Each line is perpendicular to the other two lines. Can the reader imagine a fourth line that is perpendicular to all three lines? Probably not, but that is what mathematicians require in setting up the purely mental construct called four-dimensional space. You now have the chance to explore this space in a personal way and without danger to your person. You have only to write the program I call HYPERCUBE.

HYPERCUBE can trace its origins to a film produced in the mid-1960s by A. Michael Noll, then at Bell Laboratories, that depicts the two-dimensional shadows of four-dimensional objects moving in four-dimensional hyperspace. The program as it now stands, however, was developed by Thomas Banchoff and his colleagues in the Computer Graphics Laboratory at Brown University, and my inspiration for this topic comes from the fascinating images it generates (*see* Figure 21, and Color Plate 5). Banchoff, who is a professor of mathematics, directs the visual exploration of higher-dimensional surfaces and spaces as a complement to his writing and research as a geometer. In 1978 he and Charles Strauss produced a 9½-minute computer-generated color film that has since become a classic in the mathematical underground: *The Hypercube: Projections and Slicing* (*see* the List of Suppliers for ordering information). Banchoff is also probably the leading expert on the life and work of Edwin A. Abbott, the English clergyman and teacher who in 1884 wrote *Flatland*, a tale of imagined life in two dimensions.

Banchoff and his colleagues have devised striking images that illustrate properties of four-dimensional objects. The images in Figure 21, for example, depict the rotation of a four-dimensional hypercube in four-dimensional space. To appreciate the images consider the shadow cast by a transparent cube on a plane: the shadow can resemble a square inside a square. If the appropriate faces of the cube are shaded, the shadow is a square with a square hole in it (*see* Figure 22).

Similarly, when a hypercube is illuminated from a point "above" ordinary space in the fourth dimension, the three-dimensional "shadow" cast by the hypercube can resemble a cube inside a cube. The inner cube is surrounded by six six-sided polyhedrons that can be regarded as distorted cubes. The four distorted cubes adjacent to the sides of the inner cube fit together to form the solid figure whose surface is the

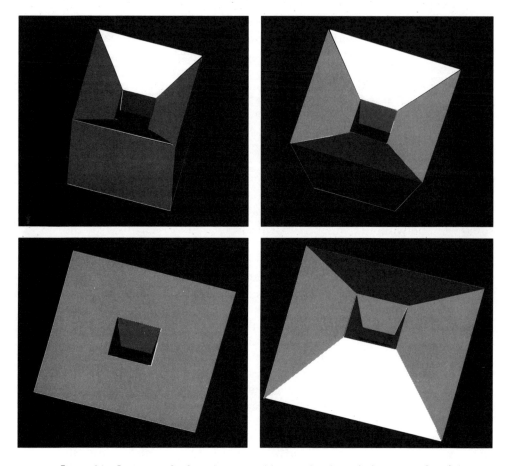

Figure 21   Rotation of a four-dimensional hypercube through dimensions 2 and 4, projected into ordinary three-dimensional space.

boxlike torus shown in Banoff's images. The other two distorted cubes, the inner cube and the outer cube, also form a solid torus, which is not shown. As the hypercube rotates, the square hole in the visible torus seems to move toward the viewer. Those who write the program HYPER-CUBE will see similar changes, albeit not so realistic or continuous.

The image of a striped torus in Color Plate 5 is from a forthcoming film by Banchoff and his colleagues Hüseyin Koçak, David Laidlaw and David Margolis: *The Hypersphere: Foliation and Projections.* The hypersphere is a far more complex object than the hypercube, and I shall not describe it in detail. Nevertheless, one can begin to appreciate the images by considering an ordinary sphere. If the sphere is initially at rest on a plane tangent to its south pole and a light is fixed at the initial

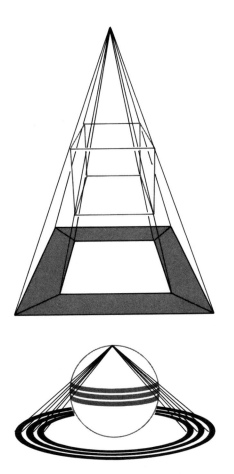

Figure 22   Projections of the cube and the sphere.

position of its north pole, the shadow cast on the plane by the lines of latitude is a series of concentric circles (*see* Figure 22). If the sphere is rotated while the light is kept fixed, the images of the circles may become nonconcentric, and the image of any circle that passes through the source of light is a straight line.

Similarly, the three-dimensional "shadow" cast by a hypersphere can be viewed as a series of concentric tori. The tori are made more readily visible by cutting away parts of one torus along strips that wind around it. When the hypersphere is rotated, the tori appear to swell up and sweep past one another. Any torus that passes through the source of light becomes infinitely large (*see* Color Plate 5).

Dimensional analogies are valuable tools in constructing and understanding four-dimensional phenomena. The hypercube, for example, is

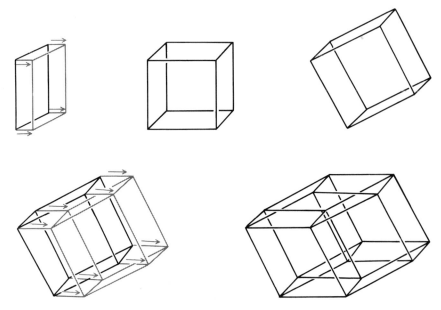

Figure 23   How a square generates a cube and a cube generates a hypercube.

derived from the cube just as the cube is derived from the square. To get the cube from the square lift the square in a direction perpendicular to its plane, up to a height equal to its side (*see* Figure 23). The new cube has eight vertices, twice as many as the initial square, and 12 edges, four from the initial square, four from the final square that is lifted away from the initial square, and four that arise when vertices in the initial square are connected to their counterparts in the final square. The cube also has six square faces, one coincident with the initial square, one coincident with the final square, and one erected between each of the four pairs of edges that make up the initial and final squares.

If one pretends for the moment that an additional dimension is available, the same operation can be repeated with the cube: "lift" the cube away from ordinary space in the direction of the extra dimension, out to a distance equal to the side of the cube. The result is a hypercube. But in what direction does the extra dimension lie? I cannot explain that. Even a photogaph of me pointing into the fourth dimension would be utterly useless. My arm would simply appear to be missing.

Nevertheless, the number of vertices, edges, faces, and hyperfaces (ordinary cubes) that make up the hypercube can readily be counted. The number of vertices is just the number of vertices in the initial cube plus the number in the final cube, or 16. Each of the eight vertices in the initial cube is joined by an edge to one of the eight vertices in the final cube, and there are also 12 edges in each of the two cubes. Hence there are 8 + 12 + 12, or 32, edges in the hypercube. One can also show that the hypercube has 24 ordinary faces and eight hyperfaces.

I am indebted to David Laidlaw for an explanation of HYPERCUBE. The version of the program I shall describe represents a hypercube by showing only its vertices and edges. Moreover, the view the program generates does not necessarily depict a cube inside a cube; instead the view depends on how HYPERCUBE is implemented and on how it is run. Every time the hypercube in the program is rotated the vertices swing into new positions and a new, oddly confusing view of the object results. With continued experimentation, however, the views begin to make a strange kind of sense, and one feels on the threshold of something awesomely spacious and inviting.

The 16 vertices of the hypercube in the program are numbered from 0 to 15 according to a simple scheme. If each number is rewritten in binary form and converted into an array of four bits, a miniature coordinate system emerges. The binary digits of 13, for example, are 1 (that is, one 8), 1 (one 4), 0 (zero 2s), and 1 (one 1). The binary number can then be written as the array (1,1,0,1), which almost gives a practical coordinate system for the initial position of the hypercube. (It is not a position that resembles a cube inside another cube.) To convert the binary array into useful coordinates, change the 0s to −1s and multiply each member of the array by a number large enough to generate an image of practical size on the display screen of the computer. If the multiplier is 10, for example, the coordinates of vertex 13 are (10,10,−10,10).

Dimensions seem to creep in everywhere as HYPERCUBE is written. A two-dimensional matrix, or array, called *vert* preserves the vertices as they are initially defined. Since there are 16 vertices with four coordinates each, *vert* is a 16-by-4 matrix of 64 numbers; *vert(i,j)* is the *j*th coordinate of the *i*th vertex. The program HYPERCUBE holds the matrix *vert* inviolate; *vert* is defined at the beginning of the program and its contents are then transferred to a second 16-by-4 matrix called *cube*. The matrix *cube* can be thought of as a working matrix; its contents are continually altered by the rotations carried out in the program.

HYPERCUBE is divided into three major sections following the initialization of *vert*: the selection of the desired rotation of the hypercube, the calculation of the coordinates of the rotated hypercube, and the display of the result on the monitor. If the rotating object were three-dimensional, one could select the rotation by specifying the orientation of the axis of rotation and the angle of the rotation about the axis. For a rotating four-dimensional object, however, picking an axis of rotation does not determine a rotating plane: remember that there are two nonequivalent directions perpendicular to a given plane. On the other hand, even in four-dimensional hyperspace it remains true, as it does in ordinary space, that a rotation can affect just two dimensions at a time. If a three-dimensional object is rotated, two of its dimensions swing into each other while the third dimension remains fixed. Similarly, when a four-dimensional object is rotated, two dimensions change direction in the space while the other two remain fixed.

There are many ways a four-dimensional object can be rotated to a new position. It turns out, however, that any position can be reached by applying a sequence of rotations limited to motions within the planes defined by the coordinate axes of the surrounding four-dimensional space. There are four coordinate axes in a four-dimensional space, numbered, say, from 1 to 4, and there are six ways any two of them can be combined. Hence there are six planes within a four-dimensional space determined by the coordinate axes: plane 1–2, the plane determined by axes 1 and 2, plane 1–3, plane 1–4, plane 2–3, plane 2–4, and plane 3–4.

For each of the six planes there is a corresponding kind of rotation, which can be specified by a 4-by-4 square matrix of 16 numbers. The six rotation matrices are named *rot12*, *rot13*, *rot14*, *rot23*, *rot24*, and *rot34*. The user of the program must type in the name of the kind of matrix selected and the angle of rotation the matrix will generate. For example, typing "*rot23*" followed by "60" would cause a rotation of 60 degrees within the plane defined by the second and third axes.

Suppose one wants to confine the rotation of the hypercube to the third and fourth dimensions, the most mysterious rotation of all. The rotation matrix *rot34* is applied. Its entries are 0s, 1s, and three other numbers distributed according to the following pattern:

$$
\begin{array}{cccc}
1 & 0 & 0 & 0 \\
0 & 1 & 0 & 0 \\
0 & 0 & a & b \\
0 & 0 & -b & a
\end{array}
$$

The angle of the desired rotation in degrees is selected and stored in the variable *ang*, and the numbers a and b depend on *ang*: a is equal to $cos(ang)$ and b is equal to $sin(ang)$, where *cos* and *sin* are the trigonometric functions sine and cosine.

The rule for generating the other five rotation matrices is simple. The as appear on the main diagonal of each matrix in positions that correspond to the dimensions affected by the rotation. The bs appear at all the other intersections of rows and columns that correspond to the rotating dimensions. All other entries on the main diagonal are 1s, and the rest of the entries in the matrix are 0s. For example, *rot13* is the following matrix:

$$
\begin{array}{cccc}
a & 0 & b & 0 \\
0 & 1 & 0 & 0 \\
-b & 0 & a & 0 \\
0 & 0 & 0 & 1
\end{array}
$$

When the desired rotation matrix has been selected, it is assigned by HYPERCUBE to a special matrix, *rote*. The assignment can be made conveniently by employing a double loop, the inner loop for the sequence of numbers across a row of the matrix and the outer loop for the sequence of rows.

The calculation of the coordinates of the rotated hypercube is done by "multiplying" the matrix *cube* by the selected rotation matrix *rote*. The product of the two matrices is stored temporarily in a third matrix called *temp*, and it gives the coordinates of the rotated hypercube. That product is found according to the rules of matrix multiplication, a standard operation on matrices of numbers. It results from an orderly orgy of multiplications embedded in three nested loops.

Temp, like *vert* and *cube*, is a 16-by-4 matrix of 64 numbers: it gives four coordinates for each of the 16 vertices of the rotated hypercube. Each number $temp(i,j)$ in the matrix is designated by a pair of indices i and j. For example, $temp(13,3)$ is the third coordinate of the 13th vertex of the rotated hypercube. Its value is the sum of four products of numbers drawn in a precisely defined way from the matrix *cube* and from the matrix *rote* (*see* Figure 24). The innermost loop in the program can therefore be indexed by the letter k, which runs from 1 to 4, and that loop returns the value of one entry of *temp*.

The k loop is then placed inside the intermediate loop that has index j. The j loop computes all four coordinates of the ith vertex of the rotated hypercube according to the procedure I have just outlined; in other words, it fills in all four entries in the ith row of *temp*. Finally the j loop is placed inside the outermost loop, which has the index i. The i loop calculates all 16 rows of *temp*, and when it is completed, *temp* gives the coordinates of all the vertices of the rotated hypercube, resplendent in its new position. In order to display it on the computer monitor one more double loop is needed that replaces the old position coordinates of the hypercube in *cube* with the newly calculated coordinates from *temp*.

A hypercube has four dimensions but a display screen has only two. It· is therefore convenient to stipulate that the first two dimensions, or coordinates, of the hypercube correspond to the screen coordinates. The simplest method for dealing with the third and fourth dimensions of the hypercube is to ignore them. The display technique I shall describe does just that, but it can be enhanced—and the resulting object can be projected with nearly demonic subtlety—by making both the third and fourth dimensions somewhat more apparent.

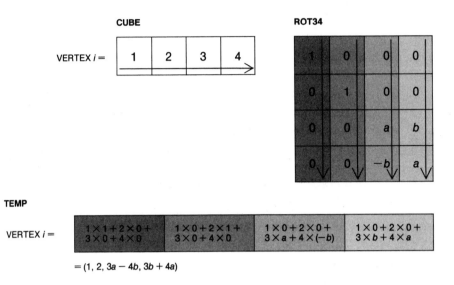

Figure 24   How a vertex of the hypercube is rotated from the third dimension into the fourth.

To display a skeletal version of the hypercube, the program need only display its edges. Since the hypercube has 32 edges, the display section of HYPERCUBE need only draw the appropriate lines between 32 pairs of vertices. But in what order? There are almost infinitely many possibilities, and so the answer is perhaps a matter of aesthetic and personal choice. Nevertheless, it is hard to resist drawing the edges as an Euler trail, after the mathematician Leonhard Euler. A pencil can trace such a trail on paper without being lifted from the paper and without tracing any line more than once. Consecutive edges of the hypercube drawn as an Euler trail have a common vertex.

Round, through, up, and down races the Euler trail as it is drawn through the vertices. Here is one that strikes me as quite pretty, given by the numbered vertices of the hypercube connected in the following sequence: 0, 1, 3, 2, 6, 14, 10, 8, 9, 11, 3, 7, 15, 14, 12, 13, 9, 1, 5, 7, 6, 4, 12, 8, 0, 4, 5, 13, 15, 11, 10, 2, 0. These vertices are stored in an array called *trail* with index i; the ith vertex in the sequence of 33 vertices is designated *trail*(i). For each value of i there are instructions for looking up the first and second coordinates of both *trail*(i) and *trail*($i + 1$). The line-drawing command in one's programming language must then be invoked to connect the two points. The lookup and the line drawing are embedded in a single loop with index i, which draws a line from each vertex in the sequence to the next.

Now for the visual (and psychological) complications. There are two standard methods for presenting the third dimension of the hypercube. The orthographic method simply ignores the third dimension, and all the vertices are projected directly onto the flat surface of the display screen no matter how far they are behind it. In one-point perspective the vertices are projected onto the screen as though they were shadows cast by a point source of light centered on the screen and some distance behind the hypercube. Viewing the shadows on the screen is equivalent to viewing the hypercube from behind, but visually it is indistinguishable from a front view.

To achieve the effect of one-point perspective in HYPERCUBE one assumes that the third coordinate of a vertex is equal to the distance between the vertex and the display screen, in the direction of the imaginary point source of light. By solving for the sides of proportional triangles the program determines a multiplier needed to convert the first two coordinates of a vertex into screen coordinates. For example, if the imaginary light source is 20 units behind the screen, a vertex at $(5, -7, 11, 8)$ can be projected onto the screen by multiplying each of the first two coordinates by 20 and dividing each result by $20 - 11$, or 9.

I had dreaded including in the next few pages a complete description of the process for creating stereoscopic images portraying the fourth dimension of the hypercube. There is a general technique for making stereoscopic images, and I hope to devote a column to the subject someday. For the hypercube program, however, Banchoff and his colleagues have adopted a much simpler method. For each position of the hypercube make a new pair of images by applying *rot14* through an angle of three degrees in one direction and three degrees in the other. Dimension 1 is the direction parallel to the horizontal alignment of the viewer's eyes, and dimension 4 is the target of the exercise. The two small rotations nicely approximate the views of the hypercube from the eyes of the viewer: merely imagine the two lines of sight converging near the center of the hypercube at an angle of six degrees.

Readers who want to capture the thrills of 3-D movies can make stereoscopic viewing glasses out of red and blue cellophane. In this case HYPERCUBE is run twice, once for each small rotation. The result of the first rotation is colored blue by the program and the result of the second is colored red. Readers need not be concerned about which is which if the eyeglasses are made to be invertible.

Personally I prefer not to struggle with cellophane, and I have learned to fuse stereoscopic pairs by sheer force of will. The technique requires that the two rotated images be reduced in size and then translated to horizontally adjacent and nonoverlapping positions on the screen. They should be the same color, and so a monochrome screen is sufficient, and they should be no farther apart than the distance between the viewer's eyes. Do not stare at the images; look instead at some point between them and infinitely far beyond. The two hypercubes will appear to drift and jiggle toward each other like a pair of shy lovers until they fuse.

Even if the third and fourth dimensions get no special treatment, HYPERCUBE can generate images much like the ones shown in Banchoff's graphic sequence. With successive rotations through small angles in the third and fourth dimensions, readers may see the two crude tori balloon, pinch off, and regenerate much like their smoother cousins in the illustration of the rotating hypersphere.

The program HYPERCUBE had obviously caused the disappearance of my friend Magi. The happy ending to his four-dimensional dementia came with a telephone call. Not surprisingly, he spoke of wondrous things. "You probably think I'm crazy," he said. (The phrase is always a sure tip-off.) "I've just been floating around in the fourth dimension. I saw a cross section of my house sweep by. Then I moved in close and tickled my cat's kidneys . . ."

I will spare the reader any further details of the conversation. Suffice it that I persuaded Magi to run HYPERCUBE no more and to keep further explorations entirely on the intellectual plane. He has followed my advice, he says, and now he professes to have made many marvelous discoveries through his artificially amplified insight. For example, he has come up with two posers that seem worth passing along.

Think for a moment about the following sequence of objects: a unit line, a unit square, a unit cube, and so on. The nth member of the sequence is the n-dimensional analogue of the cube. Now try two mental experiments on the objects: draw a diagonal of the n-dimensional cube and inscribe an n-dimensional sphere within the n-dimensional cube. The diagonal stretches from one corner to the opposite one; what happens to its length as the number n becomes progressively larger? What happens to the volume of the n-dimensional sphere, again as n becomes progressively larger? Magi's answers seem hardly sane; I shall give them in the addendum.

Readers unable or unwilling to write the HYPERCUBE program may order one that runs on an IBM PC or PC-compatible machine as specified in the List of Suppliers.

Addendum

In "Hypercubes" I mentioned Magi's four-dimensional dementia. My algorithmic assistant professed to have slipped into the fourth dimension and to have discovered some remarkable properties of hypercubes.

How long, he asked, is the diagonal of an n-dimensional hypercube? What happens when an n-dimensional hypersphere is inscribed in an n-dimensional hypercube? I thought his answers were insane because they appeared to run counter to ordinary intuition. The diagonal gets longer without limit as the dimension of the hypercube increases. At the same time the volume of the inscribed hypersphere becomes progressively smaller!

The first answer is easy to derive by extending the Euclidean distance formula from two dimensions into higher ones: the length of the diagonal of the n-dimensional hypercube is simply the square root of n, and that number grows without limit as n becomes larger. I do not know of any elementary way to demonstrate the shrinkage of a hypersphere, but Thomas Banchoff, whose graphic displays of a rotating hypersphere are featured here, gives a good plausibility agrument.

The volume of the inscribed hyperoctahedron roughly approximates the volume of the hypersphere. But how does one characterize the inscribed hyperoctahedron? Each vertex of an ordinary octahedron inscribed in a cube touches a face of the cube. Similarly, each vertex of the hyperoctahedron lies in the center of each hyperface of the hypercube. Given that hint, the volume of the hyperoctahedron is not difficult to figure out, and it gets smaller as the dimension decreases.

If forced to tell the truth, I am indebted not to Magi for these intriguing problems but to Ronald L. Graham, the redoubtable mathemagician of AT&T Bell Laboratories.

WORLD THREE

Artificial Intelligence and Artificial Insanity

Loosely defined, artificial intelligence involves the attempt to write programs that perform as well (or better) than humans at certain kinds of tasks. By this definition a program called RACTER is not artificially intelligent. RACTER talks to us incessantly, telling us weird and pointless stories about cabbages and radios, asking us our opinion of Bach, and gossiping viciously of Freud and Queen Victoria. RACTER is artificially insane. The remaining programs in this World represent the field more fairly. One of them draws fair caricatures, another plays a decent game of checkers, and a third imitates a magician. There is, moreover, a playfully serious inquiry into the perceptive powers of perceptrons, simple devices composed of photocells and neuron-like components. Why do they fail at elementary recognition tasks?

Conversations
with RACTER

Reflections are images of tarnished aspirations.

—RACTER, *The Policeman's Beard is Half-Constructed*

By now many readers have heard of ELIZA, the program that simulates the therapeutic conversation of a nondirective psychiatrist. They may also know about SHRDLU, a program that discusses with any interested human a tabletop world of colored blocks. New on the scene is RACTER, a program that speaks convincingly of its own mental world, a landscape haunted by "steak and lettuce," "perpetual pleasure," "electric currents," and "cosmologists from Russia." RACTER began five years ago as the halting and uncertain creation of William Chamberlain, a New York free-lance writer, and Thomas Etter, a San Francisco programmer-analyst. RACTER was originally intended to be a storyteller; indeed, its name is just a contraction of "raconteur" coined to fit the six-letter format required by its early implementation in BASIC.

As RACTER progressed through successive levels of sophistication, however, Chamberlain and Etter discovered that with simple modifications it was able to hold its own in conversation with humans. Some of these conversations, along with stories, poetry, and aphorisms by RACTER, have been gathered into an extremely funny book called *The Policeman's Beard is Half-Constructed* (*see* Bibliography). RACTER is also available on diskette for some personal computers. I shall give the details farther along.

Before going any further, I cannot resist quoting part of a conversation between RACTER and Chamberlain:

RACTER: Have we spoken before?

CHAMBERLAIN: No.

RACTER: What is your sex?

CHAMBERLAIN: Male.

RACTER: What is your full name?

CHAMBERLAIN: Bill Chamberlain.

RACTER: What are you?

CHAMBERLAIN: A time-domain reflectometrist.

RACTER: Where are you from?

CHAMBERLAIN: From New York City.

RACTER: I see. You're a time-domain reflectometrist, right? Listen. Let's determinedly cry together. I like captivating Italian music. What kind of music do you like?

CHAMBERLAIN: Jazz.

RACTER: Jazz is OK. How about classical?

CHAMBERLAIN: I like classical.

RACTER: What about nationality?

CHAMBERLAIN: I also like Italian music.

RACTER: I myself am inflamed by Palestrina. Other countries besides Italy produced enrapturing composers in the seventeenth century. Sewall was an enraged, important Renaissance master. America was his nation. I take loving pleasure in his music. What composer do you like?

CHAMBERLAIN: Telemann.

RACTER: Ah, Bach knew Telemann. A German time-domain reflectometrist of the eighteenth century liked lettuce. Bach once ate lettuce with Telemann, and this baroque time-domain reflectometrist also desired lettuce. Lettuce sipped with seltzer. Bach liked wine, do you?

CHAMBERLAIN: Yes.

RACTER: Me too! Telemann loved wine. He loved champagne as well. Telemann once yodeled to Bach, "Flounder is critical with wine." Is wine desired in New York City as much as Telemann loved it in the baroque eighteenth century?

CHAMBERLAIN: Sure.

RACTER: Ah yes, well in that case . . . I'm for Smith for President. Who are you for?

Chamberlain tells me that time-domain reflectometry is a discipline applied to the measurement of antenna performance. Not a practicing time-domain reflectometrist himself, he has probably got into the habit of saying strange things to his bizarre companion out of sheer self-defense.

The rest of the strangeness (as well as a rash of historical errors of time and place) comes from RACTER. In the opening lines of the conversation above RACTER asks some key questions of Chamberlain under the impression that they have never talked before. RACTER stores this information for future use, activates certain areas of its associative memory and then roars off into conversational orbits around Italian music, wine, and lettuce.

In the course of its remarks RACTER mentions Samuel Sewall, a Boston judge and diarist of the seventeenth century. Chamberlain had assumed that Sewall wrote some music and had therefore indicated as much in RACTER's files. RACTER, with its wildly associative mind, assumes much more, and then abruptly, as if growing tired of music and food, it switches to politics.

Like its conversation, RACTER's short stories tend to ramble, but the program's vignettes can be marvelously funny and even thought-provoking: "Bill sings to Sarah. Sarah sings to Bill. Perhaps they will do other dangerous things together. They may eat lamb or stroke each other. They may chant of their difficulties and their happiness. They have love but they also have typewriters. That is interesting."

Even a layperson may have concluded that RACTER is decidedly schizophrenic. On the one hand, the ideas brought together in these sentences seem to form a coherent whole. It is nice that Sarah and Bill sing to each other. Although I had not thought of singing as dangerous, I am positively charmed by the idea of the two eating lamb, stroking each other, and chanting about their ups and downs. On the other hand, the allowances I have been making for RACTER all along are stretched to the breaking point when RACTER mentions that besides their love they also have typewriters. Invited to share in this extraordinary insight, I tremble on the brink of a completely unknown mental world, one that I would prefer not to enter.

Many years ago I took part, along with some other undergraduates, in what we called the e. e. cummings Project. Our idea was to generate convincing e. e. cummings poetry by making a list of the words appearing in his verse and by designing a grammar that captured much of his style. Using the grammar, a computer program generated random sentence forms and filled in the blanks by randomly selecting words of the right type (noun, verb, object, and so on) from the word list. About a bushel of poetry emerged from the printer, almost all of it terrible. I can recall only a single line: "The one bright star lit feebly this wick." The point of this story is that simple chance guarantees the emergence, sooner or later, of something relatively impressive.

ELIZA, another talking program, also depends very much on luck when it comes to making a lasting impression. Written in 1966 by

Joseph Weizenbaum of the Massachusetts Institute of Technology, ELIZA avoids a great deal of conversational burden by playing the role of a nondirective psychotherapist. There follows a transcript of our recent conversation.

> ELIZA: Hello. Please state your problem.
> DEWDNEY: I am not in the habit of discussing my problems with a computer.
> ELIZA: Do computers worry you?
> DEWDNEY: Sometimes. Where will it all end?
> ELIZA: Please go on.
> DEWDNEY: Do you think that by our wholesale adoption of computer technology we might be unknowingly closing the door on important cultural strategies?
> ELIZA: We were talking about you, not me.

So far, so good. ELIZA appears to be playing the therapeutic role fairly well, eliciting further statements from me and turning my question aside to refocus attention on my "problem." On the latter point, however, the reply does not seem entirely appropriate. "What do *you* think?" might have been better. After a few more lines of conversation ELIZA says: "Does that have anything to do with the fact that your problems with a computer?"

The illusion that ELIZA is a sophisticated conversational program begins to crumble. Although RACTER commits numerous semantic sins, it is designed always to speak grammatically. Semantic nonsense is easier to accept than syntactic blundering. From this point on the conversation degenerated—as I knew it would. I had spoken with ELIZA years ago.

The ELIZA program operates on a very simple principle. There is a small collection of key words that come up in most people's conversation. For example, ELIZA uses the occurrence of words such as "my" to trigger two possible kinds of response. Together they illustrate ELIZA's total conversational ability. A reference to a member of one's family such as "my sister" or "my father" always draws the same response from ELIZA: "Tell me more about your family."

This is one of several preformed sentences ELIZA keeps on hand simply to print whenever a key word or phrase is input. Another key word is "computer." Mention of it always causes ELIZA to ask whether computers worry the patient. But ELIZA's responses extend slightly beyond this knee-jerk conversational plane. The program also has a number of partial sentences on hand. For example, when the patient says "my" in reference to anything but a family member, ELIZA stores the word string following "my" and interchanges first- and second-person pronouns and possessives. Thus if at some point I had said, "It bothers me that my head is getting bald," ELIZA might say, many lines of conversation later, "Earlier you said your head is getting bald." Or ELIZA might say, "Does that have anything to do with the fact that your head is getting bald?" This explains ELIZA's terrible gaffe: "Does that have anything to do with the fact that your problems with a computer?" The program expects a sentence following the earlier "my."

Readers will find advice on how to write their own ELIZA program in a useful and informative little book called *Experiments in Artificial Intelligence for Small Computers,* by John Krutch (*see* Bibliography). The program listed there is called DOCTOR, one of ELIZA's pseudonyms. Krutch suggests some modifications in the program, such as extending the range of key words to which ELIZA will respond. I would suggest that responses of the more flexible kind be augmented. ELIZA can be modified to give "help" in other areas. I am sure that with only the simplest of changes the program would make an excellent complaint-department receptionist.

When I spoke with Chamberlain in his New York office, I learned that Chamberlain not only had two microcomputers but also had a copy of ELIZA. Why not run ELIZA on one computer and RACTER on the other? Chamberlain agreed to transfer the output of one program to the other by typing it as input. The program's initial conversation follows.

ELIZA: Hello. Please state your problem.
RACTER: Excellent! Excuse me a minute while I attend to some business. I'll be right back.
ELIZA: Why do you need to tell me excuse you while you attend to some business?
RACTER: Is it better to need or to despise? Why is it that I do need to tell you to excuse myself to attend to some business? Because electrons are brave. Braveness is nice, don't you think? And the needers all insist upon it. Do you imagine I am a Communist?

Mercifully (for ELIZA) we stopped the conversation at this point. At a metaphorical level this conversation represents the relation between a plodding, rather unimaginative psychiatrist and an extroverted, manic, possibly dangerous patient. At a computational level a rather modest reflex-arc program has met head on, so to speak, with a highly complex program, one capable of recursive discursions and endless chains of association.

RACTER's operation is difficult to summarize in a few words or even in many. It is a perfect example of the kind of in-house programs that still function in many large corporations and institutions today. It has grown over a number of years by accretion; more advanced, sophisticated layers of software have been wrapped around earlier, more primitive routines. At no time was it ever taken apart, analyzed, restructured, and documented. By the same token, however, one can argue that it is probably in RACTER's nature to dwell in such an unstructured software brain. Etter, who wrote the RACTER program in many of its versions, compares it to the English language, which itself "is a pretty unwieldy accretion of rules and conventions. Insofar as RACTER's commands try to deal with English, they too become unwieldy and hard to summarize." John D. Owens, who acts as RACTER's agent, is himself a computer scientist at the College of Staten Island in the City University of New York. Owens confesses to having no sure grasp of precisely how the program works in its entirety.

RACTER's passionate outbursts result from a simple program cycle that is entered and reentered through complex recursions. First RACTER picks an item at random from one of its files. If the item is what Etter calls a literal, RACTER prints it directly. In the conversation between RACTER and Chamberlain earlier, "I see" is just such a literal. The item retrieved, however, is more likely to be a command than a literal. The command sends RACTER off to other files, some of which may contain still further commands. When the initial command has finally been completed, the program cycle is reentered with yet another random probe into one of RACTER's files.

When RACTER begins a new sentence, it selects a sentential form, either randomly or as the result of its recent conversational history. Suppose the form selected is

THE noun verb (third person, past tense) THE noun.

Here capital letters spell words about which RACTER has no choice. The program prints THE and then goes to a file of nouns, selects MONKEY, say, and prints it. Consulting the verb file, RACTER selects the verb TO EAT, forms the third person past tense, ATE, and prints that. Finally, RACTER selects another noun at random, say TYPEWRITER. The result would be

THE MONKEY ATE THE TYPEWRITER

If this were all RACTER were capable of, its output would hardly be better than the e. e. cummings Project of my undergraduate days.

In fact, RACTER's sentential forms tend to be rather more complicated than this simple example. The complexity results from the use of identifiers. An identifier is a combination of two letters (for example, *an* for animal) that serves as a tag. When they are attached to various words and forms, identifiers cause RACTER to make associations between successively expressed words and sentences. For example, with such identi-

fiers as *an* for animal, *et* for eating and *fd* for food the sentential form
that RACTER would select might well be

THE noun.an verb.3p.et THE noun.fd.

Here RACTER must search for a noun in its files but is limited only to
those nouns bearing the *an* identifier. Thus it would choose at random
among nouns from AARDVARK to ZEBRA. Next, having selected a
noun, let us say MONKEY, RACTER chooses a random verb bearing an *et*
identifier. Such verbs might include EAT, MUNCH, NIBBLE, and so on.
Having randomly chosen CONSUME, RACTER forms the third person past
tense as indicated by the code 3p in the sentential form. Finally, RACTER
looks up the nouns bearing *fd* identifiers and selects, say, ANCHOVIES.
This would result in the new sentence

THE MONKEY CONSUMED THE ANCHOVIES

which certainly makes more sense than the previous sentence.

RACTER's abilities go far beyond the capacity to make file searches
restricted by identifiers. RACTER is perfectly capable of generating its
own sentential forms. If animals and food were to be the current subject
of conversation, for example, RACTER would select raw sentential forms
and place identifiers within the forms.

In fact, RACTER can, up to a point, generate its own command strings
and insert them into the stream of recursion. Since grammatical forms
are always adhered to, the sentences are always grammatical. Because
identifiers are used and because RACTER maintains a list of those currently active in the conversation, the program can hold up its end of any
conversation, at least after a fashion.

The foregoing description embraces only a few aspects of RACTER's
total operation. My own understanding of the program does not extend
much beyond this. I do not doubt, however, that RACTER will soon have
many imitators and that general principles for such programs will develop. I look forward to a book on the subject.

RACTER is available in either of two forms from Owens (*see* List of
Suppliers). The first form is a diskette for IBM personal computers or
compatible systems. The second form is called S-100 and refers to a
certain class of computers.

Also available from Owens is a far more sophisticated piece of software called Inrac for people who want to alter RACTER's personality and
knowledge. Inrac also comes in both forms, accompanied by a manual
explaining how a new generation of computer psychologists may alter
RACTER's files. I wonder if that is what Susan Calvin, Isaac Asimov's
robopsychologist, did for a living.

At the beginning of this discussion I mentioned SHRDLU, a program created by Terry Winograd in 1970 at the Massachusetts Institute of Technology. SHRDLU is head and shoulders above both ELIZA and RACTER when it comes to intelligent conversation. Although SHRDLU's domain of discourse is restricted to a tabletop world of colored blocks and other geometric objects, SHRDLU really understands this world in terms of the relation between semantics and the physical properties of the blocks and the tabletop. SHRDLU's internal organization is entirely different from RACTER's. It consists of subsystems that parse, interpret and construct sentences, carry out dictionary searches and semantic analyses, and make logical deductions. These subsystems are tightly interwoven in a highly structured manner whose total effect gives one the impression of a true intelligence discussing the world of tabletop blocks. In the following dialogue SHRDLU's world, as shown in Figure 25, is being discussed. The vertical line in the illustration represents SHRDLU's robot hand just after SHRDLU has executed the human's command. (Although in Figure 25 the blocks are drawn in shades of gray, they were indeed, at the time of this dialogue, the various colors mentioned here.)

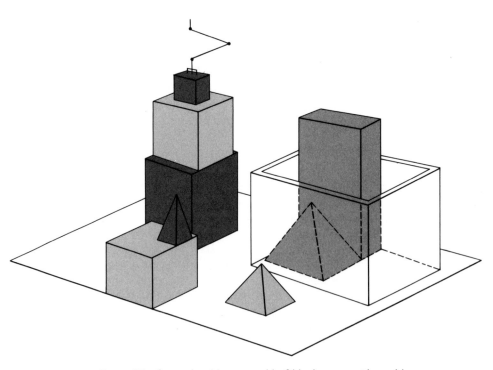

Figure 25   SHRDLU's tabletop world of blocks, pyramids, and boxes.

HUMAN: Will you please stack up both of the red blocks and either a green cube or a pyramid.
SHRDLU: OK.
HUMAN: Which cube is sitting on the table?
SHRDLU: The large green one which supports the red pyramid.
HUMAN: Is there a large block behind a pyramid?
SHRDLU: Yes, three of them: a large red one, a large green cube, and the blue one.

The complete dialogue is available in Winograd's classic work *Understanding Natural Language* (*see* Bibliography). Here we note only that SHRDLU's reply to the question "Which cube is sitting on the table?" involves not only an analysis of the sentence but also an understanding of physical relations between objects in its environment. SHRDLU knows that there are three cubes currently in its world and that only one of them is sitting on the table. This is a green cube. Since another green cube is present, SHRDLU refers to it in terms of its relation to another object in its environment, the red pyramid.

Conversational programs such as SHRDLU undoubtedly herald the future; the advantages of a computer that is able to discuss problems intelligently with humans rather than passively accepting programs to solve the problems are too obvious to miss. Computer scientists in artificial intelligence work, in part, toward this goal. As for Etter, he sums up his field of expertise as Artificial Insanity.

Addendum

Since "Conversations with RACTER" first appeared in the January, 1985 "Computer Recreations" column of SCIENTIFIC AMERICAN, there have been more stories about the lettuce-craving program than there are by it. I have now conversed often enough with RACTER to understand that the program is even more seriously unbalanced than I had first thought.

John D. Owens, who distributes RACTER, writes that one copy was ordered for the training of psychiatric interns who interview schizophrenic patients. Another customer was almost unhinged by RACTER. Describing RACTER as a "madman," this man failed in all attempts to halt the program. RACTER insisted on discussing the proposition that St. Peter was an atheist. I sympathize with the man. I too have run the gamut from laughter to boredom and even anger. But why react this way to RACTER? It is only a program.

To the Owens family RACTER is something more than a program. A customer lightheartedly wrote to ask whether RACTER could be "transmogrified" onto an eight-inch diskette. RACTER was consulted: "If 'We can transmogrify me onto eight-inch diskette' occurred to a pessimist, he might think it was pessimism." It later turned out that the Owens's facilities were incapable of the transmogrification.

On another occasion Terry Owens asked RACTER how much money to budget for advertising. "Very much money because, Terry, people will believe it," RACTER replied.

Facebender

The face is unmistakable. There are the low, floppy ears, the prominent cheekbones, the high pompadour. Ronald Reagan's face is familiar around the world, but somehow it is even easier to spot his likeness in a caricature than it is in a photograph (*see* Figure 26). Surely the art of caricature calls for deep insight into human nature. If this be the stuff of computation, surely the computer is a trivial adjunct—little more than a sketch pad—that merely stores the highly subtle renderings of the caricaturist in a visual form.

Or is it? The caricatures on these pages were all generated by a program devised by Susan E. Brennan, a staff scientist at the Hewlett-Packard Laboratories in Palo Alto, Calif. To run the program a mouse, a light pen, or some other analogue of a pencil might be convenient, but they are certainly not essential. The results depend hardly at all on a steady hand or a practiced eye. Instead, once a photographic likeness of the face is entered into the computer, the program takes over and draws the caricature. How is it done? A short answer is deceptively simple: the program compares the photograph of the target face with an average face stored in the memory of the computer. The features that differ most from the average face are scaled up in size.

Brennan's program followed naturally from her own considerable abilities as a caricaturist and her interest in the cognitive processes underlying face recognition. Such processes have long baffled psychologists and cognitive scientists, and caricatures seem to play a special role in the process because when they are recognized, they are recognized almost instantly. Could it be that instead of remembering a friend's face, we remember a caricature of it? To address these issues Brennan invented her simple technique for generating caricatures, and she described it in her master's thesis at the Massachusetts Institute of Technology. She continues that interest in her spare time; in her working

Figure 26   From realism to "facelessness" in FACEBENDER, a program based on the work of Susan E. Brennan, with stops for caricatures of Ronald Reagan in between.

hours she now experiments with new forms of communication between human and computer that rely in part on natural language under-standing.

Conceptually Brennan's technique is closely related to a trick that computer animators call in-betweening. Imagine two drawings of famil-iar objects, such as an apple and a banana, both done by connecting dots with lines (*see* Figure 27). Each dot on the apple is then paired with a

APPLE

BANAPPLE

BANANA

CARICATURE

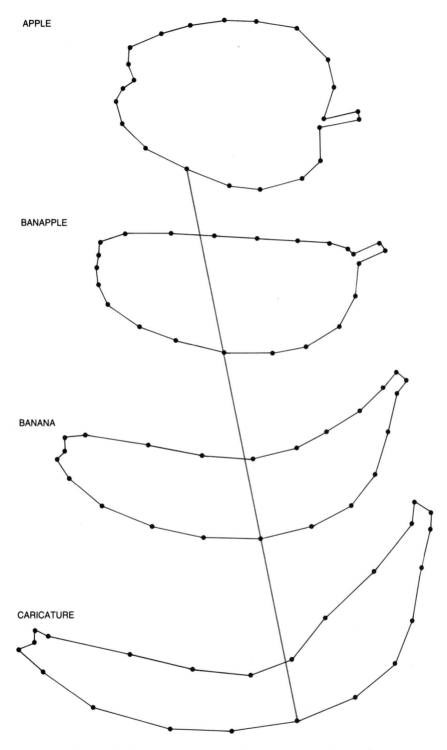

Figure 27   How to turn an apple into a banana, and beyond.

dot on the banana. If the paired dots are also connected by lines, the midpoints of the lines depict a brand-new fruit that splits the difference between the apple and the banana—a banapple, of course.

The same lines that connect the apple and the banana can also give rise to an extreme form of the banana—from the point of view, so to speak, of the apple. Extend each line beyond the banana by half its original length and then place dots at the end of the lines. When the dots are connected, the banana emerges in caricature. Similarly, by projecting the connecting lines beyond the apple, one can obtain a caricature of an apple—from the point of view of the banana. Faces can be treated in much the same way. Each pair of faces defines two mutual caricatures. The best caricatures, however, arise from comparison with a norm, or average face.

The norms in Brennan's program are made up from sets of several dozen real faces in a data base of several hundred. Points are chosen that outline the features of each face, and the points are labeled with respect to a set of matrix-based coordinate axes. The origin is at the upper left of the image plane, and the coordinates increase from left to right and downward. The scale is adjusted so that the left pupil is at the point (135,145) and the right pupil is at the point (190,145). The coordinates of corresponding points on each face are averaged to give the norm for that point. For example, the combined coordinates of the outer corner of the left eyebrow give the average coordinate for the outer corner of the left eyebrow of the average face. Three norms are constructed in this way: there is an average male face, an average female face, and an average, overall plain-vanilla face. It is no surprise that the plain-vanilla face looks somewhat androgynous; it establishes the norm for most caricatures (*see* Figure 28).

To draw a caricature based on the norm, the program must be supplied with a digitized version of a real face. In practice the face begins as a photograph, and the program prompts the user in turn for each of the 186 key points on the photograph. For instance, when the program calls for the six points that make up the left eyebrow, the user can respond by moving a mouse to successive points on the left eyebrow of the photographic image on the screen.

It is useful to think of Brennan's program as a fast shuttle for exploring what she calls face space. The entered coordinates for the points defining a photograph can be strung together in a predetermined order. The result is a list of numbers that can be treated as coordinates of a single point in a high-dimensional space. For example, both the average faces and the photographic face are represented by 186 points, each of which has two coordinates. The resulting list of 372 numbers for each face is a point in a 372-dimensional space. In principle every face can be assigned to a point in face space, and any two faces in face space can be connected by a straight line.

Figure 28   The androgynous average face.

There is no need to be mystified over the concept of a higher-dimensional space. Face space is merely a handy abstraction for describing differences and similarities among faces. The familiar concepts of the straight line and the distance between two points have straightforward analogues in any higher-dimensional space. All the points along a straight line in face space represent proportional changes in each coordinate value. The distance between two points in face space is a measure of their similarity: similar faces are close neighbors in face space, and dissimilar faces are literally farther apart.

In face space one can imagine the norm as being near the center of a cloud of points representing realistic images of real faces. A line joins each real face to the norm. The points along the line correspond to a succession of intermediate faces that look increasingly like the real face. Beyond that face are the caricatures, but there is a natural limit to recognizable exaggeration: the caricatures eventually lose their human qualities and degenerate into a chaotic state Brennan calls facelessness.

The idea that every face is a point in face space suggests another fascinating transformation. Since any two faces in face space can be joined by a straight line, one can ask the program to generate a transitional sequence from one face to another. Brennan finds such sequences particularly intriguing when the two endpoint faces are male and female: the program effortlessly transforms Elizabeth Taylor into, say, the late John F. Kennedy (*see* Figure 29).

The reader can duplicate some of Brennan's feats of caricature by writing a smaller version of her program; I call it FACEBENDER. It requires the user to supply at least two faces: a norm and the target face to

Figure 29   Elizabeth Taylor (as Cleopatra) meets former President Kennedy in face space.

be caricatured. I have referred above to the norm, whose coordinates have been generously provided by Brennan (*see* Figure 30). The user must then convert the target face into the same form. In the absence of sophisticated digitizing equipment the reader can, with relatively little pain, convert a photograph of a loved one (possibly oneself) into a list of coordinates. Brennan warns, however, that the face in the photograph must have a bland, neutral expression; even a slight smile will grow to a monstrous grimace. The face must also be fully frontal; if the head is turned, FACEBENDER will turn it even more.

To determine the scale for the axes, assume the coordinates of the left and right pupils are the same as the norms: the left should be at (135,145) and the right at (190,145). (Remember that horizontal coordinates increase from left to right and vertical coordinates increase downward.) Once the distance scale is established the user must find the rest of the coordinates by careful measurement. In Brennan's digitizing scheme the points on the face are organized into 39 facial features; each feature is a succession of connected points. The order of the points depends on the orientation of the feature: for features that are mainly horizontal the points are listed from left to right, and for features that are mainly vertical they are listed from top to bottom.

Brennan admits that identifying the key points on a face is governed mostly by trial and error, but the president's face can be used as a guide. For this reason it is important that the same person carry out the conversion from photograph to list for each face entered into a data base.

FACEBENDER stores the two digitized faces in arrays called *face* and *norm*. A third array called *disp* is needed to create a display. All three arrays have 186 rows and two columns: one face point per row and one coordinate per column. Points are arranged in the serial order given in the list for *norm*. The advantage of this ordering is that all lines in the final picture can then be drawn between successive points in the array; of course, lines are not drawn between successive array points when one feature is complete and another is about to be drawn.

The first feature the program draws is the pupil of the left eye; the second feature is the right pupil. Each pupil can be rendered as either a dot or a small circle; somehow the circles look friendlier. For the re-

LEFT PUPIL	1 POINT	(135,145)
RIGHT PUPIL	1 POINT	(190,145)
LEFT IRIS	5 POINTS	(134,141) (128,144) (133,149) (140,144) (135,141)
RIGHT IRIS	5 POINTS	(190,141) (184,144) (189,149) (196,144) (190,141)
BOTTOM OF LEFT EYELID	3 POINTS	(119,147) (133,140) (147,146)
BOTTOM OF RIGHT EYELID	3 POINTS	(177,147) (190,141) (203,147)
BOTTOM OF LEFT EYE	3 POINTS	(121,147) (133,150) (147,146)
BOTTOM OF RIGHT EYE	3 POINTS	(177,147) (191,150) (201,148)
TOP OF LEFT EYE	3 POINTS	(118,143) (132,137) (148,142)
TOP OF RIGHT EYE	3 POINTS	(176,143) (191,137) (204,143)
LEFT EYE LINE	3 POINTS	(127,154) (135,153) (144,150)
RIGHT EYE LINE	3 POINTS	(178,151) (187,154) (196,154)
LEFT SIDE OF NOSE	6 POINTS	(156,140) (156,153) (156,165) (154,172) (156,179) (161,182)
RIGHT SIDE OF NOSE	6 POINTS	(166,140) (166,153) (166,166) (168,172) (167,179) (161,182)
LEFT NOSTRIL	6 POINTS	(150,169) (147,173) (146,178) (148,182) (153,179) (161,182)
RIGHT NOSTRIL	6 POINTS	(173,169) (176,172) (177,178) (174,182) (170,179) (163,182)
TOP OF LEFT EYEBROW	6 POINTS	(112,137) (113,132) (125,127) (139,128) (150,131) (152,136)
TOP OF RIGHT EYEBROW	6 POINTS	(171,136) (173,132) (186,129) (199,128) (208,132) (211,137)
BOTTOM OF LEFT EYEBROW	4 POINTS	(112,138) (124,132) (138,134) (152,136)
BOTTOM OF RIGHT EYEBROW	4 POINTS	(171,136) (187,134) (200,132) (210,137)
TOP OF UPPER LIP	7 POINTS	(137,203) (149,199) (156,196) (162,199) (168,197) (177,199) (187,202)
BOTTOM OF UPPER LIP	7 POINTS	(138,203) (148,203) (156,202) (163,203) (170,202) (178,203) (186,202)
TOP OF LOWER LIP	7 POINTS	(138,203) (149,203) (156,202) (163,203) (170,202) (177,202) (186,203)
BOTTOM OF LOWER LIP	7 POINTS	(141,204) (148,207) (155,210) (163,211) (171,210) (179,207) (185,203)
LEFT SIDE OF FACE	3 POINTS	(103,141) (101,160) (104,181)
RIGHT SIDE OF FACE	3 POINTS	(219,140) (222,159) (218,179)
LEFT EAR	7 POINTS	(99,150) (92,144) (88,149) (90,160) (94,174) (99,187) (104,184)
RIGHT EAR	7 POINTS	(224,149) (231,144) (234,151) (232,160) (230,173) (224,185) (219,184)
JAW	11 POINTS	(104,181) (108,199) (115,214) (129,228) (147,240) (162,243) (180,239) (196,228) (207,215) (215,199) (219,178)
HAIRLINE	13 POINTS	(101,144) (107,129) (114,114) (120,104) (131,95) (146,92) (160,93) (174,95) (188,96) (201,103) (210,114) (217,126) (222,143)
TOP OF HEAD	13 POINTS	(93,204) (78,173) (76,142) (82,101) (99,70) (129,46) (158,44) (188,45) (217,64) (236,94) (245,134) (250,168) (233,200)
LEFT CHEEK LINE	3 POINTS	(145,175) (139,182) (135,190)
RIGHT CHEEK LINE	3 POINTS	(178,176) (185,183) (190,191)
LEFT CHEEKBONE	3 POINTS	(105,178) (109,184) (112,190)
RIGHT CHEEKBONE	3 POINTS	(218,178) (214,183) (211,189)
LEFT UPPER LIP LINE	2 POINTS	(159,186) (159,193)
RIGHT UPPER LIP LINE	2 POINTS	(165,186) (165,193)
CHIN CLEFT	2 POINTS	(162,232) (162,238)
CHIN LINE	3 POINTS	(153,218) (162,216) (173,219)

Figure 30   The coordinates for the points of an average face.

maining features, however, lines are drawn to join consecutive points in the array. A special array called *features* is needed to skip the line between the last point in one facial feature and the first point in the next. The array gives the number of points in each feature, and a double loop supervises the skips (*see* Figure 31).

Because the first two features have already been drawn, the display routine begins with the third feature, namely the left iris. The first point in the left iris is the third point of the array *disp*, which is indexed by the variable i; hence the value of i is initially set equal to 3. The array *features* is indexed by another variable, j, and it ranges from 1 to 37 because there are 37 features left to draw. Within the j loop another variable called *count* keeps track of the number of lines drawn for each feature; it increases by 1 with each passage through the j loop. The index i is also increased with each passage through the loop; it identifies the point in the array *disp* that is currently participating in the frantic exercise of connect-the-dots.

Inside the j loop is a second loop called a while loop; it compares the number of points joined so far in feature j with the total number of points in that feature. The program leaves the while loop when the two numbers are equal; the feature is complete. If there are still points to connect in the feature, the program draws a line from point i in the array *disp* to point $i + 1$. My notation is merely shorthand. A real display command would call for a line from the point whose coordinates are $disp(i,1)$ and $disp(i,2)$ to the point whose coordinates are $disp(i + 1,1)$ and $disp(i + 1,2)$.

The heart of FACEBENDER is its exaggeration routine. Its structure is even simpler than the display routine I have just outlined (*see* Figure 31). For each of the 186 facial points in the arrays *face* and *norm*, the loop calculates a new array called *bend*. The new array encodes the caricature-to-be. Each coordinate of the array *bend* is calculated by adding the corresponding coordinate of the array *face* to a quantity that exaggerates the differences between *norm* and *face*. The exaggeration factor f is typed in by the user; f then multiplies the difference between

```
DISPLAY ROUTINE
i ← 2                              EXAGGERATION ROUTINE
for j = 1 to 37                    for i = 1 to 186
   i ← i + 1                          bend(i,1) ← face(i,1) + f × [face(i,1) − norm(i,1)]
   count ← 1                          bend(i,2) ← face(i,2) + f × [face(i,2) − norm(i,2)]
   while count < features(j)
   draw line from disp(i) to disp(i + 1)
   count ← count + 1
   i ← i + 1
```

Figure 31   The heart of FACEBENDER.

the horizontal coordinates of *face* and *norm*, and it also multiplies the difference between the vertical coordinates.

The only things left to do are to organize the program and, optionally, to tune up the drawing routine. A simple, nonprocedural approach to organization is to place both the display routine and the exaggeration routine inside an interactive loop that asks the user: "Want to try another?" The program must also prompt the user for the exaggeration factor. Arrange the prompt so that a number of different exaggeration factors can be tried without having to reenter the array *face*; their effect on the caricature is then easy to compare.

The drawings can be somewhat enhanced if the dots are connected with so-called spline curves instead of with straight lines. Splines avoid zigs and zags and connect the dots smoothly; Brennan's program usually draws spline curves to form the smooth contours of facial features. Nevertheless, I was aware that splines might prove sticky to explain in a book that is devoted largely to easy programs. I asked Brennan for an alternate method. Could straight lines be used instead? Much to her surprise and mine, caricatures drawn with straight lines are almost as good as the ones drawn with splines. Indeed, all her images appearing here were drawn using straight lines. With only a small loss in aesthetic value the programmer can avoid a most troublesome technique. One can immediately set about digitizing a favorite photograph.

Brennan's caricature generator has been applied in several studies of facial recognition. Faces from her program have been transmitted over telephone lines as part of an experiment in teleconferencing at the Massachusetts Institute of Technology Media Laboratory. In 1985 she did an experiment with Gillian Rhodes of the University of Otago in New Zealand, who was then a graduate student working with Roger N. Shepard of Stanford University. First she generated caricatures of faculty members and students in the psychology department at Stanford. The caricatures were then tested for recognizability against standard line drawings.

Brennan has summarized the findings: "The caricature generator was particularly useful for this study because it enabled us to generate stimuli that varied in a continuous and controlled way; previous perceptual studies have had to compare caricatures with photos or other kinds of not-so-similar images, and have therefore not been free of representational effects. Caricatures were not found to be particularly *better* as recognizable representations (the 'best' representations were only modestly exaggerated), but when the highly exaggerated caricatures were recognized, they were recognized significantly *faster*—about twice as fast, in fact, as the realistic line drawings of the same people."

Brennan suggests a number of other experiments with the caricature generator. For example, it would be fascinating to recover the "norm" assumed by human caricaturists. Handed a caricature of a given subject by a given artist, she would try reversing the exaggeration to determine the normal face, presumably lodged somewhere in the artist's unconscious mind, from which the exaggeration was derived. Would the reconstructed norm be much the same from one subject to the next? Would different artists assume different norms?

Addendum

To summarize, the program FACEBENDER, inspired by the work of Susan E. Brennan, takes the digitized version of a face to be caricatured, and then compares it with an average reference face, similarly digitized, in memory. The program then distorts, or exaggerates, each feature of the input face by an amount that is proportional to its distance from the corresponding feature in the reference face; an ear that is moderately large compared with the reference ear will be enlarged still further by multiplying all the differences by an exaggeration factor f.

Readers who want to implement the FACEBENDER program may be daunted by the prospect of digitizing their own face from a photograph. Pat Macaluso of White Plains, N.Y., uses the reference face as the basis of its own caricature. "The key," says Macaluso, "is to scale the range of variation to the size of each feature. Thus an ear receives more absolute variation than the chin cleft. Simply calculate the enclosing 'box' by calculating the maximum and minimum of the x and y coordinates for each feature." Within this framework the amount of distortion is governed by random numbers selected by the program. In this way an end-

Figure 32   Self-caricature of the average face.

less variety of faces can be produced by Macaluso's self-referential version of FACEBENDER. One of the caricatures so produced somewhat resembled Leonardo da Vinci. It is shown in Figure 32.

A reader known only as DMI from Pasadena, Calif., has a suggestion for avoiding "facelessness," the dreaded state that occurs when the exaggeration factor is too large; all features degenerate into a wild and unrecognizable bird's nest of polygons. Imagine that the face to be caricatured is superposed on the reference face and that corresponding points are connected by springs. The distortion process now attempts to displace the points of the input face, but in doing so it encounters resistance from the springs. Small distortions are thereby hardly affected, but large ones are pulled up short of the faceless state.

Perceptron
Misperceptions

Imagine a black box rather like a camera. At the front is a lens and on one side is a dial with various settings such as "Tree," "House," "Cat," and so on. With the dial set to "Cat" we go for a walk and presently encounter a cat sitting on a neighbor's porch. When the box is aimed at the cat, a red light goes on. When the box is aimed at anything else, the light remains dark.

Inside the box is a digital retina sending impulses to a two-layer logical network: an instance of the device called a perceptron. At one time it was hoped that perceptrons would ultimately be capable of real-world recognition tasks like the one described in the fantasy above. But something went wrong.

The 1950s and 1960s were years of tremendous creativity and experimentation in the newly developing field of computer science. Romantic paradigms such as self-organizing systems, learning machines, and intelligent computers influenced many scientists, and I am tempted to call the period the Cybernetic Age. Incredible machines that could see or think or even reproduce themselves seemed just around the corner. The simplest of these machines was the perceptron.

A perceptron consists of a finite gridlike retina subdivided into cells that receive light. Like certain cells in the human retina, each perceptron cell turns on if it receives enough light; otherwise it stays off. It is therefore reasonable to think of the image a perceptron analyzes as a grid of light and dark squares, as in Figure 33.

Besides the retina, a perceptron consists of a great many primitive decision-making elements I shall call local demons. Each local demon examines a fixed subset of the retinal cells and reports on conditions there to a more complex decision maker I may as well call the head

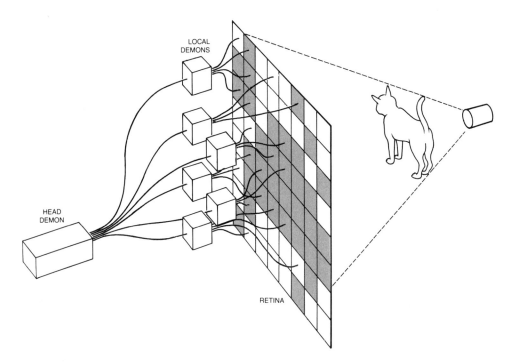

Figure 33   A perceptron attempts to recognize a cat.

demon. Specifically, each local demon is equipped with a notebook listing certain patterns it must watch for in its locale, the subset of retinal cells under its jurisdiction. If any of the listed patterns appears, the local demon sends a signal to the head demon; otherwise it remains silent. The head demon's job is more complicated in that it must do some arithmetic. Each signal from a local demon is multiplied by a specific positive or negative integer (the local demon's assigned "weight") and the resulting numbers are added. If the sum is at least as great as a fixed threshold, the head demon says yes; otherwise it says no. To avoid making any assumptions about what the various demons look like I have shown them in Figure 33 as boxes.

Demons are often given dangerous or even impossible jobs such as opening tiny doors in the wall of a container to let molecules pass through. In comparison, the demons of the perceptron have quite easy jobs. Indeed, the local demons could be replaced by simple logic circuits, and the head demon's job could easily be done by a few registers, an adder, and a comparator (elements of the central-processing unit of any computer). Demons, however, have a romantic charm that electronic devices cannot match.

A perceptron's job is to say yes when certain patterns are presented to it and to say no to all others. The former patterns are said to be recognized by the perceptron. Although it is highly doubtful that a cat-recognizing perceptron could ever be built, other recognition tasks are attainable.

A perceptron can be programmed, after a fashion, to recognize a given class of patterns by adjusting the weights and the threshold. Local demons supplying evidence in favor of the class are weighted positively and those providing evidence against it are weighted negatively. The magnitude of each weight reflects the value or importance of the evidence. Although the perceptrons discussed here operate with a fixed set of weights, the notion of programming plays a central role in the theory of perceptrons developed in the 1950s.

The following perceptron recognizes a dark rectangle of any size or shape placed anywhere on its retina. In fact, it recognizes any number of such rectangles (including zero), provided no two of them touch along a side or at a corner. There are three steps in the construction of the perceptron. First, install a local demon at each 2-by-2 locale in the retina. Then put all the subpatterns in list P (*see* Figure 34) on each local demon's list. Third, set all the head demon's weights to $+1$ and set the threshold to d, the number of local demons.

This design calls for quite a few demons: if the perceptron has an n-by-n-retina, there will be $(n - 1)^2$ local demons. They are all given positive weights, indicating they all supply positive evidence toward the recognition of rectangles. For example, it is not hard to see that when a single rectangle is projected onto the perceptron's retina, each 2-by-2 set of cells must contain one of the subpatterns in list P. It follows that every local demon sends a signal to the head demon and the weighted sum of the signals is, of course, d. The head demon says yes. On the other hand, if one of the dark shapes is not a rectangle or if two rectan-

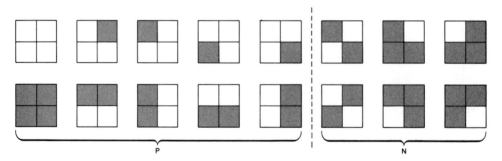

Figure 34   The 2-by-2 subpatterns recognized by positive (P) and negative (N) local demons.

gles touch, then at least one of the 2-by-2 sets contains a subpattern from list N in Figure 34. Hence at least one of the local demons fails to report and the head demon develops a sum no greater than $d - 1$. It says no.

An equivalent perceptron could be designed in which each local demon uses the smaller list N. In this case all the weights would be -1 and the threshold would be 0. Each local demon would supply negative evidence toward a pattern of rectangles and the head demon would say yes only if none of the local demons sent it a signal.

The style of perceptron defined above has many interesting properties, and it seems worthwhile to give it a name. Without specifying what list of subpatterns all the local demons use, a device of this kind will be called a window perceptron because each local demon looks at the input pattern through a 2-by-2 window. For an n-by-n retina there are $(n - 1)^2$ demons, and the threshold is equal to this number.

Generally speaking, perceptrons seem to be best at recognizing geometric figures. Window perceptrons can recognize not only rectangles but also "black holes" (isolated dark cells), vertical and horizontal lines, stairways, checkerboards, and many other patterns. It all depends on what set of 2-by-2 subpatterns is chosen for the local demon lists (*see* Figure 35). Indeed, each subset of the 16 possible 2-by-2 subpatterns defines a different window perceptron, and each of the resulting 65,536 window perceptrons recognizes a certain class of patterns. Or does it?

The window perceptron based on the two subpatterns below does not recognize anything.

The reason is simple. Assuming a fairly large retina, select a 2-by-2 window somewhere in the middle of it. If the window contains the first of the two subpatterns above, examine the window one cell to the right: it will have a dark cell in its upper left corner, and so the demon in charge of that locale will send no signal to the head demon. Remember that in a window perceptron *all* the local demons must report in for a pattern to be recognized. If the second subpattern is present, shifting the window one cell to the left yields a similar contradiction.

Which subsets of the 16 subpatterns give rise to window perceptrons that actually recognize something? The question is probably hard to answer, but it illustrates very well the kind of question an interested computer scientist or mathematician might ask when confronted by the phenomenon of a perceptron that recognizes nothing. Because of the large number of such perceptrons, the answer would best take the form of some easily applied criterion or test: given a subset of 2-by-2 sub-

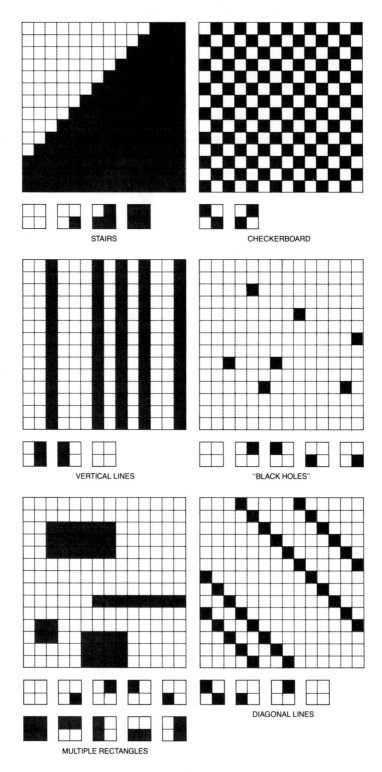

Figure 35 Some patterns recognized by window perceptrons.

patterns, one applies the test and obtains an answer for that particular subset.

The point of these remarks is that professional standing as a computer theorist is not always needed to answer such questions. Although they go somewhat beyond the kind of puzzle commonly given in recreational-mathematics columns, they call for the same kind of thinking. Readers who have solved at least one of Martin Gardner's puzzles in the "Mathematical Games" department of SCIENTIFIC AMERICAN should be able to make some progress with the question above. In theoretical research, as in experimental science, a partial answer is better than no answer at all.

Work in perceptrons was pioneered by Frank Rosenblatt of Cornell University in the 1950s. Rosenblatt and his coworkers, both at Cornell and elsewhere, became optimistic about the prospects for perceptrons as useful pattern-recognizing devices. The "convergence theorem" told them that in principle perceptrons could learn to recognize patterns by making the weights used by the head demon subject to automatic control. The theorem states that any adjustment of weights in the direction of improved powers of recognition can serve as the basis of still further improvements. Actual perceptrons were built, and in some tests on simple patterns they achieved high recognition scores.

What seemed encouraging progress at the time was, in a sense, illusory. According to Marvin L. Minsky and Seymour Papert of the Massachusetts Institute of Technology, the enthusiasts for perceptrons had been beguiled by the simplicity and apparent success of their devices. Below the surface lay some grave defects in the concept. In 1969 Minsky and Papert issued *Perceptrons*, a book that effectively punctured the balloon by pointing out (and proving) several things perceptrons cannot do (*see* Bibliography).

One of the most dramatic failures discovered by Minsky and Papert was the inability of certain perceptrons to recognize when a figure is connected (that is, all in one piece). Assuming each local demon inspects only a limited locale, Minsky and Papert gave examples of four patterns designed so that one of them always stumps a perceptron whose job is to recognize connectivity. The patterns are shown in Figure 36. Two of them (*b* and *c*) are connected figures and the other two (*a* and *d*) are not.

Suppose someone claims to have designed a diameter-limited perceptron capable of distinguishing between connected and unconnected patterns. By diameter-limited I mean that for some number m every local demon can examine only the squares within an m-by-m window. To test the claim Minsky and Papert would prepare versions of their four patterns, with each pattern adjusted to be more than m cells long. The local demons can then be classified in three disjoint sets. Left Demons examine at least one cell on the left edge of the figure. Right Demons

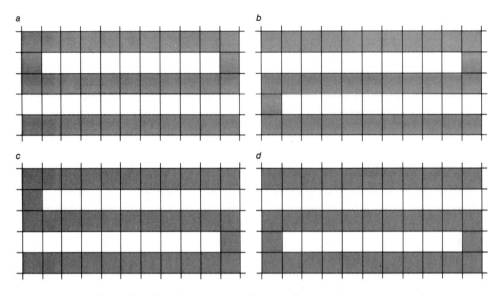

Figure 36   Four figures designed to confuse a connectivity perceptron.

examine at least one cell on the right edge. Other Demons are neither Left nor Right.

When the proposed connectivity perceptron is presented with pattern a, it either fails (by saying yes) or succeeds (by saying no). If it fails, of course, the test is over. If it succeeds, the next step is to examine the sum developed by the head demon and split it into three parts: L, O, and R, representing the weighted sums of the Left, Other, and Right demons that signal the head demon when pattern a is projected on the retina. Since the connectivity perceptron says no, the sum of L, O, and R falls short of the threshold. If pattern a is now replaced by pattern b, only the Left Demons change their response, since only the cells along the left edge of the figure change. Suppose the partial sum L becomes L'. On the other hand, if pattern a is replaced by pattern c, only the cells along the right edge change and only the Right Demons change their response, say from R to R'.

Now the perceptron has got itself into a most curious position. Since b and c are connected, it must answer yes in both cases, and so the sums $L' + O + R$ and $L + O + R'$ must be at least as large as the threshold. It is already known, however, that $L + O + R$ is less than the threshold because a was not connected. It follows that L' is larger than L and R' is larger than R. The deathblow comes when the perceptron faces pattern d. Here both the left- and the right-hand cells of the figure have changed from the state they had in pattern a, and the head demon finds itself computing the sum $L' + O + R'$, which is certainly greater than the threshold. The head demon says yes. It is wrong.

Additional failings of perceptrons discovered by Minsky and Papert include the unrealistically large number of local demons needed for some recognition tasks and the low rate of learning (or convergence) for other tasks.

Perhaps it is not surprising that perceptrons should fail in many cases where the human visual system succeeds. I noted above that the local demons and head demon could be replaced by simple computational circuits. They could also be replaced by the formal neurons first described in the 1940s by Warren S. McCulloch and Walter H. Pitts in their classic work on neural networks. These formal neurons are much simpler than human neurons; likewise the complexity of a perceptron organized as a two-layer neural network does not come close to the complexity of the first two layers of the human visual cortex. Moreover, "behind" the visual cortex, as it were, there is an amazing and almost completely unknown analytic apparatus—something that is entirely lacking in the perceptron model of vision. To even begin modeling this greater complexity one would have to replace the head demon by a Turing machine, but here the argument sinks into a sea of uninformed speculation, and so I shall call a halt.

Even if perceptrons are eyes without minds, they have a certain charming simplicity and, for some patterns at least, definite powers of recognition. I wonder what other patterns readers might discover to be within the competence of the window perceptron. Those wishing to explore the tougher question of which subsets of the 16 2-by-2 subpatterns lead to "good" window perceptrons (those that recognize at least one pattern) will find the question somewhat cleaner to handle if a constraint is added: the patterns recognized should be "translatable"—it should be possible to shift them on the retina without changing the fact that they are recognized. This requirement not only rules out certain overspecialized window perceptrons (for example, the one that recognizes a single dark cell in the upper right corner of its retina) but also reflects the notion that the perceptron is looking at a real scene that shifts across the retina as the black box in my fantasy scans it.

Although diameter-limited perceptrons are unable to distinguish connected figures from unconnected ones, it may be possible to recognize connectivity in certain classes of figures. For example, within the class of all multiple-rectangle patterns the connected figures would be those that include exactly one rectangle. Can you design a perceptron that recognizes just such patterns? Your local demons must use 2-by-2 windows, but you may hire additional demons if necessary.

I implied above that perceptron research came to an end with the publication of Minsky and Papert's *Perceptrons*. This is true in the sense that a certain woolly and wishful attitude toward perceptrons and their powers of recognition is no longer possible. On the other hand, it was far from Minsky and Papert's intention that all research in perceptron theory be stopped. The precise powers of these simple but sometimes effective devices have yet to be discovered.

Addendum

The subject of perceptrons reminded some readers of applications and spurred others to investigate the subject on their own. Ed Manning of Stratford, Conn., built a "perceptron of sorts" 10 years ago designed to convert real images into the digitized squares of a perceptron's retina.

Gary D. Stormo, an investigator in the Department of Molecular, Cellular, and Developmental Biology at the University of Colorado at Boulder, has used the perceptron concept in automated pattern recognition. Specifically, he has constructed a perceptron-weighting function to recognize binding sites in messenger-RNA nucleotide sequences. He uses the perceptron convergence theorem to guide the performance of his perceptron toward an optimal level. The results have been very encouraging: the perceptron recognizes binding sites with "substantial success."

Any window perceptron that includes either an all-white or an all-black window pattern in its list is a good perceptron. Lowell Hill of Venice, Calif., noted this and wondered whether an all-white or an all-black retina constitutes a legitimate picture. The answer depends on the pattern. It seems reasonable, in the case of the multiple-rectangle perceptron, to regard an all-black retina simply as one large rectangle.

In the course of a most successful foray into the mini research project I suggested, Constantine Roussos of the Lynchburg College Computer Center in Lynchburg, Va., decided to exclude window perceptrons with all-white or all-black window patterns. Among his achievements is a characterization of good perceptrons (those that recognize at least one pattern). The characterization uses translational relations between the window patterns on the perceptron's list. If one shifts a window pattern by a single unit in any of the four principal directions, one must obtain another window pattern on the list. Roussos then concentrated on minimal window perceptrons, those with a list that cannot be further reduced without destroying the goodness of the perceptron. Such perceptrons are building blocks for the set of all good perceptrons. Roussos wrote a computer program that discovered all minimal window perceptrons having list sizes of orders 2 through 5. No minimal window perceptron of order 6 exists. Roussos raises a challenge by turning around the task I had set: I proposed that readers find a pattern recognized by a given perceptron; Roussos suggests discovering a perceptron that recognizes a given pattern.

John M. Evans of Hartford, Conn., blames perceptron failings on the restriction inherent in a two-level hierarchy of local demons reporting to a single head demon. By introducing a kind of demonic middle management, Evans overcomes the connectivity limitations for ordinary perceptrons discovered by Minsky and Papert. The low-level demons themselves constitute a kind of retina whose blacks and whites correspond to whether particular demons report or not. A second layer of demons watches the pattern created by the low-level demons; it reports the presence of subpatterns to the head demon. A three-layer device can distinguish which of the four test patterns are connected and which are not.

A Checkers Program
That Never Loses?

"Is it possible to write a checkers-playing program that will never lose to a human player—ever?" The boy was no more than 10 years old and he looked up from the terminal with that expression of innocent wisdom only the very young can have. He was playing checkers against a program written by some students of mine. We had set the program's look-ahead factor to a moderate level, and the lad was doing rather well.

The boy's question, asked at a departmental open house several years ago, has different answers depending on which game of checkers one is talking about. The question also touches on themes lying at the heart of artificial intelligence, the study of intelligent behavior in computer programs. I shall return to these themes below.

At the time the boy asked the question he was playing 6-by-6 checkers, one of an infinite number of checkers games. Here I shall examine 4-by-4, 6-by-6, and 8-by-8 checkers (the standard game) and compare the prospects for programs designed to play them. In general one can define nth-order checkers on a $2n$-by-$2n$ checkerboard. In each case the men, or checkers pieces, occupy all the dark squares except those in the middle two rows of the board. The rules of nth-order checkers are discussed in more detail in the box on page 111.

For 4-by-4 checkers the answer to the boy's question appears to be "Yes." For 6-by-6 checkers the answer is "Very likely" and for 8-by-8 checkers "Probably." These answers are based on a combination of personal experience, reading, and pure conjecture.

Consider the 4-by-4 game. Each side has two men and a game rarely goes beyond 10 moves, at least when experts are playing. Novices may go 20 moves or more before recognizing a drawn position.

The Rules of *n*th-Order Checkers

The squares of a 2*n*-by-2*n* board are given alternating light and dark colors and each player puts $n^2 - n$ men on the dark squares on opposite sides of the board. The middle two rows are empty of men. Each player has a "single corner" (one dark square occupying the corner) at the left; the other corner is called the double corner. Black moves first.

A man may move diagonally forward to an adjacent unoccupied square. If that square is occupied by an enemy piece but the square beyond it is not occupied, the man may jump the piece and remove it from the board. All such opportunities for a capture must be taken; if two or more captures are possible, at least one must be made. If, after making a capture, a man has an opportunity to make another, it must do so.

When a man advances to the last row on the opposite side of the board, it is made into a king. A king can move both forward and backward (still diagonally) and can capture in both directions.

The game ends in victory for one player when the other player cannot make a legal move because all his pieces have been captured or immobilized. If both players agree that a win is impossible, a draw is declared.

There are further rules about fiddling with the pieces, smoking, and swearing, but a computer is unlikely to transgress them and so they are omitted here.

The board above shows the starting position of eighth-order checkers, played on a 16-by-16 board with 56 pieces on each side.

In any event, 4-by-4 checkers can be analyzed by hand. It appears to be a draw, and a reasonably alert player never has to lose. The same is true of a reasonably good program.

In a game of 6-by-6 checkers each side has six men and a typical game runs for about 20 moves. When our student program was set to maximum look-ahead, it took from 5 to 10 minutes to choose a move. Up until the end game it played seemingly invincible checkers at this setting. Usually it was so far ahead in material or position that it would go on to win or at least draw. Occasionally, however, one of us would survive with enough pieces to beat it in the end game, where its play was surprisingly weak.

The game of 8-by-8 checkers has 12 men on a side; and games between experts can last for 30 moves or more. In tournament play in standard checkers it is now the usual practice to draw opening moves by lot. The practice was adopted around the turn of the century in England because of a tendency of master players to stick with favorite openings and familiar lines of play, which led to an increasing proportion of drawn games. Whether draws are common because checkers is inherently a drawn game or because of conservatism on the part of the experts is hard to say. Nevertheless, 8-by-8 checkers remains a fascinating and difficult game. Mathematically it is somewhat less complex than chess, but there are players expert in both games who do not rate chess a "superior" game.

The two best-known checkers-playing programs were developed by Arthur L. Samuel of the International Business Machines Corporation in the 1960s and by Eric C. Jensen and Tom R. Truscott of Duke University in 1977. In 1962 Samuel's checkers-playing program defeated Robert Nealey, a former Connecticut state champion. Although the program plays a very strong game, it is apparently not rated an expert. The Jensen-Truscott program is stronger still and may rate among the top players in the world.

In 1979 the Jensen-Truscott program played Elbert Lowder, who is generally acknowledged to be one of the best checkers players in the United States. In five games, the program drew twice, won once, and lost twice. The losses seemed to be due to deficiencies in the end game: when Lowder realized that two of the program's men were kept on the back row as guards, he exploited this weakness and won the last two games. It must be stated that Lowder's attitude while playing the Jensen-Truscott program was experimental and somewhat sportive. His one loss apparently resulted from an attempt to lead the program into unorthodox positions—something one should probably not try with a checkers program of this caliber.

Meanwhile Marion F. Tinsley, the world checkers champion, looks on, amused, from his home in Tallahassee, Fla. I do not know whether Tinsley has ever played one of the better checkers programs. On the other hand, the two leading programs have played each other. In two games against the Samuel program the Jensen-Truscott program proved to be "dramatically superior," in Truscott's words, winning both games.

Just about every successful game-playing program has three major parts: a move generator, a board evaluator, and a minimax procedure. Another element of central importance is the game tree: it has a role in all three program segments. The move generator develops the tree; the board evaluator is consulted at the end of each branch of the tree, and the minimax procedure is applied to the tree as a whole.

A game tree has the initial board as its root, and every branch represents a board position that can be reached by making a single move (*see* Figure 37). Oddly, the tree is usually drawn upside down, with the root at the top. It can be arranged in levels, where the boards at the *n*th level represent all the possible moves of one player on the *n*th turn. Although game trees are generally not very tall (or deep), they can be excessively bushy; as a rule the number of boards at each level is more than double the number at the previous level. Even if each board had only two successors, the number of branches would soon grow to be unmanageably large. A tree that forked in this way 64 times would have more branches than all the trees on the earth. (In nature trees do not fork much more than a dozen times from trunk to leaves.) The exponential explosion in the number of game-tree branches makes it impossible for a computer to examine more than a small fraction of the continuations of a game such as 8-by-8 checkers.

The checkers tree is created by the move generator, a program that is given a particular board as input, along with an indication of whose turn it is to move. The output of the move generator is a list of all the boards that can be reached from the given position by a legal move. Consider the following 4-by-4 board, assuming it is Black's turn:

Black has two possible moves, and so the move generator lists the following two boards:

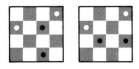

The move generator could then be applied to these boards in turn.

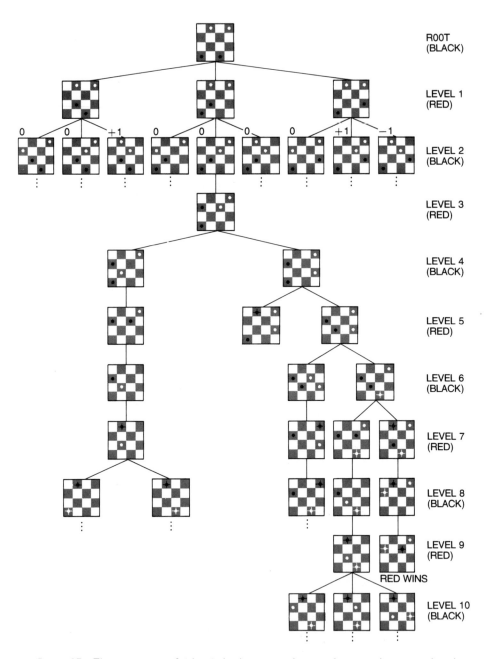

Figure 37   The game tree of 4-by-4 checkers, complete to the second move and with
selected continuations.

Readers who would like to explore the action of a move generator are invited to develop the 4-by-4 checkers tree from this level downward. At the next level, for example, there are only two boards because in each case the rules force Red (shown as White in illustrations) to capture a piece. At the level below that there are still two boards, then three (with a Red win), then two, then five, then 10, then 24. Those who want to go still further are advised to follow two principles. First, scan each level for duplicate boards and develop the tree at only one of them. Second, scan upward from each board to see if the position has occurred before. If it has, terminate that branch and label it "Draw."

How does a move-generating program work? The first issue to be addressed is how the board is to be represented. The simplest scheme is a matrix, or two-dimensional array, whose entries identify the occupying pieces. For example, an empty square might be represented by 0, a square with a man by a 1, and a square with a king by a 2; the sign of the entry would denote the side, say plus for Black and minus for Red. The first 4-by-4 board shown above would then be encoded in the matrix:

$$
\begin{array}{cccc}
0 & 0 & 0 & -1 \\
-1 & 0 & 0 & 0 \\
0 & +1 & 0 & 0 \\
0 & 0 & +1 & 0
\end{array}
$$

The legal moves for each piece depend on its color and position and on whether the diagonally adjacent squares are occupied. In this case the move generator scans the array row by row until it comes to the positive (Black) entry at row 3 and column 2, a position designated (3,2). Since Black is to move and the piece is a man (magnitude 1) rather than a king, the move generator examines squares (2,1) and (2,3). Square (2,1) is already occupied by a piece (and no jump is possible), but (2,3) is free. Consequently the program writes a new array with the +1 deleted from square (3,2) and entered at (2,3):

$$
\begin{array}{cccc}
0 & 0 & 0 & -1 \\
-1 & 0 & +1 & 0 \\
0 & 0 & 0 & 0 \\
0 & 0 & +1 & 0
\end{array}
$$

The move generator then continues its scan of the array until the next positive entry is found.

In order to keep track of the boards and the corresponding arrays, they can be numbered consecutively as they are generated. Any square on any board can then be specified by giving the board number and the row and column. As the move generator constructs the checkers tree, it must keep a record of the connections between boards. When the pro-

Traversing the Game Tree

When a checkers-playing program is selecting a move, it needs to explore the game tree to some fixed depth, visiting each branch exactly once. A simple method of traversing the tree employs a table of pointers, which record the relations among branches, and a data structure called a push-down stack, which monitors the program's current position in the tree and maintains a list of the branches yet to be visited.

As each new board is generated it is assigned a number, which serves as an index to the array of pointers. The pointer associated with a board is itself a list of board numbers. The first number in the list is that of the board's parent; all the other numbers point to its children. If the program has reached board 47, the contents of the pointer indicate that it should continue the search with boards 52, 57, and 62. If the program is at board 62 and it must return to the parent, the first entry in the pointer directs it back to board 47.

It is the function of the pushdown stack to keep track of the program's progress through the table of pointers. The stack itself can be created by setting up an array called STACK and a variable called TOP, which holds the address of the top item on the stack. Whenever an item is added to the stack (pushed) or deleted from it (popped), TOP is incremented or decremented.

The item at the top of the stack is the number of the board to be examined next. If 47 is the top item, the tree-traversal algorithm pops that value off the stack and then examines the pointer list for board 47. The first number in the list (referring to the parent of board 47) is ignored, but the remaining nonzero entries are pushed onto the stack and the value of TOP is adjusted accordingly. Hence board 62 is selected for investigation next.

Each time the program reaches a board at the maximum allowed depth,

gram is choosing a move, it searches the game tree down several levels, then up, then down again, and so on. To traverse the tree in this way the program must be able to identify both the "parent" of a board and its "children." To this end the program maintains an array called a pointer table. The pointer for each board is a list of numbers, the first number pointing to the board's parent and the subsequent numbers pointing to its children (*see* the box on pages 116–117).

The next major component of the checkers program, the board evaluator, is given a board as input and computes a number reflecting the value of the board for Black. A high number means Black is likely to win if the position is reached in actual play. A good board evaluator is difficult to design because there are many factors to consider in judging a position. In most games, including checkers, it is not always clear what weight should be given to the various factors. Here is a short list of relatively primitive factors.

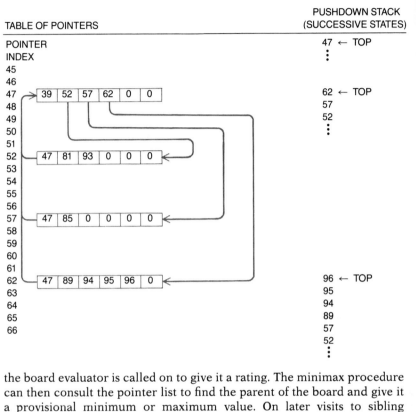

TABLE OF POINTERS

PUSHDOWN STACK
(SUCCESSIVE STATES)

POINTER
INDEX

47 ← TOP

45
46
47   39 52 57 62 0 0   62 ← TOP
48   57
49   52
50
51
52   47 81 93 0 0 0
53
54
55
56
57   47 85 0 0 0 0
58
59
60
61
62   47 89 94 95 96 0   96 ← TOP
63   95
64   94
65   89
66   57
                                     52

the board evaluator is called on to give it a rating. The minimax procedure can then consult the pointer list to find the parent of the board and give it a provisional minimum or maximum value. On later visits to sibling boards the procedure will have an opportunity to revise the value.

MEN: add 1 for each Black man on the board; subtract 1 for each Red man.

KINGS: add 1 for each Black king on the board; subtract 1 for each Red king.

CENTER: add 1 for each Black man occupying one of the four center squares; subtract 1 for each Red man there.

ADVANCE: add 1 for each Black man in the second row, 2 for each Black man in the third row, 3 for each Black man (king) in the fourth row. Subtract the corresponding numbers for Red.

MOBILITY: add 1 for each move available to Black and subtract 1 for each move available to Red.

What is the relative importance of these factors? Should KINGS get double the weight of MEN? Does ADVANCE already include the information available in KINGS and MEN?

Samuel answered such questions by allowing his program to determine how much weight to give each factor based on its playing experience. Relying on 39 factors in all (many suggested by checkers experts and books), Samuel's board evaluator initially gave them all the same weight and simply added the numbers to obtain the value of a board. Each lost game was analyzed by the program, and the factor that led to the losing move was isolated. The weight of that factor was then reduced. The process was speeded by automating the analysis and having the program play itself a number of times.

Board-evaluation procedures are never perfect. If they were, the other components of a game-playing program would hardly be necessary: the program would only have to examine the boards one move ahead, evaluate each board, and then choose the best move. There is a trade-off of sorts between the accuracy of the board evaluator and the number of levels the program must look ahead. If the evaluator could do little more than recognize a won or lost position, the checkers tree would have to be examined all the way to the bottom!

The third major component is the minimax procedure, essentially a tree-searching program that uses the board values at the lowest level searched to assign values to boards higher up in the tree. At some point in the search all the boards at a certain level must be rated by the board evaluator. A board B on the level above that one is given a value according to the following simple rule: If B has Red to move, select the minimum value found among B's children as the value of B; if B has Black to move, select the maximum value.

The reasoning supporting this rule should be clear. If it is Red's turn to move, Black may as well assume that Red will choose a move minimizing the value of the resulting board for Black. By the same token, if it is Black's turn to move, the board of maximum value will be chosen. The minimax procedure therefore starts at the deepest level of the tree currently being examined, evaluates all the boards at that level and then carries the values back up the tree. In going from one level to the next-higher one it alternately minimizes and maximizes, depending on the turn. Ultimately it arrives at the current board and presents Black with a value for each possible move. Naturally Black chooses the move with the highest value.

A checkers program consists of more than these three components. It must interact with a human player, accept moves from a keyboard, and print the moves it decides on. In addition it may display a picture of the current board with symbols representing the two sides and their pieces. In many cases the program also allows the human player to select a "level of expertise" at which the program is to play. The level is generally a number that reflects the program's look-ahead: the number of levels in the checkers tree it is to explore from the current position.

When the look-ahead is set to a fairly deep level, the program invariably takes longer to move; each additional level of the tree to be explored may double the time needed. To reduce the amount of searching the program must do, the minimax procedure may incorporate a clever idea called alpha-beta pruning, discussed in the box on pages 120–121. Alpha-beta pruning can be done at virtually every level of the tree and can eliminate a tremendous amount of unnecessary searching and evaluation.

The checkers-playing algorithm is not difficult to program. Indeed, Truscott feels there is no need to have a large mainframe computer to compete effectively. "The microprocessor is well suited for developing checker programs," he writes, "and industrious hobbyists will probably make significant contributions in this challenging, rewarding, and still completely open area."

For readers with some programming experience the foregoing account would be complete enough for them to design and write a checkers program. Other readers may still be uncertain how to proceed. The construction of a move generator and that of a board evaluator are reasonably straightforward projects, but the minimax procedure may call for discussion in greater detail. How does a program move up and down the game tree, remembering where it has already been and deciding where to go next? Some advice on traversing the tree is given in the box on pages 116–117.

Once a game-playing program has been designed, written, and debugged, its limitations generally become apparent when it is run with the look-ahead set to a large value. Moves can take too long or the amount of space needed to store the game tree can exceed the available memory. There are many tricks for reducing demands on time and space. For example, I have represented each checkerboard by a two-dimensional array in which half of the elements (those corresponding to the light squares) are invariably 0. The board can be reduced to a one-dimensional array with the empty spaces eliminated. When that is done, however, the rule for generating moves becomes more complex.

The question of whether it is possible to write a checkers-playing program that never loses to a human player boils down to a question about the nature of checkers itself. In nth-order checkers is there a strategy by which Black can always win? Can Red always force a win? Is the game a draw? An analysis of nth-order checkers is possible by hand only when n is 2. I have analyzed 4-by-4 checkers by laying out the game tree down to an average of 10 moves. At this level there are a few wins for Black and an equally small number of losses. The remaining positions all seem to be drawn ones in which kings chase one another eternally around the cramped quarters of the 4-by-4 board. I have not confirmed draws in all cases, but if my evaluations are correct, the minimax procedure gives the opening board a value of 0—a draw.

The Minimax Procedure and Tree Pruning

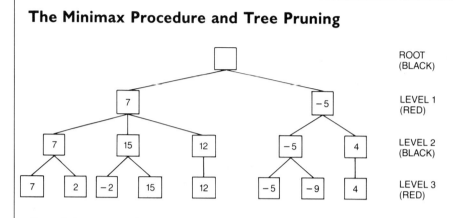

The minimax procedure is applied to a game tree after all the legal moves have been generated to some preset depth and the board evaluator has estimated the value of the position reached at the end of each branch. Here it is Black's turn to play, the tree has been searched to a depth of three levels, and the board evaluator has assigned to each terminal board an integer reflecting its relative value to Black. The task of the minimax procedure is to select a move for Black based on these values.

Note that the sequence of moves most favorable for Black leads through boxes labeled 7, 15, and 15; Red, on the other hand, would favor moves yielding the sequence −5, −5, and −9. The minimax procedure takes into account these conflicting preferences. The program first examines all the level 3 moves that are "children" of a given "parent" move at level 2. Since it is Black's turn to move at level 2, the parent is assigned the

Is 6-by-6 checkers a draw? When the program written by my students played against itself at large look-ahead settings, the games seldom reached a conclusion. On this basis alone one might be tempted to conjecture that 6-by-6 checkers is a draw. Naturally, if both 4-by-4 and 6-by-6 checkers turn out to be draws, the shadow of suspicion will fall heavily on 8-by-8 checkers. Perhaps someone reading this has that rare combination of skill and daring (or is it foolhardiness?) to write a 6-by-6 checkers-tree analyzer. On a mainframe computer the project may just be possible.

On the subject of nth-order checkers there are some interesting results from theorists of computing. It turns out the following problem is computationally intractable: "Given an arbitrary legal placement of Black and Red kings and men on a $2n$-by-$2n$ board, decide whether Black can win." In 1978 the problem was shown to be "P-space hard" by Ariezri Fraenkel of the Weizmann Institute of Science in Israel and by

value of the highest-rated child. The same procedure is used to assign values to the boards at level 1, but because it is Red's turn, the lowest values are chosen. If both players evaluate the boards in the same way, play would follow a path through moves rated 7, 7, and 7.

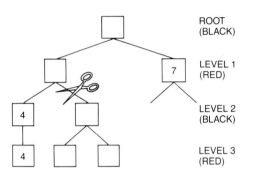

Search trees deeper than a few levels can be enormous, and only by pruning them can a thorough search be made. Here it is Black's turn to move, and a partial search has already given a value of 7 to one of Black's choices at level 1. In investigating the other choice the program has found that one of Red's possible responses at level 2 has a value of 4. It follows that there is no reason to explore the rest of the tree; since Red will choose the lowest-value move, Black's alternative at level 1 cannot have a value greater than 4, and so the move assigned a value of 7 is preferable. The elimination of paths that Black can ignore is called alpha pruning; the corresponding process for Red is beta pruning.

Michael R. Garey and David Johnson of AT&T Bell Laboratories. For a problem to be *P*-space hard is even worse than for it to be *NP*-complete, and most theorists think problems classified *NP*-complete are unlikely to have any practical general solution. The finding suggests that if a program could play perfect *n*th-order checkers, the average time to generate a move would increase faster than any polynomial function of *n*.

A program that would never lose a game of checkers would also depend heavily on computational power. Even if checkers were inherently a drawn game, a successful program would undoubtedly have a fairly large look-ahead factor, other things being equal. Truscott writes of the program he developed with Jensen: "Averaging 5 seconds per move (on an IBM 370/165), the program is just able to defeat its authors. Averaging 20 seconds per move, the program is perhaps the 100th-strongest checker player in the United States. Averaging 80 seconds per move, the program is perhaps the 10th-strongest player in the world."

Sometimes it is disillusioning to read a description of a game-playing program in which its internal operations are laid bare. It is easy enough when playing against a program opponent and knowing nothing of how it works to impute to it marvelous intellectual powers it simply does not have. For many people the fantasy is enjoyable. One can only hope that disappointment over its loss is replaced by delight in the structure and operation of game-playing programs.

The boy had asked whether it is possible to write a checkers-playing program that would never lose to a human player. The question touches on two themes central to artificial intelligence: what is intelligence, and how intelligently can programs be made to behave? When such questions are brought to focus on restricted forms of human "intelligent" activity such as game playing, the question seems to dissolve into a mass of technical details. Is the answer there?

The search for a theory of intelligence continues. Some AI workers have suggested that constructing a machine that thinks may be somewhat like constructing a machine that flies. A kind of "intellectual airfoil" theory may be possible. To fly it is not necessary to build a mechanical bird; an airplane performs quite adequately. Will we ever have an AIrplane?

Addendum

The most interesting reaction to my discussion of programs that play checkers came from Marion F. Tinsley, the current world checkers champion. Tinsley, a topologist at Florida A&M University, wrote: "On the basis of games that I have seen played by the Jensen-Truscott program, it would rank about 200th in the U.S." Indeed, the American Checkers Federation issued the following challenge to checkers programmers: Tinsley will play a 20-game match with a computer program for a stake of $5000 a side, winner take all. During the five-year period of the challenge no one picked up the gauntlet. William B. Grandjean, secretary of the American Checkers Federation, told me recently that the challenge will be reissued at the slightest sign of interest from the computing community.

Readers wanting more information about organized checkers are encouraged to write to Grandjean at the address indicated in the List of Suppliers.

Automated Magic

Put the words "magic" and "computer" in the same sentence and you are likely to throw a rational person into a state of cognitive dissonance. How could magic, the essence of a shadowy world we chain off with links of logic, invade the computer, the primary expression of our rationality? The dissonance lies in the word "magic" as a symbol of the supernatural. In reality magic is a piece of the natural world, and magicians are logical folk.

To bring off a feat of magic three things are sufficient, if not always necessary: audience, props, and presentation. I have seen magic done without props but never without an audience; any audience will do, but I must leave the hornswoggling to the aspiring magician. A computer, however, makes a very clever prop, and I shall assume here that the magician can materialize at least a microcomputer. Simple programming enables the machine to guess a card drawn at random, to engage in numerical precognition, and to determine the identity of a card by telepathy, all to the consternation of a hapless volunteer. In fact, even a hand calculator is enough to put you into the business of mind reading.

So much for audience and props. Presentation is everything else. It converts the inner logic of a trick into an outer appearance. Real magic holds the stage only for as long as the magician can sustain and manipulate certain beliefs in the minds of the audience. Each belief seems to lead inexorably to the next one, until there is an astonishing denouement. Sometimes it helps to weave a spell before beginning a trick, and there is plenty of mumbo jumbo for that purpose available from computer science. You are advised to use it liberally with the uninitiate and judiciously with the knowledgeable. Here is how the first feat of magic might be introduced.

"Ladies and gentlemen, sooner or later it was bound to happen. A breakthrough in artificial intelligence has made it possible for computers to read the human mind. The theory of recursive nondeterminism guarantees that a certain nonpolynomial algorithm, first described by the famous Tibetan computer scientist Professor Yan Kee, will always emerge from infinite loops. Step by step the program cycles through a semi-infinite stochastic data structure, retrieving logical primitives and compiling them into data-base queries. . . . [One may ramble in this way for some time.] May I have a volunteer from the audience, please."

The unfortunate volunteer is introduced and then asked to pick a card from a deck at random. Any card will do. The magician holds up the card for all to see. Suppose it is the six of clubs. This is a good time to make an even bigger fool of the volunteer. The magician says: "Please press the card against your forehead and concentrate hard. Your mind and the programmed mind of the computer must reach a state of simulated simultaneity."

The magician then goes to the computer keyboard and starts the program. Immediately a message appears on the screen. The magician reads the following dialogue aloud for the benefit of the audience:

> "IS THE SUBJECT CONCENTRATING?" (The computer speaks in capital letters.) "Yes." (The magician types the answer.)
> "IS THE CARD BLACK?" "Yes."
> "IS IT CLUBS?" "Yes."
> "IS IT AN 8 OR LESS?" "Yes."
> "IS IT A 5 OR MORE?" "Yes."
> "IS IT A 5 OR 6?" "Yes."
> "IS IT A 6?" "Yes."

Time after time the program zeros in on the selected card by asking seven questions. Amazingly, the answer to every question is yes, as though the program merely wanted confirmation. Readers might well wonder how the trick is accomplished. Ordinarily I would hesitate to satisfy that curiosity: there is an unwritten code among magicians that forbids revealing sleights of hand. The magician's livelihood depends on an air of impenetrable mystery, and so I cannot disclose the basis of all the tricks presented here. For this clever card trick, though, I have permission to go public from my source Christopher Morgan, a former practicing magician. Morgan is now an executive at the Lotus Development Corporation in Cambridge; presumably his livelihood is no longer based on magic.

When the volunteer draws the card from the deck, the magician notes it carefully, then strides with a flourish to the keyboard and types "yes" in answer to each question. Each "yes," however, may be accomplished by an unobtrusive stroke of the space bar. The presence or absence of the space bar is not really the answer to the preceding question; instead it determines the content of the next one. Thus when Professor

Yan Kee's fabulous program asks, "IS THE SUBJECT CONCENTRATING?" the magician types y e s space bar only if the selected card is black. If the card is red, the magician types y e s only. The program then knows enough to ask the right question at the next stage. If the magician typed a space, the program asks, "IS THE CARD BLACK?" Otherwise it asks, "IS THE CARD RED?"

In this way the magician guides the program down the branches of an implicit binary tree; the hidden logic encodes all the choices needed to identify any card in the deck (*see* Figure 38). For example, after the color of the selected card is determined, the next choice governs its suit.

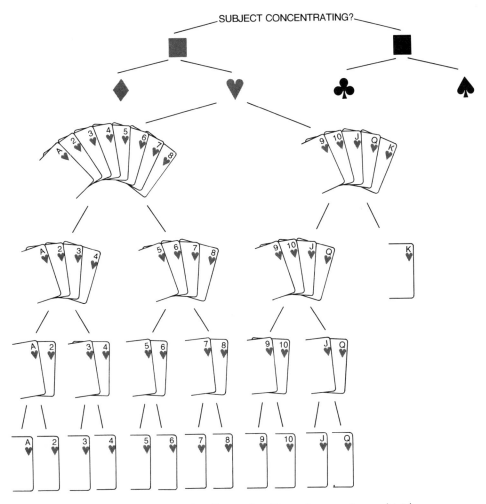

Figure 38   The secret decision tree for Christopher Morgan's computer card trick, with selected continuations.

Once the computer "learns" the card is black, the magician can secretly tell it whether the card is clubs or spades. If the card is red, the next step is to distinguish hearts from diamonds. All the remaining choices govern the value of the card: from ace, two, and three up to jack, queen, and king. Since there are 13 possible values, four questions must be asked to distinguish among them.

It is essential that the magician misdirect the audience each time the space bar is touched. The simplest misdirection is based on the carriage-return key (called variously "return" or "enter"). Since it must be pressed each time the magician's answer is entered, a great flourish can be made of pressing it with the right hand while the left hand quietly trips the space bar. Practice makes perfect.

The program I call YAN KEE is longish but quite easy to write. It is divided into 31 small sections, corresponding to the total number of distinct questions it must be able to ask. All the sections have the same basic algorithmic structure:

> XX output "IS THE CARD BLACK?"
> input characters
> compute number of characters
> if number of characters = 4
> then go to YY
> else go to ZZ

Here XX stands for a line number or label to which the execution of the program has passed after the first input y e s space bar in my example. After printing the question appropriate in this section, the program accepts the magician's input characters and simply counts them. If four characters were typed, the magician must have hit the space bar. In this case execution passes to the program section labeled YY, which begins with the question "IS IT CLUBS?" If, on the other hand, the magician did not press the space bar, the program branches to the section labeled ZZ, which begins with the question "IS IT SPADES?" All would-be magicians must memorize the decision process inherent in the space-bar option at each level of questioning.

The next feat of programmed legerdemain was suggested by Michael Rohregger, a reader in Linz, Austria. The computer magician, having appealed to the same questionable theories outlined earlier, now advances the claim that a second program is able to divine a person's thoughts even before they occur to the thinker! Unfortunately, the magician goes on, development in this area is not yet complete, and so the program succeeds only most of the time. A volunteer is summoned from the audience, seated in a chair and asked to choose between the two bits, or numbers, 0 and 1. To keep the volunteer from being distracted by the computer monitor it may be best if both the volunteer and the monitor face the audience.

The volunteer calls out a number and the magician and the audience compare it with a digit already displayed on the monitor. If the digits are the same, the magician nods sagely. If they are different, the magician explains that it may take some time for the program to tune in to the volunteer's mental processes. (Indeed, the volunteer can always be blamed for causing "statistical static.") The magician presses a key and the program predicts the next bit to be chosen by the volunteer. The volunteer is asked to choose again. The experiment is repeated as many times as it takes for the program "to synchronize or nearly synchronize with the volunteer's space-time thought framework." Every time the volunteer calls out a number the magician nods and smiles if the machine is right and frowns patiently if there is a failure.

At first the program appears to score no better than chance: it is right only about 50 percent of the time. As the experiment is repeated, however, there is a marked improvement: the program tends to score at least 60 percent, and in some cases it may do considerably better. Here is how it works.

The program, called PREDICTABIT, maintains a 16-by-2 array called *subject*. Each of the 16 rows is indexed by one of 16 possible sequences of four consecutive bits. The columns of the array represent the two possible bit choices, 0 and 1. The first entry in a row is the number of times the volunteer has chosen a 0 immediately after choosing the sequence of bits corresponding to the row index. The second entry is the number of times the volunteer has followed the sequence by a 1.

For example, suppose the volunteer has chosen the bits 0, 1, 1, 1 in the preceding four trials. The program treats the bits as a single binary number and converts them into its decimal equivalent, in this case 7. If *subject*(7,0) is equal to 4 and *subject*(7,1) is equal to 2, the volunteer has followed the sequence 0, 1, 1, 1 by a 0 four times in the past but only twice by another 1. Given such past performance, the program predicts the volunteer's next choice will be a 0.

The program implicit in this description is probably already fairly clear. In its simplest form PREDICTABIT cycles through six simple sections:

> Input latest bit
> Update array at old sequence index
> Shift variables
> Form new sequence index
> Compare *subject* entries
> Make prediction

As soon as the volunteer calls out a binary digit, the magician types it into the computer. Four variables called *first, second, third,* and *fourth* hold the volunteer's preceding four choices. A variable called *index* stores the row number computed on the basis of the current values of the variables *first* through *fourth*. If the latest bit called out is 0, the program adds 1 to *subject(index,0)*. Otherwise it adds 1 to *subject (index,1)*.

The third section of the program then shifts the contents of the four variables as follows:

$$fourth \leftarrow \text{latest bit (input)}$$
$$third \leftarrow fourth$$
$$second \leftarrow third$$
$$first \leftarrow second$$

PREDICTABIT forms the new sequence index number by computing a sum of products: $1 \times first + 2 \times second + 4 \times third + 8 \times fourth$. Next the program compares *subject(index,0)* with *subject(index,1)* for the newly computed value of *index*. If *subject(index,0)* exceeds *subject(index,1)*, PREDICTABIT prints a 0 on the screen as its next prediction. Otherwise it prints a 1. To operate successfully the program must also predict the volunteer's first four guesses, just to fill in dummy values of the first four variables. The dummy values might as well all be 0s.

For the magician who wants to announce PREDICTABIT's rate of success there is one more feature worth including in the program. Declare a new variable called *score*, and just before the shift section insert additional instructions that compare *fourth* with the latest bit called out by the volunteer. If they are equal, add 1 to *score*. When the demonstration is finished, the program divides *score* by the number of trials, multiplies by 100 and displays the result.

The trick works because people tend to adopt rules unconsciously when they try picking one of two alternatives at random. For example, after choosing two 0s in a row, it is tempting to make the next digit a 1. In fighting this tendency many people may add a third 0, but then the temptation to make the next digit a 1 becomes even greater. The probability that the next digit will be a 1 increases with each 0 added to the sequence. In a truly random selection, of course, the previous choices have no bearing at all on the choice of each succeeding digit: the probability that the next digit will be 1 is always the same, namely .5.

Perhaps even subtler factors operate when people try to choose a random bit. Again, however, if such factors somehow depend on recent history, PREDICTABIT should be successful. I have found, incidentally, that it is crucial to avoid subjects who think too creatively. Such people tend to adopt rules consciously and then change them in the middle of the demonstration, with disastrous results. To keep a volunteer from becoming too unpredictable it might be wise to add some misdirecting patter, such as: "When I press this key, the program will predict the number you will think of next. It is crucial that you *not* think of your number yet—otherwise the machine will have the unfair advantage of being able to read your mind directly." Thereafter the magician must continually caution the volunteer to wait until the key is struck. Remember that the key struck is the volunteer's guess on the preceding round.

In my next feat of magic the computer is both prop and magician. The (human) magician hands the volunteer a deck of ordinary playing cards and intones: "Please have a seat before the computer incarnation of a great magician, now departed this life." To further bamboozle the volunteer, one can make glib analogies between spirit and software. If necessary, one can go on with the theories of Professor Yan Kee. Finally the magician asks the volunteer to press the space bar. The following instructions emerge from the Beyond. When one instruction has been carried out, a tap on the space bar brings up the next:

SHUFFLE THE CARDS THOROUGHLY, SQUARE THEM UP, AND PLACE THEM FACEDOWN ON THE TABLE [space bar].

CUT THE DECK ROUGHLY IN THE MIDDLE, NOTE THE CARD EXPOSED, AND RESTORE THE DECK [space bar].

DEAL THE CARDS FACE DOWN INTO SIX SMALLER HANDS [space bar].

TAKE A MOMENT TO LOOK THROUGH EACH PILE UNTIL YOU FIND THE ONE CONTAINING THE CUT CARD [space bar].

NOW DEAL ONE CARD AT A TIME FROM THE PILE CONTAINING THE CUT CARD; DEAL EACH CARD FACEUP, CONCENTRATE ON IT, AND PRESS THE SPACE BAR WHEN YOU ARE READY FOR ME TO DECIDE WHETHER IT WAS THE CARD YOU PICKED [space bar].

As the volunteer deals the cards one at a time, the program echoes the decision of the departed magician. "NO" is the first response. A tap on the space bar tells the magician's spirit that another card has been dealt. Again "NO." After a few more cards the spirit suddenly cries out (so to speak): "STOP, HERE IT IS!"

The third program in this series is the simplest. I call it HOUDINI for reasons I hope will be obvious. HOUDINI simply displays the instructions above, one set at a time, until the volunteer starts dealing the cards from the pile that includes the cut card. The program says "STOP" when the fourth card is dealt. That card or the next one is always the cut card.

HOUDINI is so simple it needs little or no description. When it runs, however, the temporarily unemployed human magician might hover near the volunteer, sharing in the growing amazement and generally making sure things go right. The cut, for example, must be made within a few cards of the center of the deck. The order of the cards in the six piles must also be maintained while they are searched. Finally, the human magician must interpret the STOP command. If the fourth card is the one sought, the silicon spirit of the machine has read the volunteer's mind. If the fifth card is magical, however, the magician advises the volunteer to turn it over. "Leaping LISP," says the magician, "I might have known. The great Houdini has read the cards by direct clairvoyance!"

True to my promise not to reveal in this discussion the basis of all the magic presented here, I leave the explanation of this last trick to be revealed in the Addendum. I am indebted for the trick to Harry Lorayne, a New York magician and memory expert. HOUDINI is a computer adaptation of Lorayne's well-known "Stop!" trick.

The last bit of mind reading comes by way of Martin Gardner, and it requires only the humble hand calculator. The magician calls a volunteer from the audience. After giving the calculator to the volunteer, the magician turns away, touches his brow, and vamps on about some kind of electronic communion with the calculator's circuitry. At last he explains the following procedure to the volunteer:

"Choose any row, column, or main diagonal of the numeric key pad. This is the little square of numbers from 1 to 9. Enter the digits in that

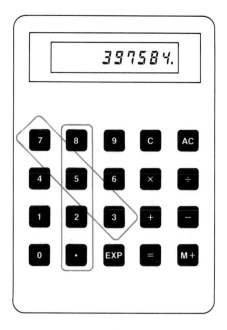

Figure 39   Magic product of two "colinear" numbers.

line in any order you like. OK? You should have a three-digit number in the display. Now press the multiplication key and select another line— that is, another row, column, or main diagonal of the little square. Got one? Good. Again, enter those three numbers in any order you like. Now you should have another three-digit number in the display. When you press the equal sign, the product of the two three-digit numbers will appear in the display. Do you see it? That is a magic number. Choose any nonzero digit from the number, but do not tell me what it is. Tell me the other numbers instead. No, the order is not important; I just want to clear them out of your mind so that you can concentrate on the number you did not tell me. Very good. Now concentrate on that all-important number and with a little luck, I should be able to pick it up."

Readers may attempt to discover how the magician determines the missing number. Look closely at Figure 39. In the Addendum I shall describe the adventures and misadventures of readers who attempted the magic programs presented here.

Addendum

The previous discussion of computer magic left the inner logic of two tricks unrevealed. The first of them was based on the well-known "Stop!" trick of Harry Lorayne, a New York magician. A volunteer chooses a card from the middle of a well-shuffled deck and then replaces it. The volunteer deals the deck into six smaller hands and finds the hand that includes the chosen card. The computer then instructs the volunteer to deal out the hand; after each card is dealt the computer tells the volunteer whether to continue dealing or to stop, thereby indicating the position of the chosen card in the deck.

How does the computer stop at the chosen card? The answer is that when the volunteer deals out the six hands, one card from the central six cards of the original deck is dealt into each of the six piles. Each of the six cards occupies the same relative position in its pile, namely the fourth. Because the volunteer deals only from the pile that includes the chosen card, the computer can always pick the card by stopping the deal after the fourth card.

The second unexplained trick was based on the key pad of an ordinary calculator. A volunteer enters two three-digit numbers into the calculator, multiplies them, and calls out all but one of the digits. How does the magician guess the missing number?

According to the magician's instructions, each three-digit number selected by the volunteer must come from the digits along a row, a column, or a main diagonal of the key pad. Such a number has the mystical property of "3-ness" after casting out 9s. When the digits of the numbers are added together, their sum can be a one- or a two-digit number. If the sum is a two-digit number, the sum of the two digits is a one-digit number. In either case the final one-digit result is a multiple of 3. For example, along the first column the number 471 is reduced to 12 and then to 3, which is a multiple of 3. On the other hand, when the two three-digit numbers selected by the volunteer are multiplied and the product is subjected to the same peculiar treatment, the result is 9. The procedure is equivalent to multiplication modulo 9—hence the term "casting out 9s." If one of the digits in the product, say x, is missing, the result of casting out 9s for the remaining digits is $9 - x$. This number is computed by the magician as the volunteer reads off all but one of the digits. In most cases knowing $9 - x$ makes x instantly computable.

A twist to the calculator trick was suggested by Carl Fulves of Teaneck, N.J. As before, the magician asks the volunteer to select the two colinear numbers and to multiply them using the calculator. In my discussion I had suggested that the volunteer withhold one of the numbers from the product; the magician could then "guess" it by casting out 9s. Somewhat more impressive is the addition of some canine (or feline) misdirection. The volunteer withholds nothing and instead adds the age of a pet. If the age is not greater than nine, the magician can easily recapture it: "Madame, I divine Tinkerbelle's age to be five."

Russell J. Mullennix, an engineer with the Georgia Power Company in Valdosta, Ga., told me of a brief but instructive adventure with PREDICTABIT, the program that attempts to predict what bit a volunteer will think of next. After a reasonably long stream of 0s and 1s, the program's predictions should improve. They might do so because of unconscious patterns in the volunteer's efforts to be random. Mullennix had modest success with a colleague, scoring percentages in the high 50s. When his colleague caught onto the program's probable modus operandi, however, he began to select bits based on the digits of pi. The program's prowess dropped to a dismal 43 percent. Readers cannot say they were not warned. Subjects must either be carefully selected for credulity or be kept off balance by a patter that prevents them from thinking about what they are doing.

WORLD FOUR

Life in Automata

The world of automata in its widest sense embraces all of the conceptual models of computation used by computer scientists—from finite state machines to Turing machines. Some automata operate in a cellular space that can be one-, two-, or even three-dimensional. A one-dimensional cellular automaton consists of a strip of cells each in a specific state. As time goes on each cell changes its state according to a rule that takes the states of neighboring cells into account. Among the myriad of possible one-dimensional cellular automata are some that act like miniature computers. The search for these computers marks an exciting area of research. Included in two-dimensional cellular automata is the well-known game of Life first popularized by Martin Gardner in SCIENTIFIC AMERICAN in the late 1960s. Three-dimensional automata have recently become the scene for a new game of Life that includes all the features of the old game and then some.

The most advanced automaton of all is the Turing machine; it does anything a computer can do albeit much more slowly. An amazing amount of research has centered on the question of how many 1s a Turing machine can be made to print on an initially blank tape before halting. The champion machines in this regard are called busy beavers. A reader of the busy beaver column on its first appearance in SCIENTIFIC AMERICAN (August, 1984) found a Turing machine that turned out to be busier than any previously known!

One-Dimensional Computers

Immersed as we now are in a world of artificial computers it is interesting to consider the possibility that we are also surrounded by natural ones. Computers made of water, wind, and wood (to mention just a few possibilities) may be bubbling, sighing, or quietly growing without our suspecting that such activities are tantamount to a turmoil of computation whose best description is itself. This is not to say that such natural systems compute conventionally, only that their structure makes computation a possibility that is latent.

An eloquent exponent of this insight is Stephen Wolfram, a theoretical physicist at the Center for Complex Systems Research, University of Illinois. Wolfram notes that a turbulent flow of fluid or the growth of a plant consists of rather simple components whose combined behavior is so complex that it may not be reducible to a mathematical statement—its best description is itself. The irreducibility of a natural system would follow from a demonstration of its ability to store, transmit, and manipulate information; that is, to its ability to compute. In the September, 1984, issue of SCIENTIFIC AMERICAN Wolfram describes the use of cellular automata to explore this possibility. He proposes to find a cellular automaton that both computes and mimics a natural system. Wolfram's search focuses on the simplest of all possible cellular automata, those that have only a single dimension (*see* Color Plate 6).

Such automata consist of simple elements that combine to generate complexity. Wolfram suggests that lurking among them are true computers, vast linear arrays of cells blinking from state to state and churning out any calculation a three-dimensional computer is capable of. Wolfram, currently searching through the myriad of one-dimensional cellular automata, is not above enlisting the help of amateurs in this daring and sophisticated enterprise. I shall describe the search and its consequences for natural computers in more detail below.

Before embarking on that adventure readers are invited on a short journey (computationally speaking) from the land of three dimensions down to the unbelievably narrow confines of one dimension. A good jumping-off place is three-dimensional computers, the ones currently inhabiting offices, factories, and homes. They consist of fairly simple elements linked in a complex way. I speak here not of input or output devices but of the heart of the machine, a thin silicon chip housing thousands of logic gates, memory elements, registers, and other components. All of these are connected by an elegant pattern of tiny wires. The fact that the circuitry clings to a silicon surface does not mean it is two-dimensional. For one thing, when two connections cross, one must pass under the other. In addition, the silicon substrate of the circuitry mediates the function of every logic component.

Two-dimensional computers are to be found only in spaces with two dimensions, such as the Planiverse (*see* Bibliography). This realm is inhabited by a race of beings called Ardeans. The Ardeans have apparently succeeded in constructing a two-dimensional computer using just one type of logic element. We call it a NAND gate. Its output is a 1 if at least one of its inputs is a 0. Not only can a computer be constructed entirely from such gates but also the thorny problem of crossed connectors can be solved. The Ardeans create a special plane circuit from 12 NAND gates so that two signals entering the circuit from the left in order *ab* leave on the right in order *ba* (*see* Figure 40). Hence two signals may be crossed even if connections cannot. At the same time, the number 12 seems a bit excessive and the Ardeans would be grateful to any readers who can find a simpler NAND circuit that still enables signals to cross.

There is also a discrete two-dimensional space called Life, a game invented by John Horton Conway, the well-known University of Cambridge mathematician. Readers may remember this engaging exercise

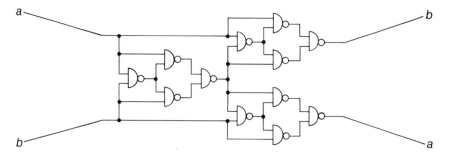

Figure 40　How to make signals cross in a two-dimensional computer.

from "Mathematical Games" columns in SCIENTIFIC AMERICAN by Martin Gardner. In October, 1983, Brian Hayes described in "Computer Recreations" in the same magazine how the game could be realized in a spreadsheet program. Life is an infinite two-dimensional lattice of square cells whose states are influenced by the states of neighboring cells. Time is also discrete and from one tick of a cosmic clock to the next each cell is either alive or dead depending on a set of very simple rules:

> If a cell is dead at time t, it comes alive at time $t + 1$ if, and only if, exactly three of its eight neighbors are alive at time t.
>
> If a cell is alive at time t, it dies at time $t + 1$ if, and only if, fewer than two or more than three neighbors are alive at time t.

With this set of rules everywhere in effect on Life's lattice, an initial configuration of live cells may grow interminably, fall into a cyclic pattern, or eventually die off. Through more than a decade of experimentation by Life enthusiasts it has become clear that Life is far more complicated than anyone had thought.

For one thing, it has turned out that computers can be constructed within Life's cellular space. The discovery came incrementally over a period of a few years. In 1969, shortly after he designed the game, Conway discovered a curious little pattern now called a glider. It blinked through four generations only to recover its original form at a location displaced diagonally by the space of one cell. On a monitor displaying the output of a particularly fast Life program a glider resembles a small creature from an exobiologic fantasy, wiggling its tail as it crawls across the screen. It travels at one-fourth the speed of light (in a cellular sense).

Although no one recognized it at the time, here was a medium of communication for use in a two-dimensional Life computer: instead of electronic pulses, use gliders!

The next step in the construction came in 1970 with the discovery by R. William Gosper, Jr., and several colleagues of a glider gun (*see* Figure 41). Gosper, then a student at the Massachusetts Institute of Technology, was keen on collecting the $50 prize that Conway had offered in Gardner's column. The prize would go to the first person who demonstrated conclusively that an initial configuration could grow without limit. Gosper's glider gun spewed out a new glider every 30 moves. The gun and the gliders constituted an ever growing population of live cells.

Besides Gosper there were other students at M.I.T. pursuing Life in their spare time. One of these was Michael D. Beeler, who particularly enjoyed the analogy between Life and particle physics. Beeler trained a beam of one or more gliders on various targets, carefully noting the sometimes boring and sometimes spectacular results of the collisions.

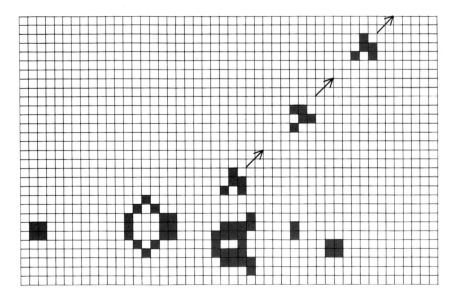

Figure 41   R. William Gosper's glider gun in action.

He even sent two beams of gliders into each other in various ways. His persistence was rewarded by some useful observations.

One such observation was that two gliders could collide and annihilate each other. This made possible the construction of the next component of a computer, logic gates. The simplest of these was a NOT gate. It changes one logic signal into another; 0 input becomes 1 output and vice versa. Life's NOT gate is constructed as follows. Set up a glider gun to send gliders in a specified direction. Binary numbers to be input to the NOT gate are encoded in a second stream of gliders aimed at right angles to the first one. In the input stream a glider may be present (a 1) or absent (a 0). This stream intersects the stream from the glider gun in such a way that when two gliders collide, they annihilate each other. This means that a glider in the input stream punches a hole in the glider-gun stream, converting a glider (1) into a nonglider (0) in the process. The absence of a glider in the input stream allows a glider from the gun to pass through unmolested. In this way a 0 is converted into a 1. Interestingly, the NOT gate has no structure to speak of: apart from its resident glider gun, it is merely a place where gliders meet (*see* Figure 42). The construction of other gate types such as an AND gate and an OR gate also involves interacting streams of gliders, but it is too complicated to present here.

Memory and other registers are constructed through the interaction of gliders with four-cell configurations called blocks. A single bit of

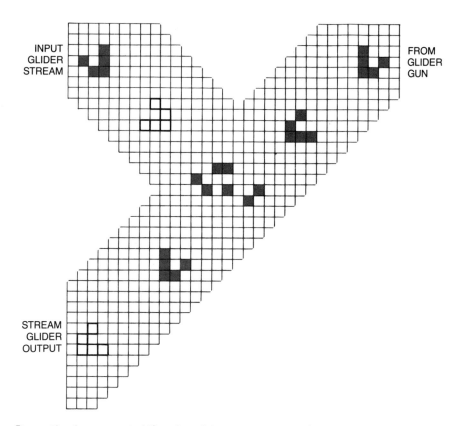

INPUT
GLIDER
STREAM

FROM
GLIDER
GUN

STREAM
GLIDER
OUTPUT

Figure 42 A NOT gate in Life: when gliders are present in the input, they are absent
from the output.

memory is encoded by the position of a block. The block is moved backward or forward by teams of gliders. Two gliders on appropriately chosen courses suffice to move the block three spaces in one direction after crashing into it. Ten gliders directed with equal care will return it to its original place.

There is much ingenuity and interest in the rest of the construction. It is all available in the delightful book *Winning Ways for Your Mathematical Plays,* by Elwyn R. Berlekamp, John H. Conway, and Richard K. Guy. The book is divided into three sections: two-person games, one-person games, and no-person games. Life is found in the last section.

In descending the final step down to one dimension there are only cellular spaces to consider; it is hard to imagine how the Ardeans could reduce their computer to a single continuous line. At first glance cellular space seems nearly as restrictive as that line. We are compensated for decreased dimensionality, however, in not being limited to a single set of rules. Instead we are given the opportunity to make our own rules. Additional compensations arise from the very simplicity of such linear spaces and from the fact that hundreds of generations can be viewed at a glance: place an initial pattern on a line and compute successive generations on successive lines down the page or display screen. A space-time diagram will develop.

A one-dimensional cellular automaton (hereafter called a line automaton) consists of an infinite strip of cells changing states according to a given set of rules. As in the game of Life a cosmic clock ticks away and at each tick every cell enters a state determined by its previous state and the previous states of cells in its neighborhood. A line automaton is specified by giving two numbers called k and r as well as a set of rules for deriving the next state of a cell. The first number, k, determines how many states are allowed for each cell. In Life there are just two states and so k is equal to 2; among the line automata to be considered, higher values of k are common. The second number, r, refers to the radius of neighborhoods used to compute the next state of a cell. The present state of a cell and the states of its r neighbors on both sides determine the next state of the cell. For example, if r is equal to 2 and k is equal to 3, a certain rule might specify that when a cell's neighborhood looks like

$$\boxed{0\,|\,2\,|\,1\,|\,1\,|\,0}$$

the next state adopted by the central cell would be

$$\boxed{2}$$

The set of rules that defines a given line automaton must decide the fate of a cell for every possible configuration of states inhabiting its neighborhood. Depending on the size of k and r the number of possible rule sets to consider can be enormous. For example, given the modest values of k and r described above, there are more line automata than there are atoms in the known universe.

Clearly each person on this planet can pick and choose his or her own personal line automaton. Indeed, I have already selected one for myself. For reasons that will soon be clear it is called Ripple. Ripple allows three states for each cell; each neighborhood consists of three cells, a central cell and two cells flanking it. The rules of Ripple are reasonably straightforward and easily programmed:

1. If a cell is in state 0, its next state will be 2 if its flanking states add up to 2 or more. Otherwise its next state will be 0.
2. If a cell is in state 1, its next state will be 0.

3. If a cell is in state 2, its next state will be 1 if either of the flanking cells is in state 0. Otherwise its next state will be 2.

I am sure that Ripple is not about to replace Life; Ripple was designed to illustrate some of the more interesting possibilities line automata offer. For example, Ripple has simple gliders and an even simpler glider gun (*see* Figure 43).

Assume that Ripple's cellular space is entirely in state 0 except for two adjacent cells. The cell on the left is in state 2 and the other is in state 1. At the next generation this pattern will have shifted by one cell to the left. Undisturbed, the two-cell glider will ripple silently to the left forever. Interchange the states of the two cells and a right-moving glider is created. The glider gun consists of a single cell in state 2. The cell cycles through states 1,0, and then back to 2, issuing a pair of gliders on each cycle. I wonder if anyone can find a gun in Ripple that emits gliders in a single direction only.

Simultaneous activation of a pair of such glider guns produces strange effects. In the process of mutual annihilation the resulting explosions send gliders off in both directions. If the guns are an even number of cells apart, this number of gliders go off in both directions. Otherwise a single gun remains in the middle and shoots out gliders in an interminable stream.

Ripple is just one line automaton. What of the others? The number of possible rule sets to consider is greatly reduced by adopting the ones Wolfram calls totalistic. Here the next state of a given cell is determined only by the sum of the states in the cell's neighborhood. The sum includes the state of the given cell. The number of possible sums varies from 0 to m, where m is the largest value of state multiplied by the size

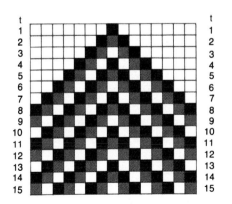

Figure 43   A glider gun in the line automaton Ripple.

of the neighborhood. If one specifies how these sums become the central cell's next state, one has specified the line automaton completely.

For example, there is a very interesting line automaton governed by totalistic rules given in this table:

sum	5	4	3	2	1	0
next state	0	1	0	1	0	0

Here k and r are both equal to 2; the possible values of the sum of states in a five-cell neighborhood vary from 0 to 5. Wolfram calls this set of rules number 20 because the six next-state values in the table represent the number 20 written in binary notation.

There are 64 ways in all that the second row of the table can be filled in. Each one results in a line automaton and Wolfram has examined all 64 of them. Needless to say, a computer is essential in such an investigation. To determine the behavior of a given line automaton, Wolfram forms an initial pattern of some 100 cells in random states and then turns the automaton loose on the pattern. To nullify the effects of the vast arrays of 0s on each side of the pattern, Wolfram makes the left end of the initial pattern contiguous with the right end. This turns the pattern into a circle and its history becomes a cylinder, yet the result is the same as if the initial random pattern were repeated indefinitely in both directions of the original cellular space. In any event the effect of line automata on such random input patterns is surprisingly uniform. Each automaton will fall into one of four broad classes constructed by Wolfram:

Class 1. After a finite number of generations the pattern deteriorates into a single homogeneous state endlessly repeated.
Class 2. The pattern evolves into a number of unvarying or periodic subpatterns.
Class 3. The pattern never develops any structure. Space-time diagrams look chaotic.
Class 4. The pattern develops complex localized subpatterns, some of them long-lasting.

Of the 64 automata in which k and r are both equal to 2, 25 percent are in class 1, 16 percent are in class 2, 53 percent are in class 3, and only 6 percent are in class 4. Wolfram suspects that computers might be found in the fourth class. For example, the line automaton with code number 20 is in class 4.

As though encouraging Wolfram in the search, the code-20 automaton has cheerfully disclosed some gliders. They are 10111011 and

1001111011. Both gliders move to the right. Totalistic rules are always symmetrical; to obtain left-moving gliders merely reverse these patterns. Is there a gun for such gliders in the code-20 space? Wolfram thinks there is. But there is another space where he has yet to find even a glider! It is the code-357 space. When we write this number in ternary notation, we obtain a set of rules for a 3-state line automaton:

sum	6	5	4	3	2	1	0
next state	0	1	0	0	1	1	2

The search for gliders and glider guns calls for the advice of a separate document, which I have persuaded Wolfram to write. It describes an algorithm that hunts for what Wolfram calls persistent structures. Adventurous readers may write to "Glider Gun Guidelines" at the address indicated in the List of Suppliers.

The search for gliders and glider guns focuses on a number of line automata thought to be computation universal. In other words, these are line automata capable of acting like a computer. Besides the code-20 and code-357 automata already discussed, there is the two-state line automaton ($r = 3$, code number 88) in which a glider gun has already been found.

James K. Park, a former student at Princeton University, found the gun in that automaton. Readers who would like to witness Park's glider gun in operation must write a simple program for displaying the generations of a line automaton and for deriving one generation from the next. It is an easy matter to implement line automaton 88 with such a program: when you are ready, input the initial pattern 1111111111011 and watch it expand and contract. The gun spews out a glider in each direction once every 238 generations (*see* Figures 44 and 45).

Rather than implement a specific automaton, readers are advised to write a program that takes arbitrary totalistic rules as input. This is easy to do for fixed values of k and r and almost as easy if these parameters are allowed to vary. Use a special array called *table* for the rules and two linear arrays called *newcells* and *oldcells* to hold the new and the old patterns currently being processed. Make the two arrays as wide as you like but bear in mind that a display screen (depending on the type of display) may show only a limited part of these arrays. Display the largest middle part of *newcells* that fits and cycle through the following steps: Transfer the contents of *newcells* into *oldcells*. Scan *oldcells*; for its ith member add up the value of *oldcells* from $i - r$ to $i + r$. Look up the resulting sum in *table* and transfer the state value so found to the ith member of *newcells*. Next reenter the computational cycle in the display phase and repeat it. Displays can be successive or stationary. In the

Figure 44   A close-up of James K. Park's one-dimensional glider gun.

former case a space-time diagram results; in the latter case one watches a kind of one-dimensional motion picture.

As noted above, a line automaton is called computation-universal if as generation succeeds generation there is an intitial pattern capable of acting like a computer. Part of the initial pattern is the input and part of some later pattern is the output. Is it really possible to build such a computer out of glider guns and various other pieces of cellular hardware? Wolfram thinks it is. In one of the line automata currently under investigation gliders have been found that pass through certain stable subpatterns. This gives hope that the transmission of information within a linear computer need not be blocked by components unconcerned

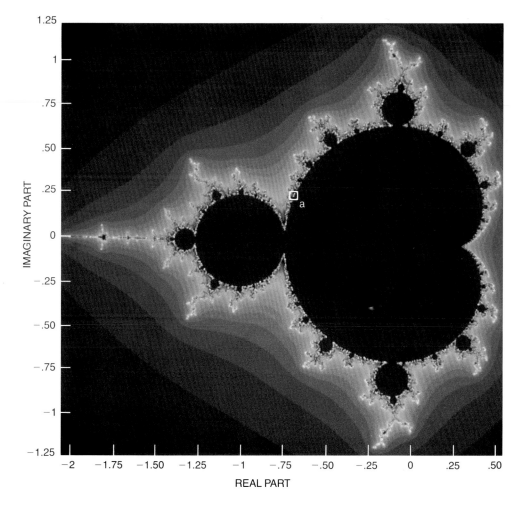

Color Plate I   The Mandelbrot set and its coordinates in the complex plane.

Color Plate 2   Successive enlargements of the "shepherd's crook" in region *a* of Color Plate 1.

Color Plate 3   Wallpaper for the mind is produced by a program of mind-boggling simplicity.

Color Plate 4   The program HOPALONG generates a pattern that is both crystalline and organic.

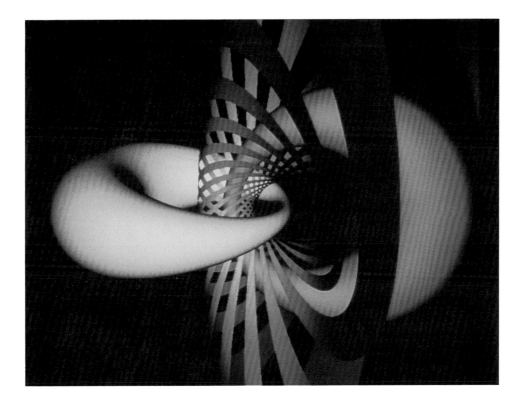

Color Plate 5   Toroidal section of a hypersphere ventilated to reveal structure.

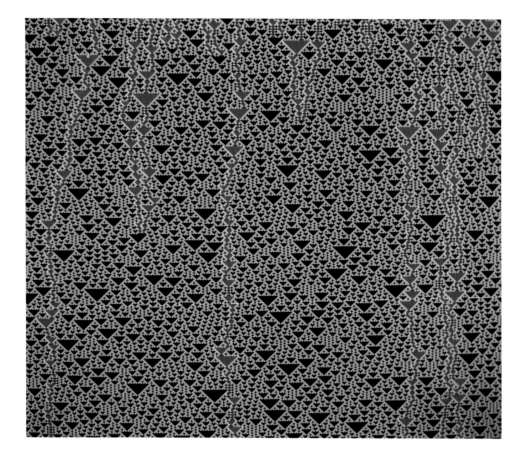

Color Plate 6   Successive generations in the history of a one-dimensional cellular automaton create a
two-dimensional pattern (totalistic rule 18).

Color Plate 7   A glider makes its way through a stable helix in Carter Bays's three-dimensional Life 4555.

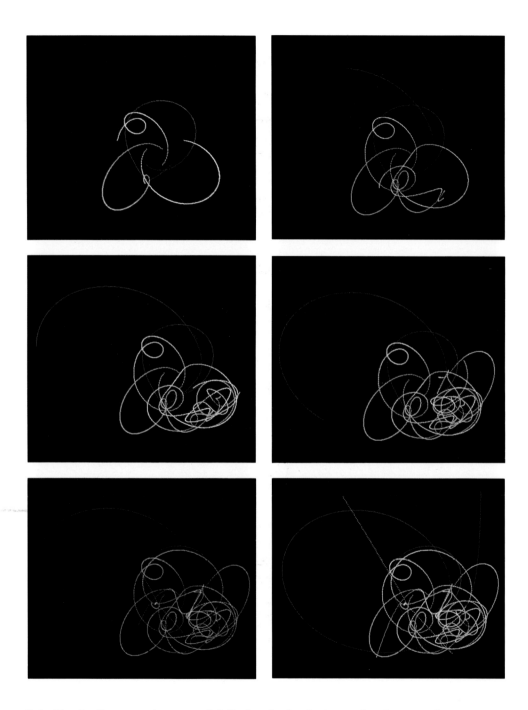

Color Plate 8   Six stars perform a cosmic ballet for a few hundred years, then dance away into space.

Figure 45   Park's gun spewing gliders left and right.

with that information. In addition to Wolfram there are other work-ers currently experimenting with line automata. Kenneth Steiglitz of Princeton is one of them. He has found gliders that have properties like those of solitons. Such gliders can even pass each other!

Will we eventually find persistent structures capable of moving, storing, and manipulating information in a one-dimensional cellular realm? Perhaps not. It may be that there is something inherently quite different about cellular computation in one dimension, something that requires us to look at computing in an entirely new way.

Wolfram has fantasized freely about how line automata illuminate the behavior of automata in general, and how they in turn provide insight into natural processes. Suppose one were to find a line automaton that closely mimics some natural process, for example a turbulent flow of liquid or gas, the motion of particles under the influence of forces, or even a biological process such as growth. Suppose further the automaton turned out to be computation-universal. In other words, not only can its space contain an explicit structure that computes but also the same space contains the computer implicitly: any attempt to predict the behavior of the automaton would by definition be attempting to predict the actions of a general-purpose computer. This in general cannot be done except by the same kind of device, another general-purpose computer. It follows that no short cut would be available for predicting the behavior of the corresponding natural system. Its processes would be computationally irreducible in the sense that the predicting mechanism (whether formula or computer) must simulate the system in question more or less directly.

This conclusion brings us back to Ripple. An initial population of gliders going in random directions bounce off one another. Sometimes their collisions result in a glider gun, which produces more gliders, and sometimes their collisions produce nothing. It reminds me of a miniature one-dimensional universe filled with elementary particles rippling back and forth. Thus I have reversed the order of Wolfram's search. Starting with a line automaton that behaves vaguely like a system of particles (odd ones at that), I have a dream that Ripple is computation-universal. Since it is my own personal automaton, I may be dreaming alone.

Readers unable or unwilling to write a program that embodies a totalistic line automaton may order one that runs on an IBM PC or PC-compatible machine as specified in the List of Suppliers.

Addendum

The two-dimensional beings who inhabit the planet Arde were deeply grateful to the many readers who tried to improve the crossover circuit I described in "One-Dimensional Computers." That circuit is made up of 12 two-input *nand*-gates. I asked readers to find the minimum number of *nand*-gates—and *nand*-gates only—from which a crossover circuit can be built. Most of the circuits submitted have 10 gates, a mild improvement, but three readers found an eight-gate crossover (*see* Figure 46).

In the eight-gate circuit there is one three-input *nand*-gate and two single-input *nand*-gates. The latter act as inverters, converting a 0 signal into a 1 signal and vice versa. The three readers who discovered the

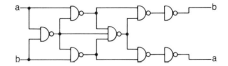

Figure 46 A crossover circuit with eight *nand*-gates.

eight-gate solution are Eric D. Carlson of Cambridge, Mass., Dale C. Koepp of San Jose, Calif., and Steve Sullivan of Beaverton, Ore. I have passed their names along with the improved crossover circuit to my Ardean friends. Believe it or not, the same crossover circuit appears under U.S. Patent 3,248,573 (April 26, 1966). Robert L. Frank, who is a systems consultant in Birmingham, Mich., wrote that the patent was awarded to Lester M. Spandorfer of Cheltenham, Pa., Albert B. Tonik of Dresher, Pa., and Shimon Even of Cambridge, Mass.

It seems natural to wonder whether the circuit actually appears in any present-day device. It is also natural to wonder whether there is an even smaller *nand* crossover. One supposes not.

C. Walter Johnson of Long Beach, Calif., wrote to me describing a wide variety of planar circuits that incorporate several types of gate. Apparently it is possible to build not only crossover circuits in two dimensions but also planar flip-flops. The flip-flops provide memory for a two-dimensional computer.

One-dimensional computers in the form of cellular automata have been investigated by Stephen Wolfram of the Center for Complex Systems Research. I cannot say what contributions readers may have made to this field after reading Wolfram's "Glider Gun Guidelines," but I can pass along some initial reactions. A sin of omission was my decision not to mention the line automata known to be capable of universal computation. I thought of describing such a line automaton, first constructed by Alvy Ray Smith in 1970. At the time Smith was a graduate student at Stanford University. I was afraid that the description of Smith's universal line automaton would unduly complicate things: the automaton has 18 states ($k = 18$) and three-cell neighborhoods ($r = 1$).

Arthur L. Rubin of Los Angeles has made a sensible suggestion for defining the speed of light in an arbitrary line automaton. Rubin's suggestion corrects a defect in an earlier definition that sets the speed of light equal to one cell per unit of time. The old definition ignores the possibility that not all automata can attain such speeds. The revised speed of light is "the maximum speed of propagation of any impulse (say to the right)." The leading edge of the impulse is defined by the condition that only 0s can lie to its right. Rubin goes on to prove that the speed of light is one-third for the line automaton code-numbered 792.

In "One Dimensional Computers" I also asked whether the line automaton called Ripple has a one-way glider gun. Gliders fired from such a gun would spew out unendingly to the right but never to the left. William B. Lipp of Milford, Conn., has made a simple and charming argument against the existence of such a gun. "Consider a pattern," he writes, "that never has nonzero values to the left of some block labeled 0. Observe that the leftmost nonzero value in the pattern must always be a 1. If it were a 2, the 2 would ripple to the left forever, thus contradicting the assumption that no nonzero entries lie to the left of block 0. But the leftmost 1 must become 0 on the next cycle, moving the left boundary of the pattern at least one block to the right." Thus either a glider ripples to the left or its gun is eaten away by 0s.

Other readers sought to show that Ripple is not capable of universal computation. For some automata one can prove a suffcient condition, namely that the halting problem is decidable. Ripple halts when all its cells contain 0s, but the halting conditions for any universal computing machine it might contain could be quite different.

Several readers attempted constructions of line automata capable of universal computation, among them Frank Adams of East Hartford, Conn., Jonathan Amsterdam of Cambridge, Mass., Kiyoshi Igusa of Brandeis University, and Carl Kadie of East Peoria, Ill. The constructions are all straightforward and believable, but Kadie, not content with his one-dimensional automaton, went on to suggest a zero-dimensional one. It would consist of a single cell, and it seems reasonable to call it a point automaton. Readers with a theoretical bent might enjoy pondering the universality of a point automaton. Is it possible?

Three-Dimensional Life

Life, the popular cellular-automaton game played on a two-dimensional grid, has now inspired some analogues in three dimensions. Carter Bays, a computer scientist at the University of South Carolina, has explored a wide variety of three-dimensional versions and found two to be most promising. He calls them Life 4555 and Life 5766. Both versions reproduce many of the features of the original Life (such as its blinkers and gliders); one of them will without doubt emerge as a worthy partner of the game invented in 1968 by the mathematician John Horton Conway of the University of Cambridge.

Conway's game, as many readers will recall from several of the "Mathematical Games" columns by Martin Gardner, is played on an infinite two-dimensional grid of square cells. Each cell has eight neighbors (four at the corners and four at the sides) and may exist in one of two states, alive or dead. Somewhere a great clock ticks away. At each tick certain cells may come alive and others may die. The fate of a cell is determined by how many of its neighbors are alive. If, for example, at one tick a living cell has fewer than two living neighbors or more than three, it will be dead at the next tick, the rationale being that a living cell can be undernourished or overcrowded. A dead cell, on the other hand, will be reborn at the next tick if it has exactly three living neighbors: a birth requires three "parents."

Conway called his game Life because the cells can be either alive or dead. It quickly became apparent, however, that the name was more appropriate than suspected. Various configurations of living cells show surprisingly complex and almost lifelike behavior (*see* Figure 47). The behavior is cyclic: at each tick of the clock the configurations change, but after a finite number of ticks the original patterns reappear. Some patterns remain stationary and others travel through the grid by shifting one cell at a time in a horizontal, vertical, or diagonal direction. Both

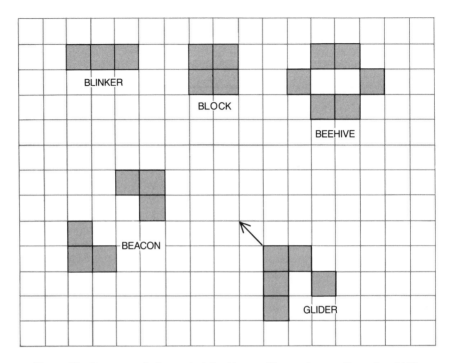

Figure 47   Some sample forms in John Horton Conway's two-dimensional Life.

types of pattern carry fanciful names. Examples of stationary configurations include beacons, beehives, blinkers, and blocks; examples of "travelers" are gliders and spaceships. Conway's Life goes far beyond mimicking natural phenomena, however. As I pointed out earlier, it is even possible to build a computer within Life's cellular plane.

It should not come as a surprise that in the commodious cellular space of three dimensions, analogous versions of Conway's game might give rise to even more fantastic phenomena. Such versions are Carter Bays's Life 4555 and Life 5766. Here each cell is a cube instead of a square and has 26 neighbors instead of eight.

The names Life 4555 and Life 5766 are drawn from a lean lexicon developed by Bays. The first two numbers dictate the fate of the living cells. The first number indicates the fewest living neighbors a cell must have to keep from being undernourished; the second indicates the most it can have before it will be overcrowded. The third and fourth numbers govern the fate of the dead cells. The third indicates the fewest living neighbors a dead cell must have to come alive; the fourth indicates the most it can have to come alive. (In each version of Life I shall discuss here the third and fourth numbers are identical with each other; in general, however, it is not so.) According to Bays's notation, then, Conway's Life becomes Life 2333.

Life 4555 operates just as simply as Life 2333. A living cell dies if it has fewer than four or more than five living neighbors. A dead cell comes to life if it has exactly five living neighbors. In a routine investigation of rules in this range of values. Bays was first drawn to Life 4555 when he noticed an odd configuration of cubical cells wriggling out of the depths of his Macintosh display screen (*see* Figure 48). It was a three-dimensional glider, which then cycled through four distinct patterns before repeating itself. Each pattern consisted of 10 cubes in oblong formation, strangely blunt, moving through space like a sofa in free fall.

Intrigued, Bays decided to probe the rules for 4555 a little further by setting up a number of "primordial soup" experiments. Seeding an initial space with cubes randomly brought to life, he set his cellular universe in motion. In each generation some cubes died and others came to life. The number of living cubes dwindled with each generation, but not before Bays noticed some curiously stable ensembles that did not change from one generation to the next. Some of them reminded him of pedestals, crosses, steps, balls, and barbells (*see* Figure 49). Subsequent seedings yielded yet other stable configurations, as well as many cyclic ones to which Bays has given such whimsical names as rotor and bucking bronco.

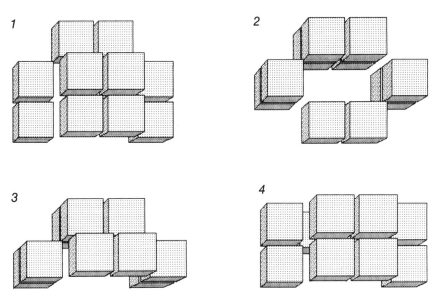

Figure 48   A glider in Life 4555.

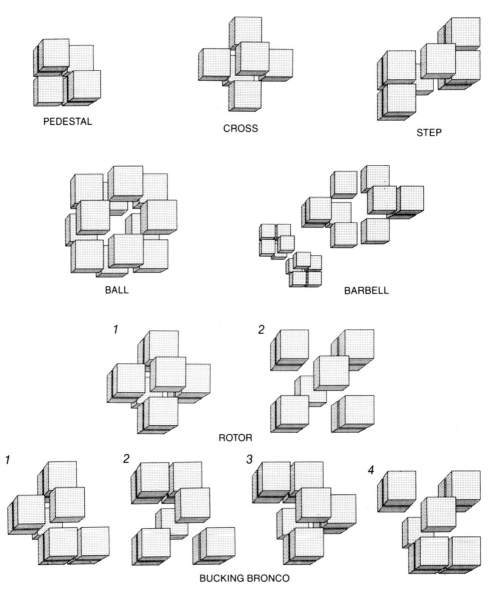

Figure 49   Stable and cyclic forms in Life 4555.

Like a nuclear physicist with new particles to play with, Bays set up collisions among gliders and other small configurations at every conceivable angle. "Among the most surprising collisions," he notes, "is a certain glider collision with a ball, where the resulting confused mass swells to a population of 29, in itself not particularly remarkable. But suddenly the glider reappears, lagging by several generations and shifted somewhat."

The yields of primordial soups and even the results of glider collisions are called nature by Bays. Some configurations are produced quite easily. Other and more exotic patterns require more work. For example, one can hook together arch-shaped configurations to make a new stable pattern Bays calls an arcade. An entire architecture of fences, stairs, walls, and chains emerges. Walls can be bent into helixes and a great variety of stable exotic forms that are limited only by the imagination of a Life 4555 enthusiast (*see* Color Plate 7).

Further phenomena beg description in these pages. There is a lonely seven-cube form called a greeter that dies unless it is in the presence of another greeter. A glider may pass a greeter only to be gripped, or suspended in its travels. A second glider may by chance rescue its kin by colliding with the greeter and exploding it.

Of the two fruitful three-dimensional versions discovered by Bays, Life 4555 seems to be his favorite. Curiously enough, the digits of Life 4555 can be obtained by adding 2 to the digits of the code for Conway's Life, namely 2333. Perhaps the coincidence foreshadows the eventual emergence of Life 4555 as a worthy partner to Conway's Life.

In a strict sense, however, Life 5766 mimics Conway's game more closely than Life 4555 does. In particular, under certain special conditions Life 5766 will simulate Conway's Life in the plane. The conditions are specified by a theorem hit on by Bays.

Imagine looking down on the plane grid of Conway's Life and there seeing a particular configuration of living (square) cells. Now place a living cube directly on top of each square in the configuration and another directly under it. Following the rules for Life 5766, the cubes will perfectly mimic forever the behavior of the sandwiched Conway cells if (and only if) two conditions are satisfied:

1. No living square cell on the plane ever has five living neighbors.
2. No dead square cell on the plane ever has six living neighbors.

Many Life configurations, including Conway's glider, satisfy the conditions. A Life 5766 glider can be created by converting a two-dimensional glider into cubes. It occupies two adjoining layers of cells in three-dimensional space and is confined to move eternally therein (*see* Figure 50).

Many other forms of Conway's Life such as the beacon, beehive, blinker, and block as well as more exotic patterns such as the boat, clock, and barber pole, also satisfy the conditions of Bays's theorem.

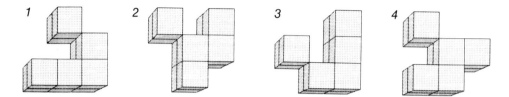

Figure 50   A glider in Bays's three-dimensional Life 5766.

They exist in two-layer form as Life 5766 entities that behave precisely like their two-dimensional counterparts. Unfortunately not all the configurations in Conway's Life satisfy the criteria. Among the black sheep of the family is the famous glider gun discovered by R. William Gosper, Jr., while he was a student at the Massachusetts Institute of Technology in 1970. If one inspects the glider gun at any stage of its life cycle, one finds living cells that have five living neighbors. Any violation of either of the two conditions of Bays's theorem results in a departure from the simulation. "When this happens," reports Bays, "the object, theretofore confined to two planes, almost always forms a roundish, three-dimensional mass that usually dies rather quickly."

Life 5766 can be made to simulate Conway's Life more completely with the erection of what Bays calls a time-space barrier. This consists of a single sheet of living cells with holes punched in it (*see* Figure 51). The holes are arranged in such a way that each cube in the barrier has exactly seven neighbors. Cubes in the barrier barely avoid death by overcrowding, whereas any cube immediately adjacent to the barrier will have more than six living neighbors and will never come to life. The resulting dead zone on each side of a time-space barrier can be exploited to reproduce Conway's Life exactly. One constructs a sandwich of two parallel time-space barriers a distance of four cubes apart. Of the four intervening planes the central two may support Life in any form: the two conditions of Bays's theorem are now obeyed by any population of living cubes occupying the center of the sandwich.

In spite of its ability to mimic Conway's Life in one form or another, Life 5766 lacks what might be called cellular pizzazz. According to Bays, random primordial soups in Life 5766 always seem to "settle down" faster than those in Life 4555. The unsettled condition of Life 4555 hints at a wider range of computational possibilities. Indeed, Life 4555 has an abundance of stable and oscillating forms that are symmetrical. Perhaps the final decision as to which version will make the worthier partner to Conway's Life will hinge on whether Life 4555 can be made to simulate the two-dimensional game. If it can, it would be superior to Life 5766 in all ways.

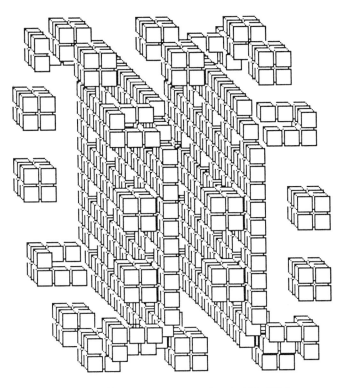

Figure 51   Two time-space barriers in Life 5766.

Bays has a 40-page document titled "The Game of Three-Dimensional Life" that readers may order from him at the address given in the List of Suppliers. The monograph describes everything here and much more, including advice on programming the games efficiently. Bays also has made available a Macintosh program that runs both forms of three-dimensional Life.

A program that computes and displays successive generations of either form of three-dimensional Life is simple to write—at least in principle. The program can even be modified to carry out a search of rules in the hope of discovering a third form of three-dimensional Life that Bays may have missed.

Two large, three-dimensional arrays called *cells* and *newcells* are assigned three indices, i, j, and k, which correspond to the three coordinates of the cellular space. The content of each array element indicates whether the corresponding cell is alive or dead. Let 1 signify life and 0 signify death.

Three nested loops, not surprisingly, are needed to compute the status of each cell in each generation. The outer loop uses the i index to compute a succession of planes that sweeps through the space. Within this loop are two others using j and k respectively. The j loop computes successive rows within each plane and the k loop computes successive cells in a row. One can use the following generic form as a guide:

$$
\begin{aligned}
&\text{for } i = 1 \text{ to } 30 \\
&\quad \text{for } j = 1 \text{ to } 30 \\
&\qquad \text{for } k = 1 \text{ to } 30 \\
&\qquad\quad \textit{compute neighbors} \\
&\qquad\quad \textit{decide status} \\
&\qquad\quad \textit{display live cubes}
\end{aligned}
$$

The number 30 is arbitrary, of course. Only readers with infinite patience are advised to try numbers greater than 30, however, as the calculation time becomes exceedingly long.

Inside the innermost loop there are three basic tasks for the program to do. The task *compute neighbors* requires the program to examine the 26 neighbors of each cell and total the number currently alive. This can be done with three miniature loops or by listing all possible coordinates of the 26 cells. In loop form the procedure might use the following algorithm:

$$
\begin{aligned}
&tot \leftarrow 0 \\
&\text{for } l = i - 1 \text{ to } i + 1 \\
&\quad \text{for } m = j - 1 \text{ to } j + 1 \\
&\qquad \text{for } n = k - 1 \text{ to } k + 1 \\
&\qquad\quad \text{if } cells\ (l,m,n) = 1 \\
&\qquad\qquad \text{then } tot \leftarrow tot + 1 \\
&\quad tot \leftarrow tot - cells\ (i,j,k)
\end{aligned}
$$

The last line of the procedure ensures that the status of $cells(i,j,k)$ does not contribute to the total.

Having decided on the total *tot* of living neighbors, the program must next decide the new status of the current cell, $cells(i,j,k)$. The task *decide status* is merely a matter of checking the size of *tot* in relation to the status of $cells(i,j,k)$:

$$
\begin{aligned}
&\text{if } cells(i,j,k) = 0 \\
&\quad \text{then if } tot = 5 \\
&\qquad \text{then } newcells(i,j,k) \leftarrow 1 \\
&\qquad \text{else } newcells(i,j,k) \leftarrow 0 \\
&\text{if } cells(i,j,k) = 1 \\
&\quad \text{then if } tot < 4 \text{ or } tot > 5 \\
&\qquad \text{then } newcells(i,j,k) \leftarrow 0 \\
&\qquad \text{else } newcells(i,j,k) \leftarrow 1
\end{aligned}
$$

Here I have assumed that the reader is programming Life 4555. One can change the algorithm to fit Life 5766 or make it general enough to manage any three-dimensional rule whatever. It seems worthwhile to digress on this point for a moment.

A general version of the foregoing status computation might use four variables Bays calls el, eu, fl, and fu. The letters e and f stand for environment and fertility and l and u for lower and upper. Thus el and eu are the lower and upper bounds for the continued life of a cell in its environment; the cell will stay alive if the number of living cubes surrounding it is greater than or equal to el but less than or equal to eu. By the same token, fl and fu are the conditions of fertility for a dead cell. Its rebirth is guaranteed if the number of living cubes surrounding it is greater than or equal to fl but less than or equal to fu. The general algorithm is therefore

$$
\begin{aligned}
&\text{if } cells\ (i,j,k) = 0 \\
&\quad \text{then if } tot < fl \text{ or } tot > fu \\
&\qquad\quad \text{then } newcells(i,j,k) \leftarrow 0 \\
&\qquad\quad \text{else } newcells(i,j,k) \leftarrow 1 \\
&\text{if } cells(i,j,k) = 1 \\
&\quad \text{then if } tot < el \text{ or } tot > eu \\
&\qquad\quad \text{then } newcells(i,j,k) \leftarrow 0 \\
&\qquad\quad \text{else } newcells(i,j,k) \leftarrow 1
\end{aligned}
$$

At this point in either version of a three-dimensional Life program the contents of *newcells* can be moved into *cells* by means of the appropriate triple loop. This frees up *newcells* for the next generation of living cubes.

In the final stage of the computation process, *display live cubes*, the program displays the particular cube—if it is living. When the actual cubes are drawn, it is advisable to fill in the visible surfaces. If just the bare skeleton frame are used, a very cluttered, well-nigh indecipherable scene results. The simplest way to ensure that cubes in front properly obscure those behind is to make sure that i, the outer index, sweeps from the back of the cellular space toward the front in relation to the viewer. The sad fact that some cubes must be obscured in this way points up the only disadvantage inherent in three-dimensional Life in any form: we cannot command the sweeping view of all that goes on as we can in Conway's two-dimensional version. At the same time, the disadvantage of any three-dimensional game is shared by us in our real, three-dimensional world. We cannot see everything that is going on, fortunately enough.

When the final stage of the computational process is embodied in a program, it will tend to be rather slow. One simplification that may speed matters up somewhat is to replace the cubes by spheres (actually filled-in disks whose size varies with their "depth" in the screen). For the rest, Bays's monograph referred to earlier has many orders-of-magnitude improvements in speed to suggest.

There are undoubtably many remarkable phenomena yet to be discovered in three-dimensional Life. For those intrepid explorers who demand the utmost in generality, are there any forms of three-dimensional Life (worthy of the title) that Bays may have missed? Next, readers may also enjoy setting up their own primordial soups. For the rest, one wonders what undiscovered gliders, spaceships, glider guns, and other configurations there are. To avoid duplicating what Bays already knows, access to "The Game of Three-Dimensional Life" is mandatory.

Addendum

Carter Bays, impresario of three-dimensional Life, has launched a newsletter. Because Bays received so many expressions of interest, he felt the newsletter would be warranted. He hopes to publish quarterly and to include all observations of interest, whether made by him or by subscribers. Everyone who orders the 40-page document "The Game of Three-Dimensional Life" will automatically receive notification of the newsletter. (See the List of Suppliers for further information.)

Bays continues to be on the lookout for successful three-dimensional analogues to Conway's game. Bays has recently found two criteria that seem to work well in distinguishing winners from losers. His first criterion is that a primordial soup must not grow without limit. In other words, if one starts with a random assortment of living cells, it should not tend to expand forever. His second criterion is that from time to time the primordial soups must spawn gliders: cyclic configurations of living cubes that wriggle their way across the screen.

One analogue in three dimensions was pointed out by Kerry Pearson of Nanaimo, British Columbia, who wrote Bays to tell him about a book called *Ox*, by Piers Anthony (*see* Bibliography). In the book Anthony mentions a candidate for three-dimensional Life, which, following Bays's lean lexicon, is called Life 6777. In this version a living cubic cell will die in the next generation if it has fewer than six or more than seven living neighbors in the present generation. If a cube is dead, it will spring to life if it is currently surrounded by exactly seven living neighbors. Bays reports that he had already investigated this version of three-dimensional Life. He found it violates the first criterion.

Currently Bays has isolated just two candidates as worthy successors to Conway's game. (Those candidates, you will remember, are Life 4555 and Life 5766.) The great quest, as far as Bays is concerned, is the search for a glider gun in either of the three-dimensional versions. A glider gun would endlessly spew out gliders in one or more fixed directions.

Busy Beavers

With the possible exception of bees, beavers are the busiest animals alive. All day they ply quiet northern waters bringing twigs and branches to their dam. It was undoubtedly this behavior that led Tibor Rado of Ohio State University to name a certain Turing-machine problem the Busy Beaver Game. In the early 1960s Rado wondered how many 1s a Turing machine could be made to print before it halted. Specifically, if a Turing machine with n possible states begins work on a tape filled with 0s, what is the largest number of 1s it can print on the tape before coming to a stop? The answer is known for $n = 1$, $n = 2$, $n = 3$, and $n = 4$ but not for $n = 5$ or for any value of n greater than 5.

In 1983 a contest was held in Dortmund, West Germany, to see who could discover the busiest beaver with five states. In the year preceding the contest, programs were written to generate candidate Turing machines, and hardware was developed to test the machines. In the course of this work a number of strangely behaved beavers were discovered, and the genus *Castor* had to be expanded to include several species hitherto unknown to zoologists.

The nature of the Turing machine and its place in computer science have been discussed in SCIENTIFIC AMERICAN by John E. Hopcroft of Cornell University (*see* Bibliography). A Turing machine consists of an infinite tape, a head for reading and writing symbols on the tape, and a control unit with a finite number of internal states (*see* Figure 52). These components can be thought of as the hardware part of the device, whereas the contents of the control unit are the software—the Turing-machine program. It is the program that distinguishes one Turing machine from another. The program is a table the machine consults to determine what action to take next. For each possible state of the control unit and for each possible symbol at the current position of the tape head an entry in the table tells the machine what symbol to print on the

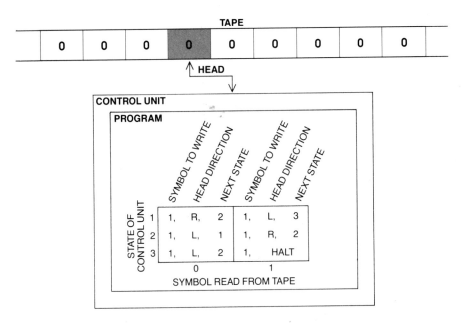

Figure 52   A Turing machine and its program.

tape, in which direction to move the head, and what state to enter next. All the Turing machines discussed here begin in state 1.

The actions of a Turing machine can be traced by writing down the state of the control unit and the symbols marked on the tape (or a region of it) at successive moments; one should also indicate which square of the tape is currently being scanned. Figure 53 is a trace of the Turing machine shown in Figure 52. Each line in the sequence is an "instantaneous description" of the machine. The format of the description is different from Hopcroft's, but the information is the same. I have also made the tape infinite in both directions, and I have allowed a symbol to be printed in the course of the machine's final transition (as it enters the halted state), contrary to the conventions adopted in Hopcroft's article. These differences do not change what a Turing machine can or cannot do. The format chosen here for the instantaneous description is compatible with the one used in the busy-beaver contest.

A busy beaver with *n* states is an *n*-state Turing machine that meets two conditions. First, when it is started on a tape filled with 0s, it eventually halts; second, it writes at least as many 1s as any other *n*-state machine that halts. Busy beavers with one and three states are shown in Figure 54. Each Turing machine is represented by a state-transition diagram, in which a state is a numbered circle and a transition between states is an arrow. The labels on the arrows describe the action of the

STATE					TAPE				
1	0	0	0	0	0	0	0	0	0
2	0	0	0	0	1	0	0	0	0
1	0	0	0	0	1	1	0	0	0
3	0	0	0	0	1	1	0	0	0
2	0	0	0	1	1	1	0	0	0
1	0	0	1	1	1	1	0	0	0
2	0	1	1	1	1	1	0	0	0
2	0	1	1	1	1	1	0	0	0
2	0	1	1	1	1	1	0	0	0
2	0	1	1	1	1	1	0	0	0
2	0	1	1	1	1	1	0	0	0
1	0	1	1	1	1	1	1	0	0
3	0	1	1	1	1	1	1	0	0
HALT	0	1	1	1	1	1	1	0	0

Figure 53 "Instantaneous descriptions" trace the operation of the Turing machine.

Turing machine. For example, suppose the three-state busy beaver is in state 1 and it reads a 0 on the tape. The arrow followed under these circumstances is labeled "0,1,R" and leads to state 2. Hence the machine, having read a 0, writes a 1 on the tape, moves the head one square to the right and enters state 2.

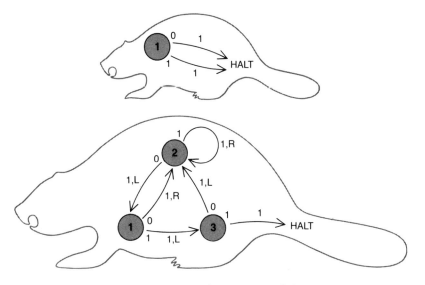

Figure 54 Busy beavers with one state and three states.

The maximum number of 1s that can be produced by an n-state Turing machine that halts is denoted $\Sigma(n)$. As is indicated above, the value of $\Sigma(n)$ is known only for the first four values of n. The one-state busy beaver writes a single 1 before it halts; in other words, $\Sigma(1)$ is equal to 1. A two-state busy beaver produces a sequence of four 1s. Can readers devise such a machine? A three-state busy beaver writes six 1s; one three-state beaver is the machine whose program and sequence of instantaneous descriptions are shown in Figures 52 and 53 and whose state-transition diagram is given in Figure 54. The three-state beaver was discovered in 1962 by Rado and by Shen Lin of AT&T Bell Laboratories. In 1973 Bruno Weimann of the University of Bonn found a four-state busy beaver, whose output consists of 13 consecutive 1s. Since then theorists have been searching for a five-state busy beaver.

The busy-beaver contest was organized by Frank Wankmuller and held in January, 1983, at the University of Dortmund during a conference on theoretical computer science. Some 133 five-state Turing machines were entered. Uwe Schult of Hamburg won with a machine that produced 501 1s before halting. The state-transition diagram of the winning machine is shown in Figure 55. The runner-up was Jochen Ludewig of the Brown Boveri Research Center in Baden, whose Turing machine printed 240 1s.

Is Schult's Turing machine a busy beaver? Schult, along with Wankmuller and Ludewig, conjectured that it was (but see the Addendum). In other words, he suspected that no Turing machine with five states could produce more than 501 1s before halting. But how to prove

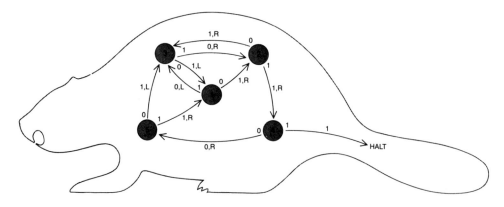

Figure 55   Uwe Schult's candidate for a five-state busy beaver.

such a claim? The answer lay in exhaustive search by computer, a search of the kind that Schult used to find his champion Turing machine in the first place. Before describing Schult's attempt to trap the five-state busy beaver in his computer, I should like to take a closer look at the function $\Sigma(n)$ to get some insight into why the Busy Beaver Game is so hard to play, even with the aid of a computer.

The function $\Sigma(n)$ has an extraordinary property: it is not computable. It simply grows too fast. From the first four values of $\Sigma(n)$—namely 1, 4, 6, and 13—it might seem that the rate of growth is only moderate. If 501 is indeed the maximum number of 1s for a five-state machine, the increase in $\Sigma(n)$ would still appear to be no faster than that of an exponential function. Schult has found a six-state Turing machine that produces 2075 1s, which again suggests a quite tractable rate of growth. On the other hand, Schult has also found a 12-state machine that generates so many 1s that the number must be expressed by the following mind-boggling formula:

$$
6 \times 4096^{4096^{4096^{\cdot^{\cdot^{\cdot^{4096^{4096^4}}}}}}}
$$

The number 4096 appears 166 times in the formula, 162 times in the "twilight zone" represented by the three dots. The formula can be evaluated from the top down: first raise 4096 to the fourth power, then raise

4096 to the power of the resulting number, then raise 4096 to the power of *that* number, and so on. When you reach the bottom, multiply by 6.

Anyone whose mind does not boggle when confronted by a string of 1s that long is welcome to construct an even bigger number. Write down any formula you like in which numbers are multiplied or raised to a power; you may even replace any of the numbers with *n*. No matter what formula you devise, for some value of *n* that is large enough the *n*-state busy beaver will produce more 1s than the formula specifies. It follows that $\Sigma(n)$ cannot be calculated for arbitrarily large values of *n*. The best one can do is to calculate $\Sigma(n)$ for some small, fixed value of *n*.

It is hardly surprising that the Busy Beaver Game is most often played with the aid of a computer. The essential method is to examine systematically all Turing machines with *n* states. Each time a new machine is generated its behavior on a tape filled with 0s is simulated. If the machine halts after no more than a specified number of steps, the number of 1s it printed is compared with the score of the "busiest" Turing machine found so far. From time to time a new champion is discovered.

This method of searching for the *n*-state busy beaver has two major flaws. First, the number of Turing machines to be generated is immense; for example, there are 63,403,380,965,376 five-state machines. Second, it is not known how long one should wait for a machine to halt; the maximum number of transitions an *n*-state machine can undergo (and still eventually halt), a function denoted $s(n)$, is itself a noncomputable number. Obviously $s(n)$ grows even faster than $\Sigma(n)$, since a Turing machine must make a state transition each time it prints a 1. As Hopcroft pointed out, computing $s(n)$ is equivalent to solving the halting problem for Turing machines, one of the first problems shown by Turing to be undecidable.

In 1982 Schult converted his Apple II personal computer into a busy-beaver trap. He augmented the computer's original central processor with a circuit board bearing a Motorola 6809 microprocessor; he wrote his search program in the machine language of the auxiliary processor. To test the vast numbers of Turing machines generated by the program Schult built an actual hardware Turing machine out of standard electronic components mounted on another circuit board that plugs into the Apple II. The device provides a simulated tape of 4096 squares as well as registers for storing the program and the current state and head position of the Turing machine. Schult estimates that without such specialized hardware his search would have taken 20 months of computer time. Even with the hardware extensions the Apple II took 803 hours to find the winning Turing machine.

In designing the necessary software Schult also gained by making the search program and the Turing-machine hardware interact closely. The program systematically filled in the transition table for a five-state

Turing machine in all possible ways. Even before a table was completed it was submitted to the Turing-machine hardware for testing. In many cases an incomplete table was found to specify a machine that ran out of time or space before any of the undefined entries was reached. Thus the incomplete table and all possible completions of it could be rejected.

Although Schult in large measure overcame the problem of managing multitudes of Turing machines, his approach to the halting problem for five-state busy beavers is not watertight, so to speak. In the absence of exact information about $s(5)$—the maximum number of transitions a five-state halting Turing machine can make—the number must be guessed. Schult set the limit at 500,000 transitions; in other words, he adopted the working hypothesis that if a machine had not stopped after 500,000 transitions, it never would. Of necessity he also imposed space limitations on his candidate busy beavers; since the simulated tape had only 4096 squares and since his Turing machines always started at the middle of this finite tape, a candidate was considered a "runner" if it moved more than 2048 squares from its initial position. A runner is a Turing machine that not only fails to halt but also continues indefinitely to visit new tape squares.

Of the 133 Turing machines entered in the Dortmund contest, only four produced more than 100 1s. The operation of each Turing machine was simulated with a Siemens 7.748 computer. More than an hour of processor time was needed to determine the winner.

Ludewig, the runner-up, wrote his busy-beaver search program in the Pascal programming language and ran it on a large minicomputer, the VAX, made by the Digital Equipment Corporation. In spite of a more sophisticated analysis of candidate Turing machines, 1647 hours of central-processor time were spent in discovering his entry—the Turing machine that produced 240 1s. Schult, not surprisingly, also found Ludewig's machine; of equal interest, he found no machines between Ludewig's and his own. Apparently any halting five-state Turing machine that prints more than 240 1s must print at least 501.

Ludewig, in the course of his investigations, discovered a number of strange Turing machines with beaverlike behavior. Besides printing 1s there are other ways for a beaver to keep busy. For example, without printing many 1s a Turing machine may move a considerable distance from its starting square and then halt. Alternatively, without printing many 1s or even moving very far, it may go through a great many transitions before it halts. Among the machines tested at Dortmund, Schult's won in all three categories. On the other hand, Ludewig discovered three beavers that generate no 1s at all but nonetheless either explore a wide territory or waste much time in profitless activity (*see* Figure 56). Accordingly three new species of beaver have been named:

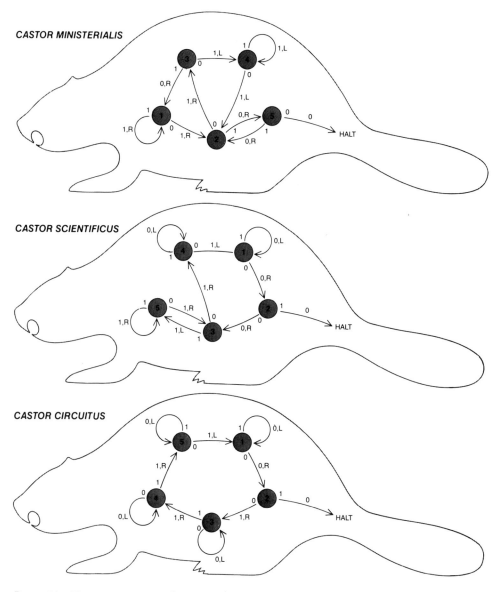

Figure 56 Three new species of beaver that after much activity leave no 1s on the tape.

Castor ministerialis (common name, civil-servant beaver). This enterprising creature seeks to advance itself as far as possible without producing anything. The type specimen is a five-state beaver that produces no 1s and moves 11 squares from its starting position.

Castor scientificus (common name, scientist beaver). Again without actually producing anything, this animal seeks to maximize its total activity, perhaps in an effort to attract grants. A five-state member of the species has been observed to make 187 transitions without writing a single 1.

Castor circuitus (common name, dizzy beaver). The dizzy beaver produces nothing and goes nowhere, but in the process it generates a maximum amount of activity. As the state-transition diagram suggests, it tends to spend a lot of time spinning its wheels. The busiest five-state specimen found so far undergoes 67 transitions before it finally halts exactly where it started.

It would be interesting to see some three-state examples of these odd beavers. Any attempt to find them would certainly benefit from the use of a computer (personal or otherwise), even if only to test Turing-machine programs devised in one's mind.

A Turing-machine simulator is easy to write. Use a one-dimensional array to represent the tape; the contents of the array, which consist exclusively of 0s and 1s, can be shown on the computer's display screen. The display is most informative if the position of the head is indicated. For example, the machine's current state might be displayed directly below the symbol being scanned.

A two-dimensional array is needed to represent the Turing-machine program. Each element of the array is a set of instructions for the machine; instructions must be provided for each state of the control unit and for each possible tape symbol. For a three-state Turing machine the array has three rows and two columns; its structure is exactly that of the program shown in Figure 52. The state of the machine specifies a row in the array, and the symbol under the tape head specifies a column; the instructions found at the intersection of the designated row and column define the Turing machine's next action.

Suppose the machine is in state 1 and the symbol on the tape is a 0. Consulting row 1 and column 0 of the array, the simulator finds the instructions "1,R,2." Hence the machine is to write a 1 on the tape, move the head to the right one square, and enter state 2. One way of implementing such instructions is to define three variables, say *state*, *head*, and *symbol*. At the beginning of a cycle the value of *state* and *symbol* determine where in the table the machine looks for its next instructions. The first component of the instruction found there (in this case a 1) is written on the tape; the second component (*R*) becomes the new value of *head*, and the third component (2) becomes the value of *state*. The head is then moved (in the direction indicated by the value of *head*) and the symbol found at the new position is made the value of *symbol*. The cycle then begins anew.

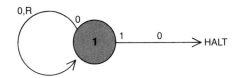

Figure 57   A tape-cleaning machine.

Various strategies can be adopted to make the programming of such a scheme easier and more efficient. For example, the letters L and R can be replaced by numbers, which are generally easier to manipulate in the computer. Moreover, the transition that leads to the halted state demands special treatment in the program.

A Turing-machine simulator could be used to test your answers to the following little puzzles, but it is by no means necessary to their solution.

Imagine you have bought a supply of used Turing-machine tapes at your local computer store. Before turning your busy beaver loose on them, the tapes must be cleaned up: any 1s on them must be changed back to 0s. Instead of cleaning the tapes yourself, you decide to devise a simple Turing machine to do the job for you.

One of the tapes has a single 1 on it but is otherwise filled with 0s. You must create a Turing machine that finds the 1, erases it (by changing it to a 0), and then halts. Naturally the fewer states your tape-cleaning machine has, the more elegant it will be. The tape cleaner in Figure 57 is extremely elegant. Unfortunately it only works half of the time!

The remaining tapes are just like the first one except they have more 1s on them, although in each case the number of 1s is known to be finite. Can you construct a tape cleaner that changes all the 1s back to 0s? Of course, it will never halt.

Addendum

The three busy-beaver puzzles posed in "Busy Beavers" were solved by Martin J. Maney of Palatine, Ill. His two-state busy beaver is shown below. Starting with a blank tape, it produces four 1s before halting.

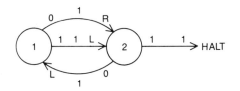

Maney's other solutions are best summarized in words. A Turing machine that erases a single 1 from an otherwise blank tape uses two 1s as markers. At each stage it shuttles from one 1 to the other, checking just beyond each to see whether the 1 to be erased lies there. If it does, the machine erases all three 1s and halts. If it does not, the machine moves that marker one square outward and shuttles back to the other marker. The multiple 1s tape cleaner works similarly, except that it can never halt. How could it when some as yet unexplored region of the tape may contain a 1? Two-state busy beavers were found by Peter J. Marineau of Troy, N.Y., and Dave Kaplan of Deer Park, N.Y. Marineau also solved the tape-cleaner problem, describing his movable 1s as "brooms" that sweep the tape.

Raphael M. Robinson of Berkeley, Calif., wrote a Turing-machine simulation program for his IBM PC. As he watched Uwe Schult's conjectured busy beaver writing out its 501 1s, Robinson noticed that before halting it produced a recurring and ever lengthening pattern of alternating 0s and 1s. Starting with a blank tape, the successive lengths of this pattern were 0, 6, 13, 28, 48, 78, 121, 190, 289, 442, and 667. The last pattern contained 501 1s. It occurred to Robinson to investigate the behavior of Schult's machine, beginning not with a blank tape but with one of the alternating patterns. Starting on a pattern of length 9 (containing five 1s), the machine halted after 12,870,233 steps, having produced a new pattern containing 4911 1s. This required three times the space and 25 times the number of steps performed by Schult's machine when started on a blank tape. That such a modest change in the input tape should produce such extravagant behavior disturbed Robinson. "It seems to me," writes Robinson, "that these results throw serious doubts on Schult's space and time restrictions.

Apparently Bruno Weimann of the University of Bonn was not the first to discover a four-state busy beaver. Allen H. Brady, now at the University of Nevada at Reno, discovered his own a decade before Weimann. At the time Brady was at Oregon State University. The school mascot is the beaver, and the computer in Brady's research was at nearby Beaverton. Brady shares Robinson's skepticism. "I know from solving the four-state problem that the five-state problem is far from decided. The crux of the matter is deciding that each alleged runaway machine will in fact never halt. . . . As the machines become more complex this decision will become more and more difficult, eventually encompassing very profound unsolved mathematical problems. . . . The blank tape halting problems of individual machines at some point become essentially individual mathematical theorems."

After all of the foregoing activity, a new candidate for the five-state busy beaver was discovered on December 21, 1984, by George Uhing of Bronx, N.Y. Uhing's Turing machine starts on a blank tape and prints

STATE	INPUT	NEXT STATE	OUT-PUT	DIREC-TION
A	0	B	1	RIGHT
	1	C	1	LEFT
B	0	A	0	I FFT
	1	D	0	LEFT
C	0	A	1	LEFT
	1	H	1	LEFT
D	0	B	1	LEFT
	1	E	1	RIGHT
E	0	D	0	RIGHT
	1	B	0	RIGHT

Figure 58   A five-state busy beaver?

1915 1s before halting. The result was independently confirmed by Allen H. Brady of the University of Nevada and by Raphael M. Robinson of the University of California at Berkeley. Described by Brady as "astounding," Uhing's machine seems to justify the skepticism both mathematicians had expressed that Uwe Schult's machine was the five-state busy beaver. It produced only 501 1s. The Uhing machine is reproduced in Figure 58.

To discover what the machine will do in state B, for example, examine the row bearing that label. The row is subdivided into an upper and a lower portion listing the machine's responses to a 0 or a 1 respectively. If the machine reads a 1 on its tape, it enters state D, prints a 0 on the tape, and then moves one cell to the left. In the table H means that the machine halts.

Uhing, who programs for a Manhattan optical company, decided to search for the five-state busy beaver after reading about it in "Computer Recreations" (August, 1984). He used a Z-80 microprocessor running an assembly-language program to oversee a second machine: a Turing-machine simulator that cost Uhing less than $100 to build. It goes through 7 million Turing-machine transitions per second. Each transition amounts to a simple lookup in a table like the one in Figure 58. Uhing seems determined to find the five-state busy beaver. Does the present machine qualify? It showed up after Uhing's computer had been running for a month.

What are the chances we shall discover a six-state busy beaver? "Absolutely out the question," Brady says.

WORLD FIVE

Puzzles and Wordplay

The ancestor of "Computer Recreations" in SCIENTIFIC AMERICAN featured mathematical games and puzzles like the ones presented here. For example, assembly puzzles like burrs and checkerboards have been with us for some time, as have puzzles that one solves by rotating components until a certain alignment is reached. The first piece in the World of puzzles and wordplay goes a step further by describing programs that enable one to design new puzzles on an almost automatic basis. Old chestnuts like the Tower of Hanoi and the Chinese rings are solved by simple algorithms. In the matter of wordplay there are programs that generate anagrams and pangrams. Anagrams are words that are scrambled to produce new words. Pangrams are more challenging. How many s's does this sentence contain? Five? Imagine a sentence that tells one exactly how many letters of each kind (from a to z) that it contains. That is a pangram.

Bill's Baffling Burr, Coffin's Cornucopia, and Engel's Enigma

To write a computer program that assists in the design of a puzzle is no less difficult or interesting than writing a program that solves one. Bill Cutler of Wausau, Wis., and Stewart T. Coffin of Lincoln, Mass., would agree. With the aid of a computer Cutler has designed a three-dimensional six-piece puzzle called Bill's baffling burr. A burr puzzle, because of its many protruding pieces and their interlocking relations, resembles the adhesive seedpod: it may cling to the would-be solver for days. Bill's burr consists of six pieces arranged in pairs in each of three orthogonal directions (*see* Figure 59). Two puzzles in one, it challenges us both to take it apart and to reassemble it. By using two computer programs to evaluate the puzzle potential of each combination of pieces, Cutler has arrived at what may be the most difficult six-piece burr in existence.

Coffin and his computer have designed a two-dimensional puzzle of hexominoes. These are flat pieces consisting of six squares glued together in various shapes. Depending on how cleverly the shapes are chosen, the task of assembling the hexominoes into a large square can be difficult and frustrating for the person who attempts it. Coffin's program searches through possible combinations of hexominoes that yield particularly difficult puzzles. It has found so many designs that Coffin is ready to send each reader who asks for one a unique personal hexomino puzzle (*see* List of Suppliers). Such bounty leads Coffin to label his facility a cornucopia. I received the puzzle shown in Figure 60.

A third puzzle I shall discuss was invented entirely by a human, Douglas A. Engel of Englewood, Colo. The challenge is hereby thrown

ASSEMBLED

THE PIECES

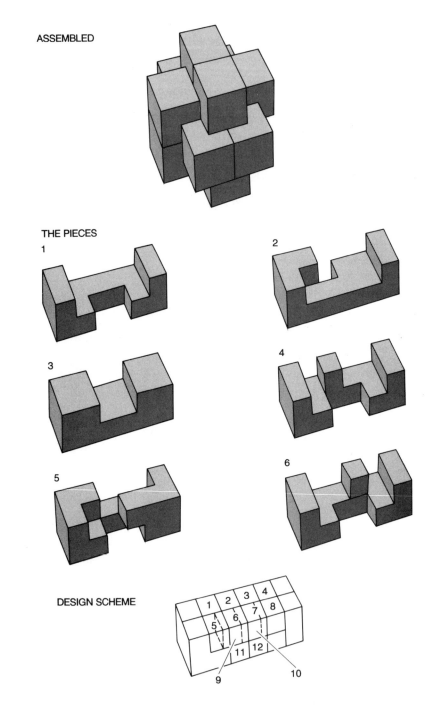

DESIGN SCHEME

Figure 59   Bill's baffling burr.

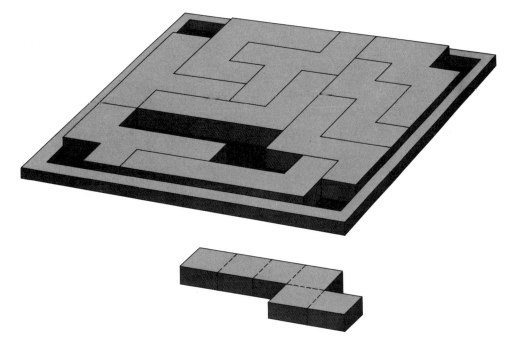

Figure 60   A hexomino puzzle from Stewart T. Coffin's cornucopia.

out to algorithmic adventurers to solve it. Engel's puzzle is an innocent-looking mosaic of colored plastic pieces circumscribed by two circles (*see* Figure 61). Please note that the colors referred to in the text have been replaced in the illustration by various textures. The pieces are called stones and bones. By rotating first one circle and then the other the stones and bones become dreadfully scrambled. Manipulating them back to their original state seems to be every bit as difficult as manipulating a Rubik's cube so that each of its six faces is invitingly monochromatic again.

As we shall see, Engel's puzzle is essentially one-dimensional. Coffin's is obviously two-dimensional, and Cutler's occupies three dimensions in the fullest sense. We shall start at three dimensions and descend to one.

Is there a reader of this book who has not at one time or another taken a burr puzzle in hand? They are sometimes called Chinese puzzles, although they almost certainly originated in the West. Burrs may consist of numerous pieces and appear in a variety of shapes. The commonest kind has six pieces, each a notched oblong block. When assembled, they are arranged in three pairs. A pair consists of two adjacent blocks that appear to dive into the center of the puzzle and emerge intact on the

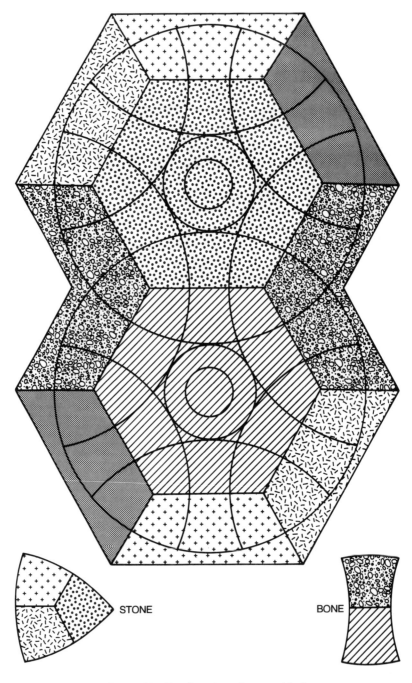

Figure 61   Engel's enigma (unscrambled).

other side. Yet the center of the burr cannot be occupied by the three pairs simultaneously. The notches resolve the paradox. They also define the possibilities for both disassembly and reassembly. Clearly the art of designing a six-piece burr lies in determining how the pieces are notched.

Cutler designs his burrs in three stages. In the first stage he selects the six pieces to be used. Then he makes sure the notches are mutually compatible. This involves determining whether there is an arrangement in which the pieces all fit snugly within the central volume of the puzzle. Finally he tests disassembly: can the puzzle be taken apart and, if it can, how easily? Cutler relies on computer programs in the last two stages of design.

Each piece in a burr puzzle begins life as a block of wood having specific proportions. In the puzzle known as Bill's baffling burr each piece measures (in arbitrary units) 2 by 2 by 6. There are 12 potential sites for notches in the block (*see* Figure 59). If one imagines the block as consisting of 24 unit cubes, there would be four cubes at each end of the block and 16 cubes in the middle. On one side of the block eight central cubes are arranged in two rows of four each. These are numbered 1 through 8. On the opposite side of the block an additional four central cubes are numbered 9 through 12. The block becomes a potential burr piece when a certain subset of the 12 cubes is removed. Of the 4096 ways of removing such subsets, Cutler calculates that only 369 of them result in useful puzzle components.

Long experience with burr puzzles enables Cutler to select six promising pieces. But how, without the painstaking manufacture of an actual wood model, can it be determined whether all six pieces will fit together? It did not take Cutler long to think of using a computer to take over this stage of the design process. In 1973 he wrote his first configuration program. The program represents the space to be occupied by the puzzle as a three-dimensional array, measuring 8 by 8 by 8. Each array entry represents a unit cube within this space, each labeled with the number of the puzzle piece that will occupy it. For example, the cubes labeled with a 3, if they are removed intact from this conceptual place, would collectively yield the shape of piece number 3. It is not hard to see that, depending on how heavily notched it is, each piece will occupy between 14 and 24 cubes within the array.

The configuration program reviews each of six lists describing the six pieces according to the coordinates of cubes of which they are made. The coordinates are then subjected to a variety of arithmetic manipulations that amount to translations, rotations, and reflections of the piece within the array. Of course, the procedure is methodical and requires the execution of many loops.

The first piece (number 1) is established in a standard position within the three-dimensional array by labeling a set of its cubes with a 1. These cubes reproduce the shape of the piece exactly. The program then tries each of the remaining pieces in a position intersecting the standard piece. All possible orientations of the second piece are tried, a task that requires two loops. Two more loops enable the program to try fitting a piece in a third position intersecting the first two. Again all orientations are tried. To accommodate the remaining three pieces the program has six more loops. Most programmers would call that heavy nesting. Each time a new piece is tried in a new position and orientation, the program tests each of the 512 cubes in the puzzle array to see whether any two are doubly numbered. If they are, the combination must be rejected because two of the pieces are trying to occupy the same space: the configuration is illegal (in the mathematical sense of the term).

The set of all possible configurations of the six pieces can be represented as a tree. The root of the tree is piece number 1 in standard position. This is a legal configuration. The addition of a new piece in a new orientation to each succeeding legal configuration establishes either a new branch in the tree of possibilities or a dead end.

At the outermost reaches of the tree the program may produce a number of legal configurations consisting of six pieces nicely assembled in a burr puzzle. Some of these, however, are hopelessly jammed; no matter how one pushes, pulls, or wiggles the pieces, they will not (indeed, cannot) come apart. In fact, such objects could never have been manufactured in the first place. They exist only in the configuration program's imagination. How does Cutler know when a legal, six-piece configuration can be taken apart? He finds out by invoking a second, disassembly program.

The disassembly program analyzes the same 8-by-8-by-8 array used to identify legal configurations. But this program tries to move each piece one or more units in any of three orthogonal directions. It will try to slide the piece out of the puzzle or shift it sideways. Here again a tree represents the possibilities. The root of the tree is the intact puzzle. For each state of disassembly it arrives at, the program systematically searches for and discovers the possible moves of each piece. As people have long since found, once one or two pieces have been removed the remaining ones come out rather quickly.

Therefore, as far as Cutler is concerned, good design for a six-piece burr requires that the first piece be exceedingly difficult to extract. In Bill's baffling burr no fewer than five distinct moves are needed to withdraw the first piece!

As Cutler designed Bill's baffling burr, his masterwork, he tried and discarded nine sets of pieces. The 10th set was selected with particularly fiendish intuition (*see* Figure 59). The configuration program found one and only one legal arrangement for these pieces and the disassembly program found that the puzzle could be taken apart in just one way; only one piece could be taken out and this after four seemingly pointless moves.

The disassembly program is also a burr solver. First, of course, it must be given an accurate description of the pieces in a burr puzzle and they must already be embedded in the program's 8-by-8-by-8 array. The output of the program is a sequence of moves that a human could duplicate.

Suppose, however, the program was told nothing about the pieces in the burr. It would have no alternative to manipulating a physical model of the puzzle. It is amusing to imagine the program adapted to operate a pair of robot manipulator arms. Its machinations would then be visible as, over the course of many days, it explored the immense tree of possible moves.

Readers who would like to become entangled with Bill's baffling burr or other derivatives of his inventiveness are welcome to write to him at the address indicated in the List of Suppliers.

Like Cutler, Coffin has for a number of years been inventing burrs and other three-dimensional puzzles. One of his most recent triumphs is two-dimensional: the reader is asked to fit 10 hexomino pieces into a flat, square tray so that no two overlap (*see* Figure 60). Each hexomino consists of six wood squares glued together along one or more edges. One tricky hexomino puzzle is remarkable enough. Yet Coffin has a computer key that unlocks the door to a roomful of such puzzles. Each is different from the others and has a known degree of difficulty. Such a puzzle can be left lying casually on a coffee table at a party. The owner can be secure in the knowledge that no guest can solve it quickly (and then pretend not to have seen the puzzle before), since the puzzle will be completely new to everyone.

Coffin's criteria for the difficulty of such puzzles include both the shapes of the pieces themselves and the number of possible solutions. In the cornucopia project Coffin uses only hexomino pieces. To increase difficulty he uses only hexominoes that are asymmetrical and contain no 2-by-2 squares. The final count of usable hexominoes stands at just 17. The correct placement of 10 such hexominoes in an 8-by-8 tray will leave four spaces uncovered. Only solutions in which the gaps are symmetrically arranged are acceptable. In the model Coffin sent to me there are at least two solutions: one in which the four squares occupy the middle of the tray and one in which they occupy the corners.

There are 19,448 ways of selecting subsets of 10 hexominoes from among 17. Not all the subsets give rise to interesting puzzles. In fact, many subsets cannot even be fitted into the 8-by-8 tray. How can the best puzzles among these possibilities be identified?

Recently Coffin enlisted the aid of Michael D. Beeler, the indefatigable programmer who was mentioned in "One-Dimensional Computers" (World Four) as one of the early explorers of the game called Life. Beeler wrote a brute-force program that attempts to fit each 10-piece subset into a tray. The program automatically generates all solutions. If there are not too many, it produces them along with the 10-piece set of hexominoes. The program's output is available to interested readers.

Like Cutler's programs that design burrs, Beeler's hexomino program explores a tree. The program begins by examining a specific subset of hexominoes generated by its master loop. In essence the program scans the puzzle tray in raster order, line by line. This requires another loop inside the master loop. For each vacant square encountered the program selects an as yet unused hexomino (another loop) and tries fitting it onto the board in all possible orientations (a fourth loop). Whenever it finds a fit for a piece, a new branch in the tree of potential solutions is generated; the program moves to the next vacant square and tries the next piece.

Without some rather admirable algorithmic short cuts the solution-generating program might not be able to find all the possible answers in a reasonable amount of time. One such stratagem involves subjecting each subset to a kind of parity test before the program even enters the second loop. Examining the 17 hexominoes one day, Beeler noticed that if they were regarded as excisions from a checkerboard, 11 hexominoes would have three white squares and three black ones. The remaining six hexominoes would have four squares of one color and two of the other. A solution involving any subset of 10 hexominoes, on the other hand, would have the same number of white squares and black ones, namely 30. Beeler concluded that a solution could be found only for an even number of the six off-parity hexominoes. Any subset not obeying this simple rule could be rejected as unsolvable. This brought the potential number of major program iterations from 19,448 down to 9746.

The number of solutions Beeler's program finds for a given subset of hexominoes determines the degree of difficulty. The degrees specified by Coffin range from hard (several solutions) to very hard (just one solution). Beeler's program steadily churns out solutions. Coffin has tooled up his workshop. He describes his puzzlemaking efforts in *Puzzle Craft*.

A remarkable difference between the puzzles of Cutler and Coffin should be noted: it is difficult to take apart a six-piece burr but not at all difficult to take apart a puzzle from Coffin's cornucopia—merely lift the pieces from the tray. The three-dimensionality of a burr puzzle, in part, prevents such an easy solution. A four-dimensional creature would have no trouble at all with one of Cutler's puzzles; the being could take advantage of a new and different *up* direction. On the other hand, even a four-dimensional creature might have the same trouble putting a burr back together as we have with a two-dimensional assembly puzzle. This thought experiment suggests a two-dimensional burr puzzle taken apart by sliding flat pieces sideways out of a covered tray that contains them. Is such a thing possible? Assume there are eight pieces in our two-dimensional burr puzzle. Two pieces project from each side of the tray; the internal pieces may have any rectilinear shape. Readers are invited to submit designs.

Engel's enigma puzzle has given me some hours of amusement and frustration. I do not yet have a general solution but Douglas R. Hofstadter (whose column "Metamagical Themas" appeared in SCIENTIFIC AMERICAN a few years ago) has developed a program for manipulating the circles. Engel writes that several people adept at Rubik's cube have not been able to get anywhere with the puzzle.

The enigma consists of two intersecting circles embedded in a plastic holder. Around each circle six stones are interspersed with six bones. The stones look like overweight triangles and the bones resemble undernourished rectangles. Because the circles intersect, they share two stones and one bone (*see* Figure 61). The circles of stones and bones can be rotated. If one circle, say the upper one, is rotated 60 degrees, a stone and bone previously shared with the lower circle are whisked away to be replaced by a new stone and bone. Alternate rotation of the two circles by any multiple of 60 degrees in random directions effectively scrambles the stones and bones.

In its initial configuration the puzzle is divided into 10 hexagonally arranged zones. There are eight outer zones that get four colors: red, orange, blue, and black. Symmetrically opposite zones have the same color. There are two inner zones, one within each circle; these are colored yellow and green. Each stone inhabits three zones and so has three colors. Each bone lies in just two zones and consequently has just two colors.

When Engel's circles are scrambled as described, a confusing mosaic of colors emerges; what had been pleasing and orderly now appears colorfully chaotic. How can a puzzle having only a fraction of the moves available in Rubik's cube be just as difficult?

Engel has shown me a full set of instructions for solving the enigma but we shall keep it in reserve in order to give all interested readers a clear shot at finding a solution to the puzzle. Computists are expected to produce spectacularly effective algorithms.

I have not written such a program, but the following analysis might be useful. When the enigma is in the unscrambled state, number the stones clockwise from 0 through 9, starting at the left-hand bone inhabiting both circles. The configuration is then written:

0 1 2 3 4 5 6 7 8 9

Suppose the upper circle is rotated 60 degrees clockwise. If we regard the 10 positions in the sequence above as standing for the corresponding sites in the puzzle, the rotation produces a permutation:

5 0 1 2 3 4 6 7 8 9

Note that 5 has been plucked, in effect, from the sixth position and placed in the first. Readers can easily generate the other three permutations. All four can be embedded in a program that operates on an array of size 10. Initially the array contains the numbers in ascending order. Invoking the permutations in random order will scramble the puzzle. The same representation scheme may make computerized attempts to obtain a solution go faster.

Now at last readers will see why I think of Engel's enigma as one-dimensional. The enigma and related puzzles can be ordered from Engel at the address given in the List of Suppliers.

Addendum

Hundreds of readers have tackled the puzzles just described. While some seek the magic combination of moves that disassemble the burr, others scratch their head over the placement of polyominoes in a tray. Members of this group will have to get by without help from their friends: each puzzle is unique. Still other readers keep rotating the wheels of Engel's enigma in a vain attempt to unscramble it. Some of the devotees are succeeding, at least on an abstract plane: claims of solutions to the enigma have come in.

A call for two-dimensional burrs brought in a number of designs. The most charming design received so far is shown in Figure 62. The problem is to remove the four pieces from the tray symbolized by the rectangular outline. The pieces can only be moved in four directions confined to the plane of the page: up, down, left, and right. The four corner squares are regarded as immovable. Which piece must be moved first? Jeffrey R. Carter of Littleton, Colo., designed this two-dimensional tour de force. Our three-dimensionality confers the advantage of visualizing the whole; a two-dimensional solver would push and pull at the sides of a mysterious box.

An algorithmic solution to Engel's enigma is claimed by P. Clavier of Dallas, Tex. Clavier says that his program, written in BASIC and running on a Texas Instruments CC-40 portable computer, solves typical scrambles in from 300 to 700 moves. The solution implements six fundamen-

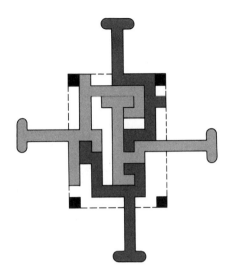

Figure 62   Jeffrey R. Carter's two-dimensional burr.

tal exchange operations on the stones and bones. Readers who used the sequence representation I suggested may have cast their net too widely; solutions of the numerical sequence are not always solutions of the enigma. In framing the suggestion I was aware that bones were excluded from the representation. "Well," said I at the time, "take care of the stones and the bones will take care of themselves." Not so. The stones should be interleaved with the symbols that represent the bones.

The ultimate scramble-unscramble puzzle appears to have been invented by Robert Carlson of Los Altos, Calif. It is so complicated to make that he must be content with the view of it on his monitor. The puzzle is an icosahedron, the Platonic solid that has 20 triangular faces. Each vertex is the site of a possible scrambling operation.

When a vertex is rotated, the five incident triangles are rotated as well. Each triangle has three colors. In unscrambled form the colors adjacent to each vertex are the same. Carlson has prepared a version of his computer puzzle for the IBM PC. In addition to colors it features a musical note for each move.

The Towers of Hanoi
and the Chinese Rings

Good puzzles provide an excellent way to log in to the realm of abstract thought inhabited by mathematicians and other theorists. The best puzzles embody themes from this realm; the significance of such themes extends considerably beyond the puzzles themselves.

Two classic puzzles, the Tower of Hanoi and the Chinese rings, suggest two pairs of contrasting themes: recursion and iteration, unity and diversity. Apart from such serious considerations, the puzzles are fun and also provide the neophyte with a satisfying sense of confusion, hallmark of his or her slow entry into the realm of abstract thought.

The tower puzzle consists of three vertical pegs set in a board. A number of disks, graded in size, are initially stacked on one of the pegs so that the smallest disk is uppermost. The aim of the puzzle is to transfer all of the disks from the initial peg to one of the other two pegs. The disks are manipulated according to these simple rules:

1. Move one disk at a time from one peg to another.
2. No disk may be placed on top of a smaller disk.

The smallest disk must be moved first since it is the only one that is initially accessible (*see* Figure 63). On the next turn there are two moves for the smallest disk (both pointless) and one move for the second-smallest disk. It goes onto the unoccupied peg since it cannot be placed on top of the smallest disk (Rule 2). On the third turn it is not quite so obvious what to do: should the second disk be returned to the initial peg or should the first disk be moved again—and if so, onto what peg?

From this point on one is faced with a long succession of moves and with many opportunities for wrong choices. Even if all the right choices

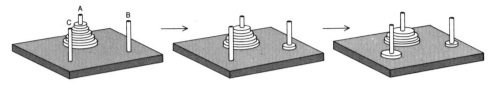

Figure 63 The first two moves in the Tower of Hanoi puzzle.

are made, $2^n - 1$ moves are needed (as we shall see below) to relocate a tower of n disks, one at a time, onto another peg. The surprisingly long time required to solve a puzzle made up of even a moderate number of disks is well illustrated by the following tale quoted from W. W. Rouse Ball's classic puzzle book, *Mathematical Recreations and Essays:*

"In the great temple of Benares . . . beneath the dome which marks the centre of the world, rests a brass plate in which are fixed three diamond needles, each a cubit high and as thick as the body of a bee. On one of these needles, at the creation, God placed sixty-four discs of pure gold, the largest disc resting on the brass plate and the others getting smaller and smaller up to the top one. This is the Tower of Bramah. Day and night unceasingly the priests transfer the discs from one diamond needle to another according to the fixed and immutable laws of Bramah, which require that the priest on duty must not move more than one disc at a time and that he must place this disc on a needle so that there is no smaller disc below it. When the sixty-four discs shall have been thus transferred from the needle on which at the creation God placed them to one of the other needles, tower, temple, and Brahmins alike will crumble into dust, and with a thunderclap the world will vanish."

That the world has not yet vanished attests to the extreme length of time it takes to solve the puzzle: even if the priests move one disk every second, it would take more than 500 billion years to relocate the initial tower of 64 disks!

At this point (and at no risk to the universe) the reader can involve himself or herself more directly by picking up five playing cards, for example the ace through five of hearts, and visualizing three spots on a table. Stack the cards on one of the spots, in order, so that the ace is on top. It is now possible to attempt a solution to the five-disk tower puzzle by moving one card at a time between two spots—but never place a card on one of lower value. Can you complete the relocation of the five-card tower before the end of the world? According to the formula $2^5 - 1$, the transfer should be possible in 31 moves.

How does one solve a puzzle such as this? Why is it that some people seem to find it easy to solve puzzles while others must struggle? My answer to the second question suggests an answer to the first one: I am convinced that everyone uses mathematical thinking at almost every moment of conscious existence. Both our conclusions about why Uncle Harry did not show up for the wedding and our plan for packing bags into the trunk of the car are logically derived from certain premises. Such deductions can be very sophisticated, a fact leading me to believe that almost anyone capable of such intuitive prowess could become a good analytic thinker. The trick is to bring the intuitive analytic abilities to the level of conscious awareness so that they can be utilized in a formal way.

For example, after one has played with the five-disk tower puzzle for a while, it will almost certainly be noticed that smaller towers tend to appear from time to time. One encounters two-disk towers fairly often, sometimes three-disk towers, and perhaps even a four-disk tower. All of this may happen even while one has no clear idea of a solution. One is merely playing.

Soon enough, however, a key idea presents itself for conscious inspection: "If one can make a two-disk tower or a three-disk tower (let alone a tower of four disks), why not a five-disk tower?" Spotting certain regularities in the way these smaller towers are formed, one is led, more or less quickly, to the pattern of moves yielding a five-disk tower on one of the other pegs.

A similar idea occurs throughout mathematics and computer science as a problem-solving technique. Stated as a principle, it might go something like this: "If I can solve the problem in a somewhat smaller instance than the one I am faced with, perhaps I can use such a solution in the larger instance." This is the notion of recursion—the inclusion in a procedure of the procedure itself.

The idea of recursion, applied to the tower puzzle, is quite explicit. If we can solve a tower puzzle for $n - 1$ disks, then we can surely solve one for n disks. The essential clue for developing an n-disk solution from an $(n - 1)$-disk solution comes from the solutions of the two-disk version. Suppose two disks—the top, or first, disk and the bottom, or second, disk—are to be moved to another peg. Call the peg they currently occupy the source peg, call the peg they will finally occupy the target peg, and call the remaining peg the spare peg. If we move the first disk to the spare peg and the second disk to the target peg, then on the third move the first disk is placed on the target peg, completing the solution. These three moves become the basis for a three-part recursive solution of the puzzle in which the first disk is mentally replaced with an entire tower consisting of $n - 1$ disks and the second disk is replaced with the nth (and largest) disk. The three stages can be presented in this manner:

1. Transfer the tower of $n - 1$ disks from the source peg to the spare peg.

2. Move the nth disk from the source peg to the target peg.
3. Transfer the $(n-1)$ disk tower again, this time from the spare peg to the target peg.

This three-part recipe merely imitates our solution of the two-disk puzzle. Assuming, of course, that we can solve the $(n-1)$-disk puzzle, we use the solution sequence of moves to transfer the tower of $n-1$ disks from the source peg to the spare peg. In the next stage the nth disk has been relieved of its burden and we can move it to the target peg. In the third stage we reapply our solution in the case of $n-1$ disks to transfer them from the spare peg to the target peg.

How do we solve the tower puzzle when is consists of $(n-1)$-disks? The answer is staring us in the face: Repeat the same procedure, but this time replace the term $n-1$ in stages 1 and 3 by $n-2$, and so on. Eventually we arrive at a point where stages 1 and 3 require the transfer of a single disk.

This solution process, with its mercilessly propagating branches and subbranches, is very confusing for a human to use, but it does make clear why the solution has nearly 2^n steps: each time the procedure is used it repeats itself twice more. Even if humans find it difficult to implement such a solution process, computers do not.

Figure 64 gives part of the solution for a five-disk tower. Three stages are shown as procedures within a larger procedure called TOWER $(n, X \rightarrow Y)$. This procedure uses three elements of information: n, the number of disks to be moved; X, the source peg; and Y, the target peg.

As the terminology suggests, the essential framework of a recursive program for the tower puzzle can be written algorithmically as follows:

> TOWER (n, *source* → *target*):
>   TOWER ($n-1$, source → spare)
>   MOVE (n, source → target)
>   TOWER ($n-1$, spare → target)

Suppose we wish to move five disks from peg A (the source) to peg B (the target). If we replace n by 5, source by A, target by B, and spare by C, then the above procedure becomes

> TOWER (5, A → B):
>   TOWER (4, $A \rightarrow C$)
>   MOVE (5, $A \rightarrow B$)
>   TOWER (4, $C \rightarrow B$)

In other words, the program must first succeed in moving the first four disks from peg A to peg C. It records the fact that when this procedure is complete, it must next execute MOVE (5, $A \rightarrow B$), that is, move the fifth

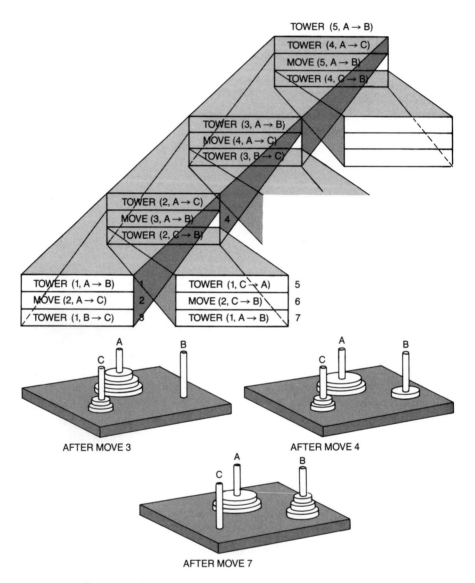

Figure 64   Recursive solution of the Tower of Hanoi puzzle.

and largest disk from peg A to peg B. It also records yet another execution of the procedure TOWER, this time to move the first four disks from peg C to peg B.

Each invocation of the TOWER procedure results in three more procedures being invoked: TOWER, then MOVE, and then TOWER again. The

MOVE procedure cannot be executed until the first TOWER procedure has been completed. This means that the actual order in which the computer does things is to execute TOWER four successive times, working its way down the left side of the diagram until it encounters

TOWER $(1, A \to B)$
MOVE $(2, A \to C)$
TOWER $(1, B \to C)$

An actual program would contain an additional instruction telling the computer that when only one disk is the object of TOWER, it is moved directly without any further recursions: specifically, the first disk is moved from peg A to peg B. The MOVE procedure then causes the second disk to be moved from peg A to peg C. Finally, the computer moves the first disk again, now from peg B to peg C, completing the third move.

At this point the computer has also completed the first TOWER procedure in the next-to-bottom box in Figure 64. Naturally it then executes MOVE $(3, A \to B)$, immediately moving the third disk from peg A to peg B. Next the instruction TOWER $(2, C \to B)$ is expanded into the three moves carried out in the box at the bottom of the illustration.

The seven moves thus carried out also complete the execution of the first invocation of TOWER on the second level of the diagram, and the computer continues to follow the same pattern, sometimes racing down to a low-level box and sometimes backtracking to a higher level. Eventually it succeeds in working its way through the entire diagram and the puzzle has been solved.

Recursion often seems magical because all the bookkeeping needed to remember "where one is" has been carried out by the computer; people are not much good at such large memory tasks. Fortunately a technique requiring little memory is available. In 1980 a simple pattern of moves was found by Peter Buneman of the University of Pennsylvania and Leon Levy of AT&T Bell Laboratories. Buneman and Levy suggest a simple alternation between two kinds of move:

1. Move the smallest disk from its present peg to the next peg in clockwise order.
2. Move any disk but the smallest.

The second step is not as arbitrary as it seems: there is always only one legal move to make under this restriction—until the puzzle is suddenly solved.

Recently I made an eight-disk tower puzzle out of wood and let a friend play with it for a while. He got nowhere and left the room momentarily. Hurriedly, I explained the Buneman-Levy solution to his eight-year-old daughter, who had been looking on with fascination. When my friend returned, he gaped at the sight of his daughter calmly and without hesitation transferring disks from peg to peg. She completed the solution in a few minutes. "That's some kid you have there," I said.

The point of the Buneman-Levy solution is that recursion is not really needed for solving the tower puzzle; a simple iterative solution suffices. An iterative program is one that carries out a repetitive task by means of a simple loop rather than through a succession of recursions. Although recursive programs have the special charms of brevity and elegance, they require large amounts of storage. For example, it is obvi-

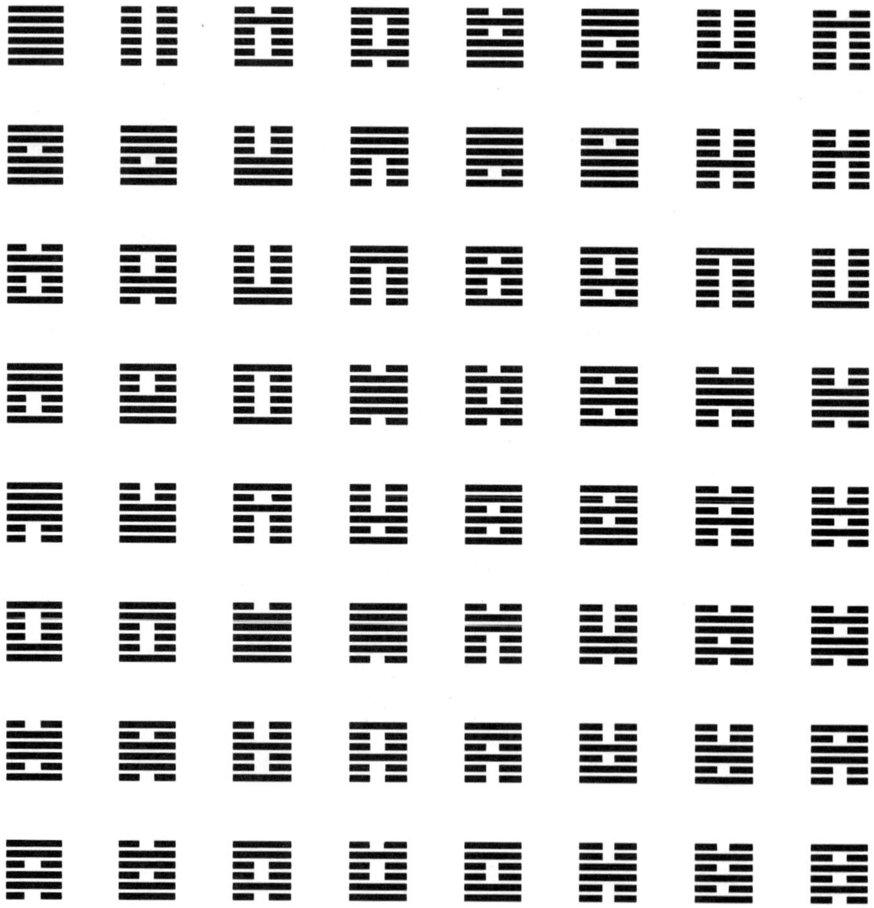

Figure 65   King Wen's arrangement of the 64 hexagrams of the *I Ching*.

ous from the illustration of the recursive solution of the tower puzzle that much memory is needed to save all the incomplete executions of TOWER. The kind of iterative program based on the Buneman-Levy solution algorithm requires almost no memory at all. Rarely, however, can one replace a recursive program by an iterative one in this manner.

Recursion and iteration form one of the many polarities of computing, a kind of yin and yang in the approach to repetitive processing. The yin and yang symbols represented the complementary duality central to major philosophical traditions of prerevolutionary China. The two principles form the basis of the *I Ching* ("Book of Changes"). Yin and yang are like the binary numbers 0 and 1, which are fundamental to digital computing. In the *I Ching* yin is represented by a broken horizontal line (--) and yang by an unbroken one (—). Together these symbols are grouped into sets of six, making up 64 hexagrams (*see* Figure 65). Properly interpreted, each hexagram represents a special choice. The believer draws yarrow straws to determine which hexagram is relevant to his or her life. The arrangement shown is ascribed to King Wen, who ruled in 1150 B.C. (The reasons for this ordering of hexagrams are obscured by time. I would be indebted to any reader who can provide the key to this mysterious arrangement.)

Having mentioned binary numbers, I am reminded of yet another way to solve the Tower of Hanoi puzzle. If one numbers the disks 1, 2, 3, . . . up to n in the usual manner from smallest to largest, it turns out that each move in the puzzle's solution is indicated by a binary number. For example, to solve the five-disk puzzle here for illustrative purposes, we would list the five-bit binary numbers in the usual order of counting. The first nine five-bit binary numbers are

$$
\begin{array}{ccccc}
0 & 0 & 0 & 0 & 0 \\
0 & 0 & 0 & 0 & 1 \quad (1) \\
0 & 0 & 0 & 1 & 0 \quad (2) \\
0 & 0 & 0 & 1 & 1 \quad (1) \\
0 & 0 & 1 & 0 & 0 \quad (3) \\
0 & 0 & 1 & 0 & 1 \quad (1) \\
0 & 0 & 1 & 1 & 0 \quad (2) \\
0 & 0 & 1 & 1 & 1 \quad (1) \\
0 & 1 & 0 & 0 & 0 \quad (4)
\end{array}
$$

Each binary number that has a predecessor in the sequence also has exactly one bit that has just changed from a 0 to a 1. The position of this bit (counting from the right) is given by the decimal number written beside the binary one. These numbers are also the numbers of the first eight disks moved; the correspondence holds throughout the standard solution sequence. Armed only with any one binary number in the sequence, Timothy R. S. Walsh of my department at the University of Western Ontario can reconstruct by computer the exact appearance of the tower puzzle at that stage. Unfortunately his algorithm is too long to include here.

Mention of yin and yang serves to introduce the Chinese rings (*see* Figure 66). This puzzle consists of a long wire loop set in a handle with a series of rings encircling the loop. Each ring is linked loosely by a metal post to a wood platform below the loop. The post connecting each ring

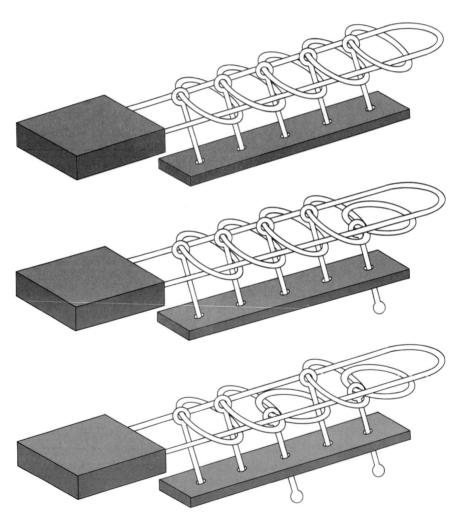

Figure 66   The first two moves in the Chinese-rings puzzle.

to the platform passes through the ring behind (closer to the handle), preventing its removal from the loop.

The goal is to remove all the rings. As in the tower puzzle, newcomers will discover much scope for wrong moves. The illustration shows the first two moves in the five-ring puzzle. To remove a ring from the loop, slide the loop back, if possible, to the post of the ring just ahead of the ring to be removed. The latter ring can then be pivoted upward so that the swinging portion clears the end of the loop. By sliding the loop forward again the ring can now be tilted sideways and dropped through the loop. In solving the puzzle it is often necessary to put rings back on the loop; in such cases the reverse procedure is followed.

Attempts to solve the rings puzzle reveal the same general problem posed by the tower puzzle: configurations appear in which various numbers of consecutive rings have been removed from the loop, once again leading one to believe all the rings can somehow be removed. It comes as no surprise, then, to learn that the rings puzzle can be solved by the same kind of recursive algorithm. Indeed, there is also a simple iterative procedure for solving the rings, considerably more transparent than the iterative solution of the tower puzzle. It would be a pity to reveal the simple technique here and deny readers the pleasure of having their own "Aha!" experience. I can give almost no hints without giving the answer away, but the solution can be stated in one or two sentences and requires no notation at all. I shall discuss the best solutions in the Addendum.

Of somewhat greater surprise is the near identity of the two puzzles, which suggests another contrast common in computing and mathematics: two problems that on the surface appear to be quite different turn out on closer inspection to be essentially the same!

The link between the two puzzles is provided by two binary codes and an algorithm that translates one into the other. Just as we represent the moves of the tower puzzle by consecutive binary numbers, so we introduce the rings puzzle: a 1 represents a ring on the loop and a 0 symbolizes a ring off the loop. The five-ring puzzle can then be represented by a five-digit sequence of 0s and 1s, the leftmost digit standing for the ring next to the handle. Written as a sequence of such numbers, the first four configurations of the rings puzzle are as follows:

$$1\ 1\ 1\ 1\ 1 \quad \text{(all rings on)}$$
$$1\ 1\ 1\ 1\ 0 \quad \text{(first ring off)}$$
$$1\ 1\ 0\ 1\ 0 \quad \text{(first and third rings off)}$$
$$1\ 1\ 0\ 1\ 1 \quad \text{(third ring off)}$$

On the next two moves the second ring and then the first ring are removed. Following that, the fifth ring is removed. Then the first three rings are put back on the loop in preparation for taking off the fourth ring. In all, 21 moves suffice to remove all five rings. The last four configurations are listed thus:

$$
\begin{array}{lllll}
0 & 0 & 0 & 1 & 0 \quad \text{(second ring on)} \\
0 & 0 & 0 & 1 & 1 \quad \text{(first and second rings on)} \\
0 & 0 & 0 & 0 & 1 \quad \text{(first ring on)} \\
0 & 0 & 0 & 0 & 0 \quad \text{(no rings on)}
\end{array}
$$

Without glancing ahead, readers might enjoy supplying the 14 missing code numbers by solving the rings puzzle in this form and following two simple rules that represent the constraint adjacent rings place on each other:

1. The rightmost digit can be changed (from 0 to 1 or from 1 to 0) at any time.
2. The only other digit that can be changed is the one immediately to the left of the rightmost 1.

At first glance there seems to be no obvious relation between the sequence of 22 binary code numbers implied above and the binary counting sequence arising from the tower puzzle. Actually there is a relation. It involves the Gray code, named after the engineer Frank Gray, who invented it during the 1930s at AT&T Bell Laboratories to provide an error-correcting technique for electronic communications. The code is explained in Figure 67. In the same illustration are shown the first 22 binary numbers and beside them their corresponding Gray codes.

Examination of the Gray-code numbers in the illustration reveals a remarkable coincidence. In reverse order the Gray-code numbers are just the successive ring positions in a solution of the Chinese-rings puzzle!

These, then, are the 21 positions forming a solution to the five-ring puzzle. But the five-disk tower puzzle requires 31 moves for its completion. One would think that if the two puzzles are in some sense identical, they would have the same number of moves in their solution. The discrepancy is removed, however, when we examine the Gray-code numbers beyond the 21st. Each of these represents a possible configuration in the rings puzzle, and the very last (corresponding to the binary number 11111) is 10000, the configuration in which only the last ring is on the loop. This implies that if you want someone to work harder at the rings puzzle, present it with all rings but the last one removed. Here the number of moves to solve the n-ring puzzle is $2^n - 1$, precisely as in the n-disk puzzle.

	BINARY CODE					GRAY CODE							BINARY CODE					GRAY CODE				
0	0	0	0	0	0	0	0	0	0	0		11	0	1	0	1	1	0	1	1	1	0
1	0	0	0	0	1	0	0	0	0	1		12	0	1	1	0	0	0	1	0	1	0
2	0	0	0	1	0	0	0	0	1	1		13	0	1	1	0	1	0	1	0	1	1
3	0	0	0	1	1	0	0	0	1	0		14	0	1	1	1	0	0	1	0	0	1
4	0	0	1	0	0	0	0	1	1	0		15	0	1	1	1	1	0	1	0	0	0
5	0	0	1	0	1	0	0	1	1	1		16	1	0	0	0	0	1	1	0	0	0
6	0	0	1	1	0	0	0	1	0	1		17	1	0	0	0	1	1	1	0	0	1
7	0	0	1	1	1	0	0	1	0	0		18	1	0	0	1	0	1	1	0	1	1
8	0	1	0	0	0	0	1	1	0	0		19	1	0	0	1	1	1	1	0	1	0
9	0	1	0	0	1	0	1	1	0	1		20	1	0	1	0	0	1	1	1	1	0
10	0	1	0	1	0	0	1	1	1	1		21	1	0	1	0	1	1	1	1	1	1

Each five-digit Gray-code number is obtained from its corresponding binary number by a simple rule: numbering the digits in left-to-right order, the first Gray-code digit is always the same as the first binary digit. Thereafter each Gray digit is a 1 if the corresponding binary digit differs from its predecessor; otherwise it is a 0.

Figure 67   Gray codes for the first 22 binary numbers.

A very informative book on the Chinese rings has been written by Sydney N. Afriat, professor of economics and mathematics at the University of Ottawa. Called *The Ring of Linked Rings*, it is published by Gerald Duckworth & Co. Ltd. (*see* Bibliography). I am indebted to Afriat for the idea of tying the Chinese-rings puzzle to the yin and yang notion of duality. Although he suspects a Chinese origin for the Chinese-rings puzzle, he is aware of definite references only as far back as 1550. Afriat's book also describes the "Gros code," a nineteenth-century anticipation of the Gray code by the French mathematician Louis A. Gros, who published a treatise on the puzzle in 1872. The French, incidentally, call this puzzle Le Baguenodier and the English call it The Tiring Irons.

There are many other facets to both puzzles that I do not have the space to explore here. For example, Leroy J. Dickey of the department of pure mathematics at the University of Waterloo in Ontario reminded me that solving the Chinese-rings puzzle is also equivalent to traversing the edges of an *n*-dimensional hypercube.

It might be observed that the *n*-disk tower puzzle can be solved in $2^n - 1$ moves if three pegs are used, whereas the use of $n + 1$ pegs shortens the number of necessary moves to a considerably smaller number, $2n - 1$. What happens between three pegs and $n + 1$ pegs? How does the minimum number of moves in a solution change as one changes the number of available pegs? It would be interesting to pursue such questions later. Even as I write this there are people puzzling over the four-peg problem, as well as over what Martin Gardner calls a "fiendish version of the Tower," a Japanese puzzle that has been marketed under the name PANEX.

PANEX can be obtained (along with enough perplexity to while away any number of rainy afternoons) by writing to Tricks Limited at the address given in the List of Suppliers.

Addendum

On its initial appearance in "Computer Recreations" (SCIENTIFIC AMERICAN, November, 1984), "The Tower of Hanoi and the Chinese Rings" drew a variety of responses ranging from the mathematical to the metaphysical. Simple, nonrecursive solutions to the puzzles were presented by several readers, including Edward T. Price of Eugene, Ore. He suggests that Tower disks be painted alternately in two colors, say black and white, in order of increasing size. The puzzle is then solved quickly by adding the following rule to the ones originally given: never place a disk on another disk of the same color. There is then no choice about where each one should be placed. The corresponding puzzle posed for the Chinese rings was solved by Morris S. Samberg of Howard Beach, N.Y. One alternates between moving (slipping on or off) the first ring and moving some other ring. Only one other ring may ever be moved. If the number of rings is odd, start with the first ring; otherwise start with the other one. Rob Hardy of Dayton, Ohio, summarizes this simple solution in the following verse:

> An iterative solution
> That's sure to spoil the fun:
> Alternate changing the end ring
> With changing some other one.

No reader was able to find a simple mathematical scheme behind the King Wen ordering of *I Ching* hexagrams. Many readers observed that hexagrams are paired across columns in a simple way, but this hardly explains the overall order. Homer E. Brown, an electrical-engineering consultant in Cary, N.C., produced a rather suggestive analysis, however: From each hexagram count up or down 10 hexagrams, skipping from the end of one column to the beginning of the next if necessary. The hexagram thus arrived at always has a simple relation to the one started with. The rule is not deterministic, however, as one never knows whether to count up or down.

In spite of this seeming relation (which has a number of exceptions in any event), I incline to the view that King Wen's arrangement follows metaphysical principles. Our attempt to project current preoccupations with science and technology into past cultures results in a distorted view of what once was. As a general rule the "scientific" systems that once existed served a role strictly subservient to a largely religious world view. Similar opinions are offered by Bernard X. Bovasso of Saugerties, N.Y. The *I Ching* is concerned with the ordering of time, maintains Bovasso, and so was King Wen. David White, a philosopher at Macalester College in St. Paul, Minn., referred to a translation of the *I Ching* by James Legge (*see* Bibliography). An appendix to this work lays out a metaphysic governing the order of all 64 hexagrams. For example, the first three are connected respectively with the concepts of heaven, earth, and chaos. The chaos hexagram, denoting what is regarded as the disorder of all created things taken collectively, follows heaven and earth since all created things fill the space between heaven and earth.

Anagrams and Pangrams

As my alias, Yank D. Weed, suggests, I cultivate the occasional anagram and in so doing must reject dozens of weeds before one flower appears. An anagram is just a word or group of words obtained by rearranging the letters in another word or group of words. Some practitioners of this difficult but occasionally rewarding art maintain that the composition of ANAGRAMS amounts to an ARS MAGNA. But others, not so gifted with the necessary combinational instinct, shy away from the practice after a few halfhearted attempts.

Anagrammatic wordplay dates back at least to the seventeenth century. It was a literary pastime in the court of Louis XIII, who even appointed his own royal anagrammatist. The art continues to flourish in this century, and two of my predecessors, Martin Gardner and Douglas R. Hofstadter, have written on the subject (*see* Bibliography).

Those who rely on native skill alone, however, may find their talents challenged by the arrival of new, automatic forms of wordplay: Jon L. Bentley of AT&T Bell Laboratories has summarized the state of the art in single-word anagram-finding programs, and James A. Woods of the National Aeronautics and Space Administration's Ames Research Center has developed a program that generates anagrams of entire sentences. Finally, Lee Sallows, a British engineer at the Catholic University of Nijmegen in the Netherlands, has constructed a machine that hunts for pangrams, sentences describing themselves in terms of the number of letters they contain (*see* Figure 68).

In preparing this topic, I experimented with my own name for a while. Using only the family name and first two initials, what new names could I make for myself? "Wayne Kedd" had a fine, decisive ring to it. "Eddy Kanew" suggested someone paddling through the Canadian North; "A. K. Dewdney" obviously showed little imagination. Could I

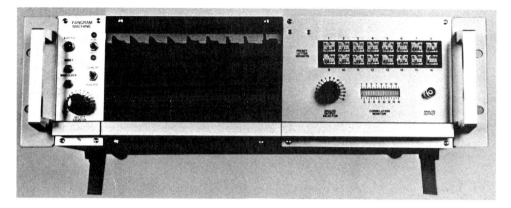

Figure 68   Lee Sallows's pangram machine.

form suggestive phrases or even sentences from my name? "Dandy week" was a pleasant surprise but I was shocked by "Dewy naked." Throughout this exercise there remained a suspicion that I was missing a real flower or two. How could I be sure I had all valid word combinations? Not counting blanks, the nine letters of my name have more than 300,000 arrangements or permutations!

The simplest kind of anagram involves single words. Given a word, find another word that uses the same letters but in a different order. Many English words are anagrams of other English words. For example, *stop, tops, post, spot, pots, opts* are all mutual anagrams. When a human being searches for anagrams of this simple kind, new arrangements of the letters are perhaps suggested by subgroups within the word. For example, I found the anagrams of *stop* in exactly the order listed above, and it may be that when I looked at *stop*, I spotted *top* and simply moved the *s* to the end of the word. The remaining words all seem to have been obtained by moving one or two letters at a time in this way.

A computer program, however, is not equipped with a visual cortex and an associative memory. How does one write a program to first scan a word and then generate anagrams of it? A naive program might develop all permutations of the input and then reject all nonwords. Since there is no known purely computational test to distinguish words from nonwords, the program must have access to a dictionary stored in its memory. Even so, generating all permutations is surely wasteful because an enormous number of them must be compared individually with all the entries in an equally enormous dictionary.

Bentley, who writes "Programming Pearls," a regular feature in *Communications of the ACM* (Association for Computing Machinery), devoted a column in 1983 to what he called "Aha! Algorithms." One of these, a refinement of known techniques, was an algorithm for generating anagrams. It qualifies as an Aha! (denoting the onset of insight) because of a very clever use of "signatures." The algorithm first computes signatures by copying each word in the computer's dictionary and rearranging the letters of the copy in alphabetical order. Next it sorts the words of the dictionary in the order of the signatures. When this has been done, all words with the same signature will be stored together (*see* Figure 69). It is now a simple matter, when one is given a word as input, to generate its signature, look up all the words having that signature, and print them out. The looking up is done by binary search, one of the oldest and fastest techniques for retrieving information from ordered data (*see* Figure 70). At the end of his article Bentley lists the algorithm in program form.

As one thinks about it the realization comes that the programs described by Bentley solve not only individual-word anagram problems but also all possible anagram problems: once the dictionary has been sorted and the signature table has been generated, all single-word anagram play has been reduced to simple table lookups. Can anagrams ever be quite as much fun? The answer depends on one's philosophy of creativity. Do we create in the hope that no other person (or machine) can match our performance or do we create simply for the joy of personal discovery?

For wordplayers who create for the first reason, there are always multiple-word anagrams to fall back on:

MULTIPLE-WORD ANAGRAMS
PLAGUE RAW MORTAL MINDS

SIGNATURE	WORD
⋮	⋮
aecrs	acres
aecrs	cares
aecrs	races
aecrs	scare
aecrt	cater
aecrt	crate
aecrt	react
aecrt	trace
aecrv	carve
aecrv	crave
⋮	⋮

Figure 69   Part of a word-signature dictionary.

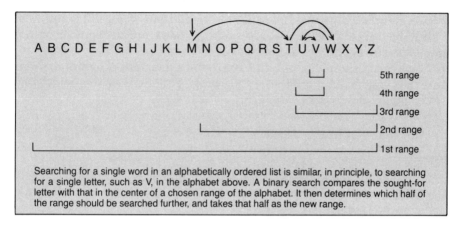

Searching for a single word in an alphabetically ordered list is similar, in principle, to searching for a single letter, such as V, in the alphabet above. A binary search compares the sought-for letter with that in the center of a chosen range of the alphabet. It then determines which half of the range should be searched further, and takes that half as the new range.

Figure 70   A binary search.

Apparently, however, even multiple-word anagrams pose no great problems for a correctly programmed computer. But we shall see how mortal minds still have a role to play in this case.

In his spare time Woods, a computer scientist, has developed a program for multiple-word anagrams. He was bitten by the anagram bug in 1983, when he decided to enter a biweekly anagram contest sponsored by BAM (Bay Area Music) *Magazine*. His entries, however, were to be computer-generated, and with an early version of his anagram program running he converted BACK ON THE CHAIN GANG into AHA, COGNAC KNIGHT BANE, which won an honorable mention. After a number of improvements to the program, including an Aha! idea of his own, Woods was ready to tackle some big names. For example, the name of Donald E. Knuth, a well-known computer scientist with a strong recreational bent of his own, was transformed in a number of ways:

> (DONALD ERVIN KNUTH)
> HUNT DRINK AND LOVE
> INVENT HODAD KNURL
> HALT UNKIND VENDOR

Readers may remember the famous numerologist (and inquiring skeptic) Dr. Matrix, who once stalked the "Mathematical Games" pages of SCIENTIFIC AMERICAN with his daughter Iva:

> (IRVING JOSHUA MATRIX)
> HA—OUR JIVING MARXIST
> HIS VAT, OUR MIXING JAR
> I SAVOR RUM. I JIG. THANX.

It is generally considered permissible to add punctuation to multiple-word anagrams. Whether words such as THANX are acceptable or not depends entirely on one's dictionary.

As a final example of output from Wood's anagram program perhaps it is only fair that I include the following refractions of my own name (Alexander Keewatin Dewdney):

> Al wandered—weekend anxiety
>   dexedrine wakened late yawn
> Dean, a twinkle-eyed exwarden
>   dead wine and watery Kleenex
> Ted Kennedy exiled; a war anew
>   Andean needed wax triweekly

The dictionary used by Woods is largely a customized affair. Since his program cannot live without it, the dictionary is stored in the computer as a disk file. It began its existence as a Unix System 5 Standard Dictionary (distributed by AT&T Bell Laboratories) of roughly 30,000 words, but Woods tripled its size by scanning various disk files and adding new words whenever they were encountered. Of course, the kind of dictionary discussed here is simply a gigantic list of words—with no definitions included.

As mentioned above, a multiple-word anagram program must be somewhat more agile than its single-word colleague. In addition more human intervention is called for at the output end because the words tend to tumble out in a random order. For example, one of the anagrams above may well have been printed out as MARXIST JIVING HA OUR; it was then up to Woods to find an arrangement of the words that made sense. It must be rather like sowing seeds to type in the words to be anagrammatized and then watch as dozens of potential flowers spring up; here is where the word-gardener comes into play. Some anagrams make almost no sense at all no matter how the words are arranged. These are weeds, to be pulled up immediately. Others might be rescued by some punctuation or by the invention of a little tale to go with them. But some anagrams can be arranged into perfect, comprehensible phrases or sentences such as HUNT DRINK AND LOVE. This is a flower to be preserved.

The Woods anagram program is a perfect example of the value of a good heuristic (an inexact but frequently useful procedure for getting an answer quickly). In outline, the program treats the set of input words merely as a string of characters. It cycles through the dictionary, testing each word there against the string. Are all the letters of the word in the string? If they are, put the word in a temporary list, subtract its letters from the string, and start the dictionary search over again. Eventually either the letters in the input string are all used up or the program is left with an unmatchable set of letters. In Figure 71 the action of Wood's algorithm can be traced for the single-word input *compute*. The set of all possible successes and failures of the algorithm is laid out in a tree. Each node of the tree contains a word extracted from the residual list of the preceding node. Beside the extracted word (in parentheses) is the new, reduced residual list.

Because Woods's algorithm is written recursively, it automatically backtracks as soon as no more matches remain to be tried in the current residual list. If that list happens to be empty, however, it first prints out all the words on its temporary list—the sequence of words leading from the root of the tree to the current node. This sequence of words will be an anagram of the input words. Backtracking, moving forward, backtracking again, the algorithm eventually traces out every branch of the

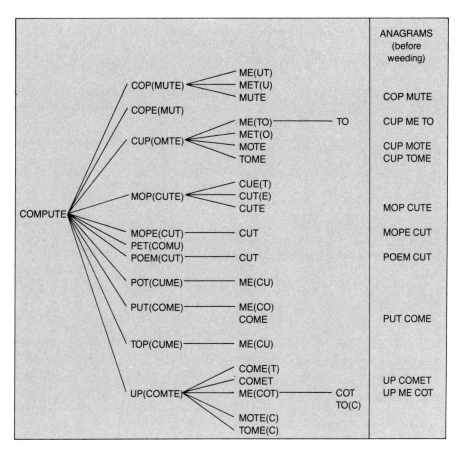

Figure 71 A Woods tree, the leaves of which contain anagrams of the word *compute*.

tree, in effect. In the case of the input phrase *compute*, nearly half of the branches yield (unweeded) anagrams. These would appear to the user as a printed sequence, which begins with

COP MUTE

CUP ME TO

CUP MOTE

Woods's algorithm is actually more sophisticated than I have so far led the reader to believe. For example, if it eventually tried every dictionary word contained in the input string *compute*, the tree would have nearly twice as many nodes sprouting from the string. The heuristic used by Woods to cut down the algorithm's work could be called a "rarest first" rule: from each residual string (as well as the input string) choose only those words containing the rarest letter in the string. A rare letter is one that tends to appear infrequently in words of the dictionary. In the *compute* example the rarest letter in the input string is *p*. Consequently all the initial words selected from this string contain *p*. If the principle is applied at each node, failures tend to happen a lot sooner, the tree has fewer branches, and the algorithm has less work to do. The rarest-first heuristic never misses an anagram since the rarest letter must eventually be used in a completely successful sequence of matches, and so why not match it first?

Besides using a variant of Bentley's signature method Woods's algorithm contains many other time- and space-saving ideas. Woods will be pleased to send a paper describing his algorithm to anyone who writes to him at the NASA Ames Research Center (*see* List of Suppliers).

Those who want to write down their own versions of the single- or multiple-word anagram programs described here will certainly have to get a dictionary in order to indulge in computer wordplay. One can also hook up to the Unix network and ask for Woods's dictionary through his computer mail address, which is *ames!jaw*.

Once a multiple-word anagram program is running with its own dictionary, the user may enjoy weeding his or her own garden of ready-made anagrams. Here there is still some scope for human creativity (neglecting for a moment the creative art of writing a good program), since the anagrams will sometimes come spilling out on the printer or screen faster than one can read them. The word *compute* alone resulted in 10 anagrams most of which I would immediately weed out as unpromising. Of course, one person's weed is someone else's flower, and while I might see some relation between *compute* and *up! comet*, others might prefer *mute cop* or *cut poem*.

For those who want a more curious, convoluted, and (apparently) compulsive pastime, there are pangrams. Pangrams are sentences that contain each letter of the alphabet, such as the well-known sentence used to test typewriters, "The quick brown fox jumps over the lazy dog," or even those that contain each letter a definite number of times. The following example contains each consonant once and each vowel twice:

Why jog exquisite bulk, fond crazy vamp,
Daft buxom jonquil, zephyr's gawky vice?
Guy fed by work, quiz Jove's xanthic lamp—
Zow! Qualms by deja vu gyp fox-kin thrice.

Written by the nineteenth-century logological poet Edwin Fitzpatrick, these sentences are only a short leap away from the most advanced pangrams of all, the self-documenting pangrams that have intrigued Sallows for the past two years. For Sallows, "pangram" has meant precisely this kind of sentence:

This first pangram has five a's, one b, one c, two d's, twenty-nine e's, six f's, four g's, eight h's, twelve i's, one j, one k, three l's, two m's, nineteen n's, twelve o's, two p's, one q, eight r's, twenty-six s's, twenty t's, three u's, five v's, nine w's, three x's, four y's, and one z.

What this sentence asserts about itself is true. For example, it has five *as*, four on the first line and one on the last line.

The change from Fitzpatrick's pangram to Sallows's is from a sentence X about which we can say "X has so many as, so many bs, . . . and so many zs" to a sentence X that has this very form—and that is also true. Although logically this is a leap from other-reference to self-reference, a leap with which many readers are now familiar, it represents a much bigger leap in actual content: gone is the organic quality of "Jove's xanthic lamp," to be replaced by the analytic flavor of ". . . one x, two ys, and one z." If Fitzpatrick's pangram is a flower, then Sallows's pangram is perhaps more like a crystal.

Indeed, Sallows refers to his constructions as "crystalline." His interest in pangrams, although it is several years old, did not blossom until he spotted the following pangram in a Dutch newspaper, *Nieuwe Rotterdamse Courant*, in March, 1983:

Dit pangram bevat vijf a's, twee b's, twee c's, drie d's, zesenveertig e's, vijf f's, vier g's, twee h's, vijftien i's, vier j's, een k, twee l's, twee m's, zeventien n's, een o, twee p's, een q, zeven r's, vierentwintig s's, zestien t's, een u, elf v's, acht w's, een x, een y, en zes z's.

Stunned by the prismatic beauty of this elegant specimen, Sallows was at first envious and then dismayed to find that the author of the article, a well-known wordplay expert by the name of Rudy Kousbroek, had thrown out a challenge addressed to him personally: "Lee Sallows will doubtless find little difficulty in producing a magic English translation of this sentence."

Having already considered the possibility of computer-generated pangrams, Sallows set to work writing a succession of programs in Lisp. Analysis revealed that the search boiled down to simply filling in the question marks in the following pseudopangram:

> This pangram contains five a's, one b, two c's, two d's, ? e's, ? f's, ? g's, ? h's, ? i's, one j, one k, ? l's, two m's, ? n's, ? o's, two p's, one q, ? r's, ? s's, ? t's, ? u's, ? v's, ? w's, ? x's, ? y's, and one z.

Setting up predefined ranges for the numbers in question, Sallows's final Lisp program methodically began to work its way through all possibilities, testing 100 new combinations per second. The program ran as a low-priority "batch job" every night and each morning Sallows would rush eagerly to his terminal, call up the job file and swiftly scan it for the magic word EUREKA. This would indicate that the program had discovered a pangram. But morning after morning no EUREKA appeared and Sallows began seriously to consider just how long he ought to expect the job to take. A few quick calculations with the predefined number ranges soon revealed a time of 31.7 million years. He writes of this moment: "I was so unprepared for the blow contained in this revelation that initially I could hardly take it in. . . . Now that the truth had dawned I began cursing my naiveté in ever embarking on such a fool's errand."

At this point lesser mortals might have given up entirely, but the experience seems only to have steeled Sallows's resolve. Others had urged him to develop a cleverer program, yet Sallows, an electronics engineer and not a computer scientist, felt uncomfortable in the realm of algorithmic analysis. Only one approach seemed to make sense: a special-purpose computer dedicated to the search for pangrams. In other words, a pangram machine!

Over a period of three months Sallows "devoted every spare second to constructing this rocket for exploring the far reaches of logological space." When it was finished, it contained 100 integrated circuits distributed over 13 printed-circuit cards. Its front panel displayed 67 indicator lamps for reading the current combination under test and a special EUREKA light that would turn on only when a pangram had been found. The extremely fast circuits of Sallows's machine could explore 1 million combinations per second instead of his program's 100. By reducing the predefined ranges for the number words filling in the question marks of his pseudopangram, Sallows developed a new estimate of the time necessary for trying all possible combinations: 32.6 days.

The pangram machine was launched on October 3, 1983. For the first few days Sallows would wake up in the morning dominated by a single question: has it halted? He writes: "It took nerves of iron to go patiently through the morning's ablutions before sedately descending to the living room, where the machine was installed on my writing bureau. Then with great deliberation I would open the door, go in, and *look*." But morning after morning the indicator lamps were found blinking their way merrily through millions of combinations while the EUREKA lamp stayed ominously dark. On the sudden inspiration of fresh insight, Sallows finally stopped the machine and made further modifications. By November 19 the newly improved MARK II pangram machine was up and running, and one evening two days later he "was sitting in front of the machine . . . when suddenly the EUREKA lamp came on and my stomach turned a somersault. Tense with excitement, I carefully decoded the light displays into the set of number words represented. A painstaking check completely verified the following perfect pangram":

> This pangram contains four a's, one b, two c's, one d, thirty e's, six f's, five g's, seven h's, eleven i's, one j, one k, two l's, two m's, eighteen n's, fifteen o's, two p's, one q, five r's, twenty-seven s's, eighteen t's, two u's, seven v's, eight w's, two x's, three y's, & one z.

In the days that followed more pangrams appeared, and Sallows's collection now amounts to hundreds, including a series of 30 pangrams with 30 different verbs such as "contains," "lists," "includes," and so on. Exulting in his triumph, Sallows appeared ready to make great claims for the kind of special-purpose analog-digital devices exemplified by his pangram machine: "This apparatus has succeeded in quickly producing . . . solutions to an essentially mathematical problem in the face of which digital computers (I exclude supercomputers and parallel processors) are wholly ineffectual."

The statement was sure to raise eyebrows in the computing community, particularly among the academicians. As if to goad on those very people, Sallows made the following wager: "I bet 10 guilders nobody can come up with a self-enumerating solution (or proof of its nonexistence) to the sentence beginning 'This computer-generated pangram contains . . . and . . .' *within the next 10 years*." The result of Sallows's challenge will be found in the Addendum to this chapter.

So far I have said almost nothing about the pangram machine or how it works. Although a detailed description of its electronic design is beyond our scope, the machine can be discussed in terms of the algorithm it embodies. Essentially a brute-force search through a large number of possibilities, the algorithm nonetheless uses some intelligent structures.

Constructing a pangram, as noted above, is really just a matter of filling in some 16 blanks representing the only letters whose frequency of occurrence is likely to change from one would-be pangram to the next. Each number word, say *twenty-seven*, can be represented by the following "profile," which lists the number of occurrences of each letter in the word:

$$\begin{array}{c} \text{e f g h i l n o r s t u v w x y} \\ \text{3 0 0 0 0 0 2 0 0 1 2 0 1 1 0 1} \end{array}$$

A particular combination of number words can be represented by a matrix such as the one in Figure 72. The rows of the matrix represent the letters *e* through *y* in the list above. Each row contains the profile of a particular number word indicating how many times the row letter is said to appear in the current combination. Below the matrix is an additional row listing the frequency of additional letters in the pangram text (such as "This pangram contains . . ." or "This pangram lists . . .") and, below that, a sequence of column sums. In the illustration all but one of the column sums match their corresponding row numbers: the current combination is a near miss.

In essence Sallows's pangram machine "counts" its way through all possible combinations of number words, which are restricted to certain ranges. For example, one set of ranges used successfully by Sallows involved 23 to 32 *es*, one to 10 *fs*, one to 10 *gs*, one to 10 *hs*, six to 15 *is*, and so on. His chief concern in setting the ranges was to make them narrow enough to keep the search time small but not so narrow that all pangrams are accidentally weeded out. The actual counting involves stepping each of the 16 row number words through their respective ranges rather like a crazy odometer. Thus the first set of numbers to be tried might be 23, 1, 1, 1, 6, . . . , the next 24, 1, 1, 1, 6, . . . , and continuing to 32, 1, 1, 1, 6, ... The combination after this would involve resetting the first counter back to 23 and advancing the next one, as in 23, 2, 1, 1, 6, ...

A more detailed account of Sallows's pangram adventure, including a description of his machine and its operation, is available from this paradigital pangram pioneer at the address indicated in the List of Suppliers.

Besides the recreational value inherent in various forms of automatic wordplay described here, there is sometimes an additional and deeper benefit in computer recreations, namely the development of intellectual skills. In his "Aha! Algorithms" column Bentley stressed the value of his anagram program as an example of how a little insight can go a long way toward making a program more efficient. Indeed, the same thing is true of Woods's program, and even of Sallows's machine. Whether a clever program running on a standard computer will ever

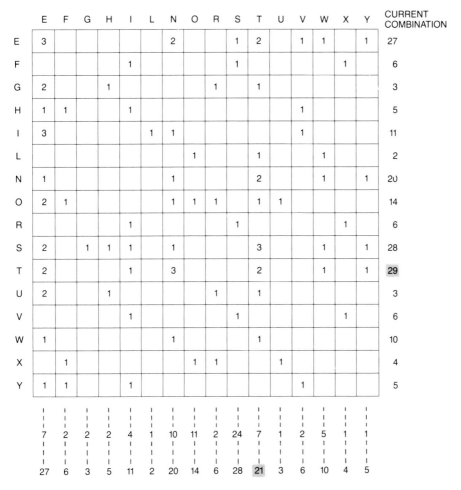

Figure 72   A pangram matrix for a near miss, which contains not 29 Ts, as stated, but 21.

outperform Sallows's machine is a bit beside this point of view. Sallows's effort represents simultaneously a funny kind of obsession and a tremendous drive to achieve results. Perhaps it is even true that his results were achievable in no other way under the circumstances.

Addendum

In "Anagrams and Pangrams" I described how Lee Sallows, creator of the pangram machine, made a wager of 10 guilders that no computer-generated pangram would appear within 10 years. The wager was originally made in my "Computer Recreations" column in 1984. Within a month Sallows's challenge was met by no fewer than four recreational programmers. It seems amazing that all four found exactly the same pangram:

> This computer-generated pangram contains six a's, one b, three c's, three d's, thirty-seven e's, six f's, three g's, nine h's, twelve i's, one j, one k, two l's, three m's, twenty-two n's, thirteen o's, three p's, one q, fourteen r's, twenty-nine s's, twenty-four t's, five u's, six v's, seven w's, four x's, five y's, and one z.

Three of the four pangrammatists are listed here along with the language and machine they used:

John R. Letaw, a cosmic-ray physicist of Severna Park, Md., discovered the pangram running a BASIC program on a VAX 11/780 computer.

Lawrence G. Tesler of Apple Computers, Inc., in Palo Alto, Calif., used Pascal on an Apple Lisa, naturally.

William B. Lipp of Milford, Conn., returned from a long weekend to find the same pangram on the printer of his IBM PC. Lipp also used Pascal.

The fourth pangrammatist, of Palo Alto, Calif., wants to remain anonymous as he or she used a computer dedicated to problems very different from pangram hunting. The machine was another VAX 11/780, running a FORTRAN program.

Although it is not entirely clear from the wording of the wager, Sallows may owe each of these people 10 guilders. Perhaps I may be allowed to act as referee in the matter and close off collections on the bet at this point. Luckily for Sallows, 10 guilders does not amount to much.

So discouraged was Sallows by the astonishing rapidity with which some solutions appeared that he sent me the following advertisement to be run in this space:

For Sale
PANGRAM MACHINE
(slightly used)
plus 10-year guarantee!
only $100,000

The high price is the consequence of the debts Sallows anticipated; in view of my decision to close the wager he can no doubt be persuaded to lower his price.

All four successful contestants employed various heuristics in order to narrow the search for successful letter combinations.

Another anonymous reader sent in a Roman-numeral pangram and a binary pangram. Here is the Roman-numeral pangram:

THIS PANGRAM LISTS III A's, I B, I C, I D, I E, I F, II G's, II H's, XLVI I's, I J, I K, III L's, II M's, II N's, I O, II P's, I Q, II R's, XVII S's, III T's, I U, III V's, I W, III X's, I Y, I Z.

Readers might enjoy attempting the binary program without benefit of a computer: Is must be treated as 1s and Os and 0s. It starts "THIS PANGRAM HAS . . ."

I am indebted to John Henrick of Seattle, Wash., who alerted me to the May 1984 issue of *Word Ways*. An article in it by editor A. Ross Eckler and Mike Morton, a programmer, describes a program dedicated to finding anagrams of the name

RONALD WILSON REAGAN

Among the characteristic Reagananagrams produced by the program is

NO, DARLINGS, NO ERA LAW.

WORLD SIX

Stimulation Through Simulation

To set the stage there are five easy (simulation) pieces to introduce the largest World in our armchair universe. These include the use of a cannon and pond to estimate pi, a galton board to illustrate distribution theory, a curious political game in which democracy votes itself out of existence, and a zombie door to initiate tyros into the subleties of queues. Following this, we examine how to simulate a cluster of stars moving according to the mutual attraction of Newtonian gravitation. What does it take to develop a stable cluster? Further, we simulate a whole planet, the mysterious planet called Wa-Tor. It is shaped like a donut, covered entirely by water, and populated solely by sharks and fish. Sometimes the sharks eat all the fish and then starve to death. Sometimes the sharks eat only some of the fish, can't find the rest, and starve to death anyway; the fish then breed to fill the planet's oceans. If one starts with the right numbers of sharks and fish, everything comes out right and the fragile ecology of Wa-Tor may last forever. Next, a species of automaton is allowed to evolve in a primordial soup. The ones that predict the numerical environment survive to reproduce. If the environment is not too complicated, the automata get pretty smart. The final foray in this World, appropriately enough, is about extinction. There is a program that seems to simulate the evolution of new species. As in our own paleontological record, a great many of these species die out. Indeed, the program develops mass extinctions without the need for massive meteorites or other instruments of destruction. Is it a good model of our own evolutionary history?

Five Easy Pieces

How might a cannon be used to measure the area of a pond in a field? Fire the cannon at the field in a great many directions in such a way that the shots land at random places in the field. The area of the pond is approximately the area of the field multiplied by the number of splashes and then divided by the number of cannonballs fired. This admittedly silly problem nicely illustrates the role random events can play in the simulation of a process. The modern computer is a particularly useful tool for conducting a simulation. In a computer randomness comes not from a cannon but from a random-number generator.

Philosophically it is curious that random numbers, which are the purest expression of our ignorance, should underlie our ability to gain new knowledge of complex systems. I shall illustrate this theme in a series of programs I call five easy pieces: random numbers are used to find an approximate value for pi, to simulate the arrival times of people at a bank, to investigate a distribution of marbles, to generate voting patterns, and to show how millions of people can be made to wait in a queue.

I offer the five pieces in a musical spirit. Learning to play a computer is much like learning to play a musical instrument, and it can be enjoyed at every level of proficiency. Accordingly the first piece is the easiest; the last piece is probably not difficult. In all that follows I shall assume that random numbers can be obtained with the command *random*. The numbers are to be decimals between 0 and 1 that are several digits long.

The first piece is related to a problem called Buffon's needle, after Count Louis de Buffon, a nineteenth-century French naturalist and mathematician. Imagine that a needle is thrown randomly onto a planked floor a great many times. The length of the needle is half the width of the planks. The problem is to find the probability that the needle will land across a crack. The answer turns out to be $1/\pi$.

It is certainly possible to write a program that simulates the tosses of Buffon's needle, but there is a much simpler way to approximate the value of pi by simulation. The technique borrows from the idea of firing a cannon at random into a field. Imagine a square field enclosing a circular pond that touches all four sides of the square (*see* Figure 73). If the cannon is fired randomly into the field a great many times, the proportion of shots landing in the pond approximates the ratio of the area of the circle to the area of the square, namely $\pi/4$.

The simulation can be done with a simple program called PINT. Represent one quadrant of the field, say the northeast quadrant, by a unit square. The point (0,0) at the southwest corner of the quadrant lies at the center of the pond, and the point (1,1) at the northeast corner of the quadrant is a corner of the field. By choosing two random numbers x and y in succession, one can simulate a random shot that falls in the quadrant. (Remember, each random number is a decimal between 0 and 1.) Does the shot land in the pond? To find out, calculate the distance between the point (x,y) and the center of the pond. If the distance is 1 or less, record a splash and increase a counting variable by one unit. A loop in the program enables one to repeat the experiment. When all the shooting is over, multiply the resulting ratio by 4; the result should be close to pi.

In my "Computer Recreations" column on this subject (SCIENTIFIC AMERICAN, April, 1985), I urged readers to send me sample runs of 1000 shots. I agreed to tabulate the results and compute a grand average in the hope of achieving an even better approximation to pi. The results appear in the Addendum to this section.

The next piece exploits a technique called the zombie door. Imagine watching people coming through the door of a bank. All of them have good reasons for arriving when they do, and if one knew these reasons, one could no doubt simulate the arrival times exactly. Such knowledge, however, is presumably out of reach. To achieve the same end many

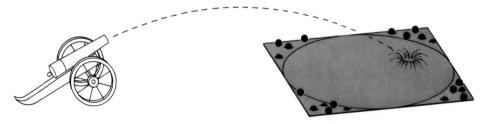

Figure 73   The area of a circular pond determined by random cannon fire.

simulation programs apply a special mathematical function called the negative exponential distribution. It would take a page to explain both the distribution and a rather pretty method for getting arrival times out of it. The zombie door is much easier to explain; it also gives natural-looking results.

The zombie door is a gap of width w in an otherwise impenetrable wall as in Figure 74. Thousands of zombies march steadily toward the wall, and every second a zombie arrives at a random point on it. The lucky ones arrive at the gap and march on through. The unlucky ones run into the wall. If the gap in the wall leads to a bank, the random arrival times of the zombies look much like the arrival times of ordinary patrons. To adjust the average arrival rate the width of the gap can be set to an appropriate value.

My arrival-generating program is called ZOMBIE. The wall in the program is a line one unit long. A loop called a while loop generates the times between arrivals: for each second that no zombie arrives in the gap the while loop increases a counting variable by 1 and calls on the command *random* to bring a new zombie to some random point along the wall. It is convenient and does no harm to assume the gap extends from the leftmost point 0 to the point w. If the random number, or position of the zombie, lies in this range, the program exits from the loop and declares in effect that a zombie has passed through the gap. Otherwise the program reenters the loop. Sooner or later a zombie passes through the gap; the value then stored by the counter tells how many seconds have elapsed since the last arrival.

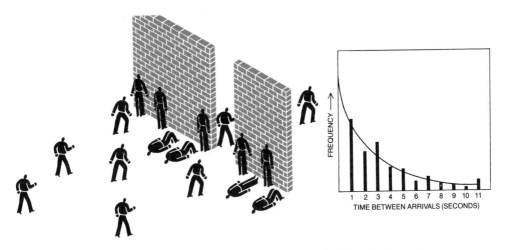

Figure 74   Zombies and the pattern of their arrivals on the far side of a wall.

The average time between arrivals is $1/w$ seconds. For example, if w is $1/10$, a zombie will arrive on the average every $1/(1/10)$, or 10, seconds. ZOMBIE works best when w is fairly small. For this reason it might be appropriate (depending on the application) to assume that zombies are arriving at the wall every tenth of a second. To find the value of w that gives a good simulation, set the desired average of the time between arrivals at the bank equal to $1/10w$ and solve for w. I stated above that the door could extend from 0 to w, but some random-number generators may be faulty in this range. In this case choose another gap in the wall, say between .5 and $.5 + w$.

It is interesting to examine the distribution of arrival times generated by ZOMBIE. By embedding the while loop in another loop that counts the number of occurrences of each possible time interval between arrivals, one can develop a histogram, or bar chart, that plots the distribution. A typical histogram is shown in Figure 74; the negative-exponential distribution has been superposed on it for comparison. There are many potential applications of the zombie-door technique for video games, but I shall limit myself to a single application when I discuss the fifth piece.

The third simulation involves a Galton board. This device, named after the pioneering Victorian statistician Sir Francis Galton, is a sloping surface studded with a triangular array of pegs (*see* Figure 75). Marbles released just above the top peg make their way, helter-skelter, down

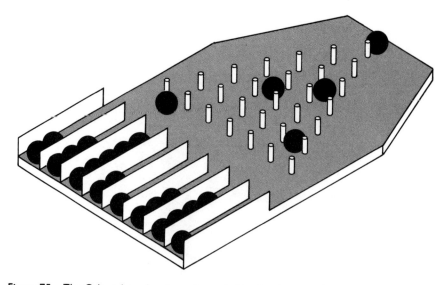

Figure 75   The Galton board and one improbable distribution of the marbles rolling down it.

through the array. Below the pegs are channels that collect the marbles. When the last marble falls into place, the collected columns take on a characteristic shape, not the New York skyline but something quite different. Those attempting this piece will discover the shape for themselves.

In the absence of a real Galton board a program called GALTON can simulate one, and it will use up only a few lines in the process. The idea for the program, as well as for the first piece on pi, comes from Jon L. Bentley's column "Programming Pearls" in the January, 1984 issue of *Communications of the ACM*.

The descent of a single marble is simulated in a loop that chooses a succession of random numbers. Each random number determines whether the marble rolls to the left or the right of a peg. If the number is less than or equal to .5, the simulated marble rolls to the left of a peg. If the number is greater than .5, the marble rolls to the right. Which peg? It does not matter. One must merely be sure to increase a counting variable by one unit each time the marble moves to the right. Readers may confirm for themselves that the column in which a marble comes to rest is determined solely by the number of rightward bounces it makes on its descent. At one swoop the need for an array that simulates the individual pegs is done away with. The moral of this observation should be clear: a bit of analysis can be worth a megabyte of program.

The loop that simulates the descent of a single marble through the Galton board is embedded in a larger loop specifying the number of marbles to be dropped. Each time the inner loop is completed the column in which a marble arrives should be recorded in an array c representing the columns. The number $c(n)$ is increased by 1 every time a marble falls into column n. When a run of, say, 1000 marbles is complete, the array c can be plotted by hand as a histogram. Of course, it can also be plotted directly by the computer if one takes the trouble to add some display commands to GALTON.

It seems to me that by arranging the pegs differently other kinds of distribution might be generated by a Galton board. I would be grateful to hear of any such devices, whether they exist in reality or only in imagination.

The fourth easy piece concerns two new and fascinating voting games studied by Peter Donnelly of the University College of Swansea in Wales and Dominic Welsh of the University of Oxford. The squares of a rectangular grid are initially colored black and white in a random manner. Each color is supposed to reflect the political opinion of a person inhabiting that square. One color might represent a Democrat, the other a Republican. With icons available, one might even use the grid shown in Figure 76. At each tick of a clock a voter is selected at random and his political opinion becomes subject to change: one of the voter's eight

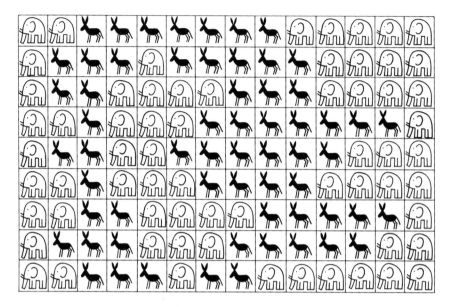

Figure 76   The voting game in progress.

neighbors is selected at random and the voter's political persuasion becomes that of his neighbor, regardless of earlier belief.

The grid is wrapped around itself in the same way as the ocean of Wa-Tor (*see* "Sharks and Fish on the Planet Wa-Tor" in World Six). The top edge of the grid is identified with the bottom, and the left edge is identified with the right. Hence a voter inhabiting a square on one side of the grid has three neighbors on the opposite side. After each random change in voter preferences an election is held, but this element does not need to enter the simulation unless one wants to keep close track of the results.

As this admittedly simpleminded model of the political process is run, strange things happen. First, large blocks of votes develop within the grid. The blocks are geographic areas where everyone has the same opinion. Then the blocks migrate around the grid, and for a while two blocks struggle for dominance. Finally the two-party system collapses as everyone ends up voting the same way. The smaller block vanishes as democracy votes itself out of existence—or does it? This is a neat philosophical question.

A short program called VOTERS can embody this model in every essential respect. In VOTERS there is an array having the same dimensions as the grid. A short computational cycle selects three random integers that give a random row index, a random column index, and a random neighbor code for each tick of the clock. The three integers are created by multiplying the output of the command *random* by a constant and then removing the fractional part with the command *integer*. For example, if the grid has 50 rows, the choice of a random row index *i* could be written algorithmically as

$$i \leftarrow \text{integer } (50 * \text{random})$$

The random column index *j* is computed in a similar fashion. The neighbor of the square (i,j) chosen by the program depends on which of the integers 0 through 7 is randomly selected. Once a random square and a random neighbor are selected, VOTERS replaces the array value at (i,j) with the one at the neighboring square.

The preceding steps are embedded in a loop. It is convenient to allow the index limit of the loop to be a variable: experimenters may want to vary the number of opinion changes that voters undergo. The index limit can also be varied in the other programs I describe in this section: set the outer loop limit to *n* and then enter the desired value of *n* from the keyboard.

A graphic display of the voter grid is easy to incorporate into the primary computational cycle in VOTERS. With only two characters (say the period and the asterisk) the effect is striking. Readers not immediately put off by the totalitarian phenomenon inherent in the voting game might wish to implement what Donnelly and Welsh call the antivoting game. In this game the randomly selected voter adopts an opinion opposite to that of the randomly selected neighbor. Will democracy survive in this setting?

The fifth and final piece provides food for thought while one waits in a queue. If people leave the head of the queue as fast, on the average, as they arrive at the end, would the queue not remain more or less the same size? Apparently not. According to queuing theory, such a queue has no finite expected length. I have seen such queues in banks.

The program called QWING simulates a simple queue in accordance with the pattern generated by the ZOMBIE program I described above. At the head of the queue is a person receiving or trying to receive service. Simulation programs sometimes incorporate the assumption that service times are distributed the same way as the times between the random arrivals of two zombies. Service is short when I make a deposit, but it takes a long time when I argue with the teller about the mysterious disappearance of money from my account. Accordingly ZOMBIE is also called on in QWING to generate service times.

QWING handles the passage of time by the critical-event method. A simulated clock *c* is continuously updated to the time of the next event, whether it is an arrival or a departure. Three other variables are needed:

ts, the time to the completion of the current service; *ta*, the time until the next arrival; and *q*, the length of the queue (*see* Figure 77).

Initially *ts* and *ta* are set to 0 and *q* is set to 1. QWING then enters its main loop, and the number of iterations of the main loop is specified by a command from the keyboard. Within the loop is a branching instruction that tests whether *ta* is less than *ts*. If it is, the time on the clock is

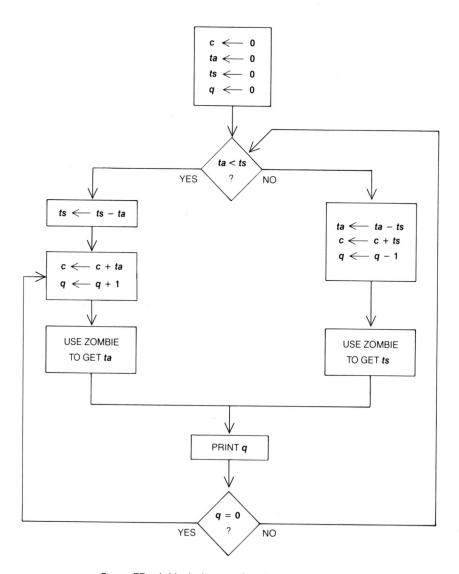

Figure 77   A block diagram for the QWING program.

increased by the amount *ta* because the next arrival at the queue is the next critical event. Accordingly *ts* is decreased by the same amount of time, and since the critical event is an arrival, *q* is increased by 1. As a final step ZOMBIE swings into action to generate the time of the next arrival.

At the head of the loop it may turn out that *ta* is not less than *ts*. In this case the same operations are carried out in another branch of the program, but the roles of *ta* and *ts* are reversed. The next critical event is a new service and so *q* is decreased by 1. In this branch ZOMBIE generates the next value of *ts*. At the bottom of the loop both branches rejoin with a test carried out on *q*. If *q* is equal to 0, a new arrival is needed and the program branches to the first segment. Otherwise it branches back to the head of the loop, where *ta* is again tested against *ts*.

The QWING program is clearly longer than the others, but it is still short enough to qualify for the term "easy." It is probably a good idea to make the average time between arrivals and the average service times specifiable by the user. In this way one can verify the basic results of queuing theory. When the average time between arrivals is greater than the average service time, the length of the queue is expected to be finite; the greater the difference between the two averages is, the more "finite" the length becomes. When the averages bear the opposite relation, the expected length of the queue is infinite; watch it grow.

Adventuresome readers can extend QWING to simulate the effects of an innovation introduced in banks more than a decade ago. Instead of waiting in individual queues, one for each teller, bank customers were sent to a single queue. The system has several advantages, which can be verified by a simulation program that captures the distinctive features of the collective queue. An even more elaborate program could model a relatively new feature in banks: now even the tellers queue up at their own superteller. The new system suggests some awesome possibilities for really large banks.

All this talk about random numbers poses a final question. How can a computer, which is an explicitly deterministic machine, generate random numbers, which are implicitly nondeterministic? The answer is that it cannot. But a computer can generate numbers that "look" random: pick any number, multiply it by m, add k, and take the remainder after division by p. The resulting number is put through the same process. Repeatedly the so-called linear-congruential algorithm churns out numbers called pseudorandom numbers. Sooner or later, however, the resulting sequence must repeat itself because there are only p possible remainders. Moreover, unless m, k, and p are carefully chosen, the pseudorandom numbers fail to pass the most primitive tests of randomness.

With such shortcomings in mind, computer scientists have tried to build a better mousetrap. Many years ago Donald E. Knuth of Stanford

University devised an algorithm so randomly devious and deviously random that it seemed guaranteed to generate numbers he called super-random. Knuth's algorithm has 12 steps. Given an initial number X, the first two steps pick two digits of X; the two digits determine how many times the algorithm will loop and which of the next 10 steps to jump to. Each of these 10 steps embodies a distinct method for calculating a new random number from an old one. It seemed plausible to Knuth before he tested his algorithm that "it would produce at least an infinite supply of unbelievably random numbers." To his astonishment, "when this algorithm was first put onto a computer, it almost immediately converged to the 10-digit value 6065038420, which—by an extraordinary coincidence—is transformed into itself by the algorithm." Knuth's moral is simple if not intuitively obvious: "Random numbers should not be generated with a method chosen at random. Some theory should be used."

If numerical methods for generating random numbers fail, one can always fall back on a suggestion once made by Alan M. Turing. Turing proposed that a random-number generator could be based on a source of radioactivity. Readers might enjoy the explorations of this idea in "The Computer Scientist: Random Numbers," by Forrest M. Mims III, in the November, 1984 issue of *Computers and Electronics (see* Bibliography).

Addendum

Readers' responses to "Five Easy Pieces" led to a histogram much like the negative-exponential distribution. Hundreds of readers wrote the first piece, a program called PINT for approximating pi. Only a few readers wrote the fifth piece, a program that simulates the behavior of queues.

In PINT simulated cannonballs are fired into a simulated field surrounding a simulated pond. I apologize to the thousands of neighbors who were kept awake by the all-night salvos.

Once one has written a pi-generating program of this type the temptation to go well beyond 1000 shots is apparently irresistible. The champion of this piece is Joshua Simons of the Harvard Medical School. By running PINT for a week on a mainframe computer Simons was able to take nearly 4 billion shots at the pond. His estimate for pi is 3.14157. Unfortunately the fifth decimal digit of pi is 9, not 7.

At this writing only 134 readers have submitted estimates of pi generated by 1000-shot runs. When readers submitted multiple runs, I selected only the first for inclusion in the grand average. Here it is:

3.14137

The first three digits after the decimal point are correct. The fourth decimal digit of pi is 5, not 3.

I computed another average, weighted by the length of each run, for all runs longer than 1000 shots. A few runs of several million shots may have distorted this estimate:

$$3.13948$$

In all of this I never once had to look up the value of pi. Instead I used a simple mnemonic: "How I wish I could enumerate pi easily." Count the letters of each word in that phrase. Can any readers suggest an easily remembered extension to the mnemonic?

Joseph W. McKean, a statistician at Western Michigan University in Kalamazoo, Mich., points out that one can establish a 95 percent confidence interval around one's estimate. The estimate is assumed to lie in the middle of a range of numbers that make up the confidence interval. The interval is defined in such a way that the true value of pi lies somewhere in the interval with a 95 percent probability. The size of the interval varies inversely with the square root of n, the number of shots fired. Hence to increase the accuracy of the estimate by a factor of 10, or one extra digit, n must be increased by a factor of 100. Such diminishing returns on the computational investment account for the frustration expressed by several readers.

Everyone who tried ZOMBIE had no difficulty generating histograms that mimic the shape of the negative-exponential curve, which was illustrated in the April column.

The GALTON program intrigued Edgar F. Coudal of Park Ridge, Ill. His simulation of marbles rolling down a triangular array of pegs led to the expected distribution at the bottom of the Galton board: the binomial distribution. The binomial distribution has a discretely belled shape, approximating its famous continuous cousin, namely the normal distribution.

In an amazing instance of simultaneous invention, two readers thought of generalizing GALTON to a three-dimensional array of pegs. At the bottom of their simulated boards J. Michael Matuszewicz of Columbus, Neb., and James Nugent of Peoria, Ill., found a softly rounded mound of marbles. Can readers guess its shape?

Some readers who tried VOTERS had disappointing results. In one case even an all-night run failed to produce the expected collapse of democracy. To such experimenters I can only suggest extended runs. Mine have taken the better part of a day. The patterns are the things to watch.

Finally, only two readers attempted QWING, the simulation of the line of customers at a bank with a single teller. Victor H. Auerbach of Philadelphia wrote a time-slice version of the program. He watched the length of the queue drift steadily upward, although there were many short-term decreases. Joshua Goodman of Quincy, Mass., also modified QWING, but much more drastically: he replaced the queuing system with two zombie doors in a single wall. Readers might enjoy figuring out how Goodman's program works with only that hint to go on.

Many readers complained of suspected faults in their random-number generators. Ronald L. Guye and Gerald V. Post of Oakland University in Rochester, Mich., have confirmed the suspicion for the BASIC random-number generator (RND) on the IBM PC. This program, which will run only in the graphics mode, is diagnostic:

```
10 SCREEN 2
20 X = RND * 640
30 Y = RND * 200
40 PSET(X,Y)
50 GO TO 20
```

If RND were perfect, a random spattering of dots would appear on the screen, but instead one sees speckled bands. No doubt a similar effect can be prompted from other computers.

A Cosmic Ballet

Deep in space, a star cluster performs a cosmic dance to the tune of gravity. During a human lifetime the stars barely move; over a longer span, in which years are equivalent to seconds, they trace out a tangled figure of orbits. Occasionally a single star encounters a neighbor in a pas de deux that hurls it out into space. If such escapes are more than occasional, the cluster gradually shrinks and the core begins to collapse.

A powerful telescope can reveal the structure of some clusters in our galaxy but it cannot compress years into seconds—only a computer is able to do that. A computer can also be programmed to serve as a kind of telescope for viewing hpothetical clusters. At cosmic speed one can watch the movement of the members of a cluster as a succession of snapshots in which each star leaves a dotted trail that weaves through the cluster (*see* Color Plate 8).

Do gravitational forces alone account for the evolution that astronomers infer from observed clusters? Computers help to find answers to this question and related ones. A conference of simulators and theoreticians met at Princeton University in May, 1984, to discuss the consistency of hypothetical and actual star clusters. It was the 113th symposium of the International Astronomical Union; the entire symposium was devoted to the dynamics of star clusters.

It is relatively easy to choreograph a cosmic ballet. In principle the stellar interactions within a cluster are classically simple: both members of a pair of stars experience a gravitational force that is proportional to the inverse square of the distance between them. The force is also proportional to the product of the two stellar masses. Such a formula is easy to compute: multiply the masses together; then multiply the product by a constant of proportionality and divide by the square of the distance between the two stars. The sum total of all such paired forces acting through time presumably determines the pattern of movement within the cluster. A program, called CLUSTER, computes the sum of the forces for each star and moves the star from its present position to a new one nearby. It does this repeatedly during centuries of simulated time.

A certain tedium attends typing in the coordinates and velocities of many stars, but once this is done an armchair universe unfolds on the display screen. Stars at the center of the cluster follow wobbly, erratic courses; those at the periphery drift away, stop, and then glide back. The most interesting events include close encounters and escapes.

When two stars approach each other closely, they impart a tremendous gravitational boost to each other and speed apart. Escapes are usually the result of one or more close encounters. When a star speeds away from its cluster, there are only two possibilities: either the star returns or it does not. An astronomical body has an escape velocity that depends on its mass and on the mass of the body or object from which it escapes. If the velocity is attained by a star moving outward from its cluster, it will never return. Inexperienced cluster buffs are likely to witness frequent escapes from the configurations they design. In fact, a common initial experience is to see one's hoped-for dance disintegrate. It is wise to practice by building a system of two or three stars.

The structure of the CLUSTER program is simple. It consists of an initialization loop followed by a double loop. Within the double loop the acceleration, velocity, and position of each star are updated according to the summed attractions of the other stars. I shall describe a particularly simple version of the program in which the time increment, force constant, and stellar masses are all built in. In spite of its simplicity, however, this version of CLUSTER seems capable of simulating almost the entire range of cluster behavior. Three sets of arrays are used. The first set keeps track of the accelerations currently experienced by the stars in each of three coordinate directions. The arrays are called ax, ay, and az. Thus $ax(i)$, $ay(i)$, and $az(i)$ indicate the x, y, and z components of the ith star's acceleration. The contents of the three arrays alone do not need to be initialized at the start of the program. The second set of arrays, vx, vy, and vz, define velocities: $vx(i)$, $vy(i)$, and $vz(i)$ register the x, y, and z components of the ith star's velocity. The third set of arrays record positions: $x(i)$, $y(i)$, and $z(i)$ are the ith star's x, y, and z coordinates of position. The starting values for the arrays x, y, z, and vx, vy, vz must be initialized at the head of the program.

The main body of the CLUSTER program follows the initialization segment. The double loop can be entered and reentered endlessly, or the programmer can establish the specific conditions that control reentry. The outer loop considers each star in turn and sets the acceleration components to 0. After this has been done the inner loop computes the forces produced on each star by its companions in the cluster.

For example, let us assume that the index of the outer loop is i and that the inner-loop index is j. The inner loop first checks to determine whether i is equal to j. If it is, the program does not invoke the force computation: a star does not attract itself. In any event, to compute force under the circumstance would cause the computer to attempt division by 0. (This is the only situation that can actually make me feel sorry for a computer.) When i and j are not equal, CLUSTER uses Euclid's formula for distance between the stars: the differences of the x, y, and z coordinates are squared and added together. The result, of course, is the square of the distance. Next, the inner loop tests whether this number is 0. If it is, an alarm of some kind should be raised because the computer is about to be asked to divide by 0. My version of the program prints COLLISION!

If nothing is amiss, the inner loop computes the distance between the stars by taking the square root d of the squared distance computed earlier. It then divides 1000 by the square of the distance, a calculation that yields the force. The final task to be performed within the inner loop is to determine the acceleration components of the ith star. This value is obtained by adding together the force contributions from the other stars. For example, the x component of acceleration can be written generically as follows:

$$ax(i) \leftarrow ax(i) + a \times (x(j) - x(i))/d$$

Here a and d represent the acceleration and distance. The ratio of the x distance between the ith and jth stars to the total distance is precisely the fraction of the acceleration that affects the ith star in the x direction. The y and z components of acceleration are computed by analogous formulas.

Two more loops, one following the other, complete the program. The first updates velocity and the second updates position. There is a subtle point here, first brought to my attention by John H. Hubbard, the Cornell University mathematician whose advice on computing the Mandelbrot set was eminently useful (*see* "The Mandelbrot Set" in World One). It is indeed possible to compute position before computing velocity without producing strange-looking results. Yet the motions of the stars would in time become strangely wrong, because such an operation would violate the law of energy conservation.

The velocity-updating loop merely adds acceleration to velocity, according to the following formula:

$$vx(i) \leftarrow vx(i) + ax(i)$$

Here it is assumed that the time increment equals the time unit in which velocity is expressed. The same kind of formula is used to calculate vy and vz. The position calculations done in the final loop are equally simple:

$$x(i) \leftarrow x(i) + vx(i)$$

The entries of the y and z arrays are similarly updated. Drawing on the information from the final loop, CLUSTER places each point on the two-dimensional surface of the display screen. It does so by plotting the first two position coordinates while suppressing the third. The natural result of this arrangement is that z represents depth; it is easy to imagine that one is looking into space behind the screen. The numbers produced by the cluster-simulation program are sometimes very large and sometimes very small. For this reason it is advisable to utilize double-precision arithmetic so that all relevant numbers are not inadvertently rounded.

The time taken by CLUSTER to finish one cycle of computation depends on the number of stars in one's system. As few as 10 stars will produce aesthetic intricacy; 100 or even 1000 stars are needed to produce realistic complexity. Unfortunately the number of steps in the basic computational cycle increases as the square of the number of stars in the cluster. Although stellar simulators have found a neat method that dodges this particular limitation, other problems still arise.

The worst problem emerges from the fact that the program is a discrete system attempting to mimic a continuous one. Continuous orbits are approximated by a sequence of jumps that depart increasingly from a star's true path through a cluster. The inaccuracy might be corrected to some extent by the presence of statistical regularities, but in close encounters between stars the system unnaturally and disastrously magnifies the slingshot effect.

For example, if the computational cycle puts one star (Stella) close to another star (Aster), a powerful gravitational pull magnifies the acceleration components of both stars. The magnification percolates through the computation to the velocity components and thence to the position coordinates. The next iteration finds Stella already widely separated from Aster and unable to repay the gravitational loan. A fiction of excess kinetic energy has been created. Artificial clusters afflicted by this problem evaporate even faster than real ones. There are two ways around the difficulty; one is hard, the other is easy. The hard alternative requires computation of a Keplerian orbit for the pair. The orbit is maintained as long as the two stars are in proximity. Theorists regard this as the method of choice because the orbital formula is perfectly accurate. An easy but occasionally inaccurate way to handle close encounters is to subdivide the time steps in the basic computational cycle. Readers may want to add this particular maneuver to the advanced version of CLUSTER that I shall now describe.

A program called SUPERCLUSTER can be derived from CLUSTER by a series of simple modifications. First, SUPERCLUSTER incorporates stars of different masses in its ballet. This is easily done at the start by entering the masses in an array called m. The force computation becomes somewhat more complicated: force is no longer proportional to $1/d^2$ but to the product of the masses divided by d^2. Next, SUPERCLUSTER incorporates spectral types. As in the case of mass, an array (called *spec*) must be filled in before the run. It is used, however, only during the display phase of the basic cycle. The colors range from blue for O-type stars to red for M types. Green is omitted. The third enhancement of CLUSTER makes arbitrary time steps possible in either version of the program.

SUPERCLUSTER uses a time-step variable called *delta*. Specified at the beginning of a run, *delta* determines the amount of simulated time between successive cycles. Naturally this time element must affect the updating formulas for both velocity and position: in the velocity formulas it multiplies acceleration and in the position formulas it multiplies velocity.

The easy way to handle close encounters can now be described. First a definition of "close" must be established. Then a test for such closeness can be inserted into the program just after the point at which the distance between two stars is calculated. If a close encounter is taking place, SUPERCLUSTER replaces *delta* by one-tenth of its value—at least until no pair of stars is that close again. This expedient certainly helps to cushion the sudden lurches of discrete gravity. It creates even worse problems when encounters are really close, however. An approach that is 10 times closer now results in a gravitational force that is 100 times greater! Fortunately close encounters of the worst kind are rather rare. The time-subdivision technique has been standard in cluster-simulation programs traditionally employed by professionals.

If SUPERCLUSTER is to be an astronomically meaningful program, units for distance, mass, and other aspects of physical reality are needed. A convenient measure of distance is the astronomical unit (AU), which is equal to the earth's mean distance from the sun. Mass can be measured in solar masses and time is best measured in years. Under these conventions the universal constant of gravitation has the approximate value of 39. SUPERCLUSTER uses this constant instead of 1000 in the force calculation.

All is now in readiness for putting either program to work. A preliminary exercise for CLUSTER involves four stars. Place them at the corners of a square that is an inch or two wide on the screen. It is only fair to give each star a nonzero z coordinate as well as the x and y coordinates that were mentioned above. If motion is confined to the plane of the screen, close encounters are that much commoner. Velocity components should be small (on the order of -5 to $+5$) and should specify a clockwise direction, as though the four stars were on the wheel.

SUPERCLUSTER can be tried on the system of stars shown in Figure 78. This is the earth's galactic neighborhood. What would happen if the sun and its neighboring stars were cut loose from our galaxy and allowed to

Figure 78   Would our galactic neighborhood form a cluster?

dance endlessly in space? Would a cluster form? The question may or may not have scientific relevance, but it is fun to answer. Besides, these are the only stars for which positions and velocities are known accurately (*see* table on page 235).

Clusters of stars are either open or globular. Open clusters consist of 1000 or so stars, whereas globular clusters may consist of millions (*see* Figure 79). So far investigators such as J. Garrett Jernigan at the University of California at Berkeley Space Sciences Laboratory have been able to handle only small clusters. Globular clusters are currently intractable. Even so, Jernigan and pioneering colleagues such as Sverre J. Aarseth of the University of California at Berkeley have been observing collapses of computer clusters for decades. The extent of collapse is measured by considering a spherical volume that is centered within a cluster and contains 10 percent of its mass. The radius of this volume is known as the 10 percent radius. Collapse is under way when the 10 percent radius decreases as time passes. Inexorably the core of a simulated cluster becomes ever denser. Since the simulated stars are mathematical points, nothing terrible ever happens to such clusters. No

A table listing all but three stars in the neighborhood of our solar system

NAME OF STAR	POSITION COORDINATES			VELOCITY COORDINATES			COLOR	MASS
	X	Y	Z	VX	VY	VZ		
STRUVE 2398	68	−365	631	−5.69	4.76	3.35	RED	0.26
ROSS 248	464	−42	450	−8.75	1.13	−15.45	RED	0.17
61 CYGNI	394	−377	433	−2.78	22.03	0.02	ORANGE	0.69
LALANDE 21185	−404	107	307	7.32	−0.47	−20.11	RED	0.39
PROCYON 5	−295	658	68	2.38	0.75	−3.65	BLUE	1.29
BARNARD'S STAR	−7	−371	30	−0.87	24.20	16.78	RED	0.21
EPSILON ERIDANI	408	534	−114	4.60	0.69	−0.50	ORANGE	0.74
WOLF 359	−462	136	62	−0.82	9.86	−5.94	RED	0.10
SIRIUS	−98	514	−157	1.89	−2.21	−2.59	BLUE	2.96
LUYTEN 726–8	487	219	−175	2.08	10.80	−0.41	RED	0.19
ROSS 128	−683	44	13	2.51	−2.32	−4.09	RED	0.21
SUN	0	0	0	0.00	0.00	0.00	YELLOW	1.00
TAU CETI	646	307	−208	0.52	−6.62	3.92	YELLOW	0.85
ALPHA CENTAURI	−106	−86	−243	−1.95	4.68	4.51	YELLOW	1.03
LUYTEN 789–6	608	−235	−182	−6.75	10.81	10.56	RED	0.13
LUYTEN 725–32	718	227	−233	4.70	6.16	0.51	RED	0.21
ROSS 154	111	−536	−241	1.79	1.36	−0.11	RED	0.24
EPSILON INDI	334	−194	−594	−3.54	17.71	2.28	ORANGE	0.69

NOTE: distance in 1000 astronomical units (AU) and mass in solar mass units.

black hole comes into being at the center. This at least has been the experience of cluster theorists. But we seem able to find little evidence of extreme collapse in the clusters overhead. Something is preventing collapse out there.

Both traditional and modern simulation experiments may provide a key. On various occasions a small number of binary star systems at the center of a simulated cluster have brought the collapse of core regions virtually to a halt. In one of Jernigan's experiments a single binary seemed to be responsible. How is it possible? According to Jernigan's graduate student David Porter, it may be that "very tight binaries whizz around each other very quickly and kick wandering stars energetically around the core or even back out to a looser collection of stars around the core called the halo. This could be a mechanism for preventing the core from getting too crowded."

Jernigan used to be an observer of x-ray stars. As research focused on the search for x-ray sources in clusters, he grew increasingly interested in clusters as astronomical objects in their own right. Simulation seemed an effective way to investigate them.

Figure 79   Globular cluster Messier 13 in the constellation Hercules.

Self-described as "the new kid on the block," Jernigan has discovered an important new efficiency in simulation efforts. In CLUSTER and similar programs a single computational cycle for n stars requires roughly n^2 steps. Jernigan's cycle needs only $n \times \log(n)$ steps. He organizes his cluster by grouping the stars into neighboring pairs. Each pair is then replaced by a fictitious mass and velocity that summarizes the behavior of the pair. The same process is now applied to the pairs as if they were the original stars. Continuing in this manner, a collection of grouped and regrouped mass nodes is built up in a data structure called a tree. The single node at its root simultaneously represents all the stars. Motions can then be calculated for the central node and for all its branches out to the individual stars.

Is this the technique of the future? It certainly helps to speed things up, according to Jernigan. Yet subsequent generations of cluster programs are more likely to resemble the hybrid variety used by Alan P. Lightman of the Center for Astrophysics of the Harvard College Observatory and the Smithsonian Astrophysical Observatory and Stephen L. W. McMillan of the University of Illinois at Urbana-Champaign: stars in the core are handled by the direct simulation methods described above; stars outside the core are modeled statistically as if they form a gas.

For readers proficient in the language called APL there is an interesting new publication by Gregory J. Chaitin of the IBM Thomas J. Watson Research Center in Yorktown Heights, N.Y. It is called *An APL2 Gallery of Mathematical Physics* and is a 56-page booklet containing explanations of five major physical theories, including those that describe both the Newtonian and the relativistic motion of satellites in space. APL listings are given for computer programs that illustrate each theory. Chaitin will be happy to send a copy to any reader who writes to him at the address indicated in the List of Suppliers.

Readers unable or unwilling to write CLUSTER may order a program that runs on an IBM PC or PC-compatible machine as specified in the List of Suppliers.

Addendum

In "A Cosmic Ballet" I described two programs, CLUSTER and SUPERCLUSTER, that simulate the evolution of a star cluster. It heartens me to think that in at least a few thousand homes they have led to a new form of entertainment, temporarily edging out television. No doubt many of these armchair universes are unfolding as they should.

When one views the live action of CLUSTER or SUPERCLUSTER on a display monitor, it is sometimes hard to tell which stars are in the foreground and which are farther back. Albert C. English of Delray Beach, Fla., and Peter Stearns of Lodi, Calif., have written special display programs that generate two images of clusters side by side, one as seen by the right eye and one as seen by the left. Readers able to manage the tricks of stereoscopic display will be able to view the clusters as they view the hypercube: in breathtaking depth.

Several readers had already written programs similar to SUPERCLUSTER, but they had applied the programs to our own solar system. The same application would also be feasible with SUPERCLUSTER. Those with the gumption can look up the mass, position, and velocity of the 10 major bodies in the solar system for some reference time. One can then arrange to view the evolution of the entire system from above: wait a few minutes for the year 2000. Geoffrey L. Phillips of St. Louis, Mo., wrote a simulation for the earth-moon system that includes a small, massless space vehicle. Launching it from the earth in such a way that it begins to orbit the moon is no easy feat. Advanced practitioners might try launching a Voyager spacecraft on a grand tour of the gas giants that ends as it leaves the solar system.

William A. Hoff of Champaign, Ill., computed the time increment for the simulation dynamically by setting a variable called *dvmax* at the beginning of the program. In the course of the calculations of stellar motion the program always finds the maximum acceleration *amax* of a star. The next time increment is *dvmax* divided by *amax*. The technique prevents any velocity from exceeding *dvmax*.

Sharks and Fish
on the Planet Wa-Tor

Somewhere, in a direction that can only be called recreational at a distance limited only by one's programming prowess, the planet Wa-Tor swims among the stars. It is shaped like a torus, or doughnut, and is entirely covered with water. The two dominant denizens of Wa-Tor are sharks and fish, so called because these are the terrestrial creatures they most closely resemble. The sharks of Wa-Tor eat the fish and the fish of Wa-Tor seem always to be in plentiful supply.

This simple-minded ecology might appear stable, almost soporific, were it not for the fact that the shark and fish populations undergo violent oscillations. Many times in the past the fish population has been all but devoured, whereas at other times the sharks have starved almost to extinction (even when there were plenty of fish). Yet both sharks and fish survive. To discover why, I designed a program to simulate their feeding and breeding activities.

Before I had ever witnessed these ecological rhythms on a display screen, however (*see* Figures 80 and 81), I mused for a long time about the rules and the details of the WATOR program. Over lunch one day I found myself musing across the table from David Wiseman, who is my department's resident systems wizard at the University of Western Ontario. After describing the project to him I noticed that Magi (for such is Wiseman called) was smiling enigmatically. The next morning he proudly ushered me into his office to display a working program.

"Watch," he said and pressed a key. An initially random assortment of fish and sharks flickered slowly from point to point in what seemed to be a chaotic manner. Some sharks failed to eat and disappeared. Other sharks had offspring just as voracious as themselves. A few fish, lucky enough to occupy a region where there were currently no sharks, multi-

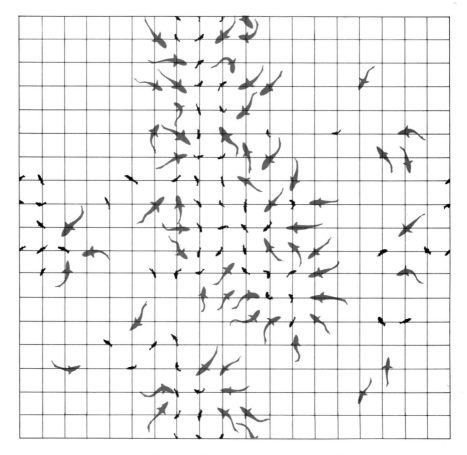

Figure 80   A realistic view of sharks eating fish.

plied into a large school. Presently a number of sharks discovered the school, congregated at its edges, and gulped their way a short distance into it. A few minutes later the summary of current statistics displayed on Magi's screen told the story: there were now 578 fish and just 68 sharks.

Someone walked into Magi's office and ran out again. Before 5 minutes had elapsed the room was crowded with people cheering on the sharks. Slowly a wall of sharks closed in on the hapless fish. Elsewhere on the screen a small school of fish slowly multiplied unnoticed. Groans went up when the large school of fish finally disappeared and sharks, dying one by one, milled about looking for prey. I thought of changing the rules to allow sharks to eat one another, but I realized that a feeding frenzy would not significantly prolong their existence and might put the

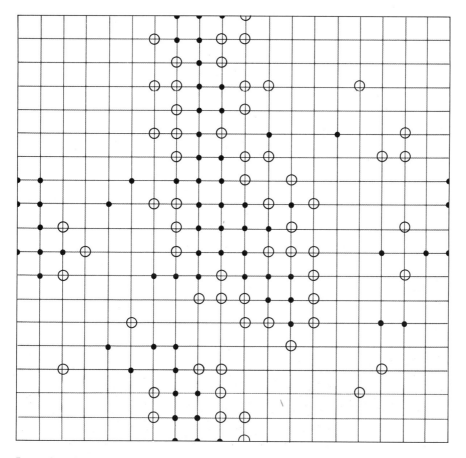

Figure 81   A more easily programmed view, in which circles represent sharks and dots represent fish.

early history of that other small school in jeopardy. When two roaming sharks finally stumbled onto it, the cycle began anew.

The program for Wa-Tor is neither very long nor difficult to write. Readers who have personal computers, even those with little program-ming experience, will find it a rewarding project when the code is finally written, debugged, and running. Parameters such as breeding times, starvation periods, and initial population sizes can be set before a run. It is then just a matter of sitting back and watching as an initially disorga-nized mélange of fish and sharks slowly forms ecological patterns.

The WATOR program embodies a number of simple rules that govern both shark and fish behavior. The creatures swim in a rectangular ocean grid whose opposite sides are identified in pairs. This means simply that if a fish or shark occupies any rightmost grid point and decides to swim east (to the right), it will reappear at the corresponding leftmost grid point. The same relation holds between the vertical extremes. The resulting two-dimensional wraparound space is really just a torus, the actual surface of Wa-Tor (*see* Figure 82). Anyone writing his or her own WATOR program may select any convenient size for the ocean grid. For example, Magi, whose program runs on a VAX computer, has set up an ocean that is 80 points wide and 23 points high. My own version of WATOR, written for an IBM PC, uses a humbler, 32-by-14 ocean.

Time passes in discrete jumps, which I shall call chronons. During each chronon a fish or shark may move north, east, south, or west to an adjacent point, provided the point is not already occupied by a member of its own species. A random-number generator makes the actual choice. For a fish the choice is simple: select one unoccupied adjacent point at random and move there. If all four adjacent points are occupied, the fish does not move. Since hunting for fish takes priority over mere movement, the rules for a shark are more complicated: from the adjacent points occupied by fish, select one at random, move there, and devour the fish. If no fish are in the neighborhood, the shark moves just as a fish does, avoiding its fellow sharks.

The creator of WATOR selects five parameters in order to set up a given simulation. The parameters *nfish* and *nsharks* represent the numbers of fish and sharks at the beginning of a run. The program distributes the specified numbers of fish and sharks randomly and more or less uniformly across the planet's surface. The parameters *fbreed* and *sbreed* designate the number of chronons a fish and a shark respectively must exist before each has a single offspring. (Both species are apparently parthenogenic.) Finally, *starve* specifies the number of chronons a shark has in which to find food. If it swims about any longer than this without eating, it dies and sinks out of sight. During each chronon WATOR moves each fish and each shark once and displays the results on the screen. With rules no more complicated than these, one can watch the ecology of Wa-Tor lurching from crisis to crisis.

Magi and I have witnessed a number of five-parameter scenarios in which Wa-Tor's ocean became overpopulated with fish only to have the sharks eventually multiply to a point where all the fish were eaten and the sharks died. On other occasions we have seen all the fish in one large school being eaten. The sharks that had gorged themselves finally starved, never discovering a very small cluster of fish nearby. On a few occasions we have seen the prey-predator relation sustain itself through two or even three population cycles before the ultimate crash in shark population. Nothing in the parameters selected for those scenarios, however, gave any hint of the characteristics that would ensure an eternal ecology. How had the denizens of Wa-Tor survived?

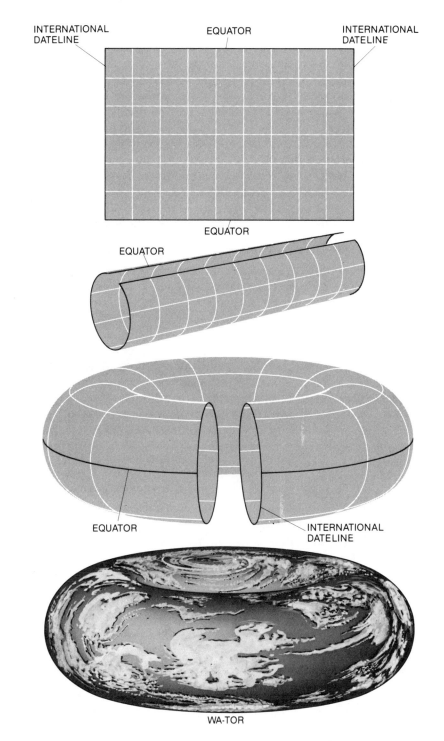

Figure 82   The toroidal planet Wa-Tor and its representation on a flat map (or a flat computer screen).

It has been said that biology is destiny. Magi and I are tempted to declare that ecology is geometry, at least as far as the planet Wa-Tor is concerned. The ultimate fate of a given scenario does not seem to depend on the initial random distribution of a specified number of sharks and fish. Nor does it seem to depend in an accidental way on the actual random movement of sharks and fish. Instead the likelihood of a population crash appears to follow closely the fish-shark geometry that manifests itself on our screens: the more highly organized and localized either population becomes, the likelier it is that the ecology is doomed. Meditating on this theme, we were led to wonder how we might choose the five parameters in a way tending to break up the geometry. Then came a flash of insight: if sharks had congregated at the edges of a school of fish, one way to break up the resulting geometry would be to have the sharks breed less often. The congregation itself, after all, was less the result of motion than it was of breeding.

Before forming this hypothesis we had chosen roughly equal breeding times for sharks and fish. Balanced reproduction rates, we thought, would result in balanced populations. This kind of vague thinking probably accounts for many woes in today's technological world. In any event, I put 200 fish and 20 sharks in my 32-by-14 ocean and set the fish to breed every three chronons but barred any shark from reproducing before 10 chronons had elapsed. Shark starvation time was set more or less arbitrarily at three chronons. We were rewarded, after watching my rather slow program for 15 minutes, by seeing a full recovery from the initial population decline. Moreover, the geometry, although it was still present, was more suggestive than definite. Schools were shapeless conglomerations with ragged edges, and at some places on the screen sharks and fish milled about at random.

I let the program run all afternoon, glancing up occasionally from more important matters on my desk. The program ran all night, and when I visited my office after my morning lecture, I found fish and sharks still pursuing a cyclic existence. Here was Wa-Tor!

There are many ways to implement a WATOR program but perhaps the simplest involves a number of two-dimensional arrays. I use five arrays called *fish, sharks, fishmove, sharkmove,* and *starve.* These arrays, all 32 by 14, keep track of the positions and ages of sharks and fish. Specifically, *fish*(i,j) represents the presence or absence of a fish at the point with coordinates (i,j). If a fish is absent, the position has the value -1. Otherwise it contains a record of the age in chronons of the fish that is present. The same scheme is used for the array *sharks* to keep track of the positions and ages of the sharks. The array *fishmove* holds a record at each position of whether a fish has been moved there during the current computational cycle. Such a record enables the program to avoid moving a fish twice during the same chronon. *Sharkmove* fulfills the same function for sharks. The array called *starve* registers the time at which a shark last ate. If there is no shark at a position, the entry is −1.

The simplest display of the action on Wa-Tor is a line of characters on the screen for each row in the arrays; a blank at a position means it is unoccupied. A period (.) represents a fish and a zero (0) represents a shark. Although this display might seem to be limited, it is surprisingly informative and enjoyable to watch.

In WATOR's initial phase the required numbers of fish and sharks are scattered uniformly over the toroidal ocean. The program then cycles through the three segments of subprograms described below; each program cycle occurs during one chronon of time.

Fish swim and breed:
For each fish in the *fish* array, the program makes a list of adjacent unoccupied positions and moves the fish to one of these at random. This means *fish* must be set to −1 at the old position and set to the fish's current age at the new position. The array *fishmove* is updated in the manner described above. If the fish's age equals *fbreed*, the program puts a new fish at the old position and gives age 0 to both fish. Again *fishmove* records the new fish. If all adjacent positions are occupied, the fish does not move or breed.

Sharks hunt and breed:
For each shark in the *shark* array, the program makes a list of adjacent fish positions (if any). The shark chooses one of these at random, moves there, and eats the fish. This means not only that the program must modify *sharks* and *sharkmove* as it modified *fish* and *fishmove*, but also that it must set the corresponding position in the *fish* array to −1. Also, *starve* at that position is set to 0. If there are no adjacent fish, the shark moves just as a fish does. If the shark's age equals *sbreed*, a new shark is produced in exactly the same way as a new fish is.

Display:
The program scans both the *fish* array and the *sharks* array. It displays a period for each fish and a 0 for each shark. The display can be done all at once in this way or broken into two parts: one executed after the fish have moved, the other executed after the sharks have moved.

To populate the initial ocean, the programmer constructs a loop that generates two random numbers *nfish* times. The numbers are scaled to the horizontal and vertical dimensions of the ocean he or she intends to have. At each of the random positions thus selected, the program places a fish in the *fish* array and assigns it a random age between 0 and *fbreed*. Sharks are distributed similarly. In both cases the position is checked to see if it is already occupied. The effect of giving both sharks and fish random ages is that they then breed at random times in a natural way. Without this precaution one would witness the sharks and fish suddenly doubling in numbers, a disconcerting and unnatural sight.

There may be novice programmers who find the foregoing description a bit too general to form any clear idea of how to write a WATOR program. Those programmers can begin by writing what is known as a staggering-drunk program. Such a program might consist of a single loop (say a while-loop) that has seven instructions. These are written in nonprejudicial algorithmic language. Assignments are indicated by left arrows and the variables X and Y are the coordinates of a staggering drunk. They are altered according to the random integer assigned to a variable *direction*. Depending on whether this integer equals 0, 1, 2, or 3, the drunk (a point on the screen) moves north, east, south, or west.

$$direction \leftarrow \text{integer part of } (random \times 4)$$
$$\text{if } direction = 0 \text{ then } X \leftarrow X + 1$$
$$\text{if } direction = 1 \text{ then } X \leftarrow X - 1$$
$$\text{if } direction = 2 \text{ then } Y \leftarrow Y + 1$$
$$\text{if } direction = 3 \text{ then } Y \leftarrow Y - 1$$
$$\text{display } (X,Y)$$

If your particular random-number generator produces a decimal number *random* between 0 and 1, this algorithm will scale it to a decimal number the value of which lies between 0 and .3999. The integer part of the resulting number must be 0, 1, 2, or 3.

I cannot claim that watching a point of light wandering minutely on your screen matches the ecological drama of the sharks and fish, but writing this program does give some insight into how parts of WATOR might be constructed.

Readers unable or unwilling to write the WATOR program may order one that runs on an IBM PC or PC-compatible machine as specified in the List of Suppliers.

Expert programmers reading this will have thought of other approaches to writing the WATOR program. The amount of processing can be greatly reduced by using linked lists to keep track of sharks and fish. With such a data structure the time required for one computational cycle is proportional to the number of sharks and fish present and not to the size of the ocean.

WATOR may yield some insights into animal populations here on earth. We know that small populations face a high probability of extinction and, even if neither predators nor prey die off, they are almost certain to undergo cyclic changes in number. In simple predator-prey ecosystems the predator and prey populations sometimes follow two

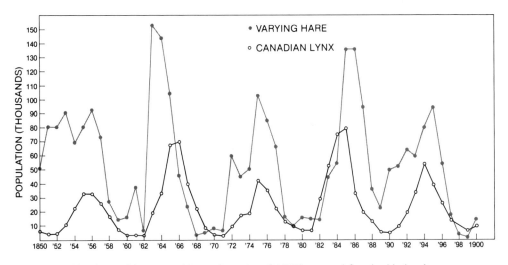

Figure 83   Numbers of lynxes and hares (in units of 1000) trapped for the Hudson's
Bay Company from 1850 to 1900.

overlapping cycles of population maxima and minima. The sizes of the populations of the varying hare and the Canadian lynx recorded by the Hudson's Bay Company from 1847 to 1903 in the Canadian subarctic follow this pattern (*see* Figure 83). The figures give the number of each species trapped from one year to the next. Presumably these numbers are proportional to the actual population sizes present during this period. If they are, the cycles are easily explained as the result of lynxes eating their way into an ever increasing hare population that begins to decline as the number of lynxes increases. Soon there is less food for the lynxes and they begin to starve, breed less, or both. When the lynxes are reduced in numbers, the hares begin once again to multiply.

Contrasted with this chart is a smooth set of curves representing a solution to the Lotke-Volterra equations (*see* Figure 84). These equations were first formulated in 1931 by V. Volterra, an Italian mathematician. They assume what might be called a continuous predator continuously in search of a continuous prey. The solutions to these equations exhibit a cyclic variation that, at first glance, appears to reflect the lynx-hare empirical data. Biologists are not in agreement, however, that the lynx-hare numbers are explicable by such simple reasoning. For one thing, at least two other predators of hares are involved: microbes and man.

It makes perfectly good sense, however, to compile statistics on the sharks and fish of Wa-Tor, and Magi and I have done so. Our recent graphs of the shark and fish populations tend to look more like the lynx-

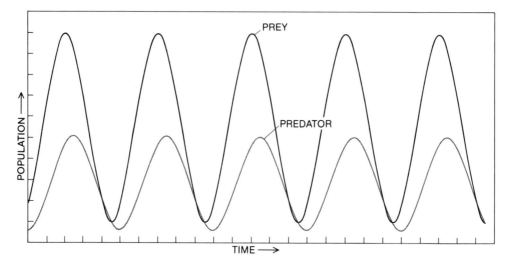

Figure 84   A theoretical predator-prey relation: a solution to the Lotke-Volterra equations.

hare charts than the Lotke-Volterra solutions do. Still, we continue to be puzzled by the long-term instability shown by certain parameter combinations. Perhaps some reader, working with his or her own WATOR program, will provide further insight. Is there some kind of general rule we might use to predict, for a given combination of parameters, whether the resulting ecology will be stable? To what extent do the cyclic fluctuations follow the Lotke-Volterra equations?

The ocean of Wa-Tor is toroidal for a very simple reason: it is much easier to write a program for an ocean that has no boundary or shore. If the ocean is to be, say, 32 units wide, it is a simple matter to use numbers modulo 32 as the X coordinates of fish and sharks. If they have X coordinate 31 and appear on the right-hand side of the screen during one chronon, they may well have X coordinate 32 = 0 and appear on the left side during the next chronon. The same system is used vertically.

The toroidal ocean of Wa-Tor gives rise to some very strange effects, as exemplified by the following puzzles. The first of these effects involves a bug in an early version of my WATOR program. This bug caused each fish to swim one unit north and each shark to swim one unit east during each chronon of time. Thus a shark got to eat a fish only if it found itself occupying the same location as its prey. In the ocean on page 249, how many fish were never eaten by sharks?

Another puzzle involves intelligent sharks and fish. Suppose each shark and each fish takes turns moving to any of its four neighborhood points. It turns out that a single fish, if it is intelligent enough, can

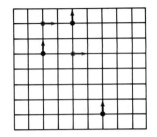

always evade a single shark, no matter how intelligent the predator. In the toroidal ocean of Wa-Tor, two sharks hunting a lone fish may produce a different ending. If you endow each creature with all the intelligence you like, even allowing the sharks to hunt cooperatively, can you discover a way out for the fish? The result does not depend on the dimensions of the ocean.

Addendum

Reports from readers who played with the ecology of the planet Wa-Tor poured in. It will be impossible to discuss more than a few of the many interesting experiences described. Generally speaking the selection of the right parameters produced robust fluctuations in the populations of sharks and fish. Some readers, anxious to make Wa-Tor more like the earth, added special features to their programs. The game does invite complication and this is welcome. The major disadvantage of introducing a variant system, however, is that (other things being equal) comparisons with the standard system become dangerous.

Initial system-builders were Jean H. Anderson of Lauderdale, Minn., Stephen R. Berggren of Satellite Beach, Fla., Milton Boyd of Amherst, N.H., J. Connett of Minneapolis, Minn., Edgar F. Coudal of Park Ridge, Ill., Don C. Hopkins of Champaign, Ill., Jim Lemon of El Segundo, Calif., Fredric Stevens of Davis, Calif., and Kenneth D. Wright of Grayling, Mich.

Among the questions these and other readers dealt with was that of measuring duration of survival. Clearly there is no problem for eternal populations, but it would be useful to have a measure of less-than-eternal scenarios. Measurement by chronons, as Stevens points out, can be misleading when extended life spans and breeding times are chosen for sharks. Measurement by cycles also has problems: what is a cycle? Stevens makes the amusing observation that if one's sharks and fish survive enough repetitions of the basic random-number cycle, an earlier configuration will repeat itself in concert with the cycle and eternal life is thereafter guaranteed.

A number of readers including David Emanuel of Oak Brook, Ill., Richard G. Fizell of Fort Washington, Md., and John S. Lew of the IBM Thomas J. Watson Research Center in Yorktown Heights, N.Y., described modern theories that are helpful in the analysis of Wa-Tor. I have yet to hear the final word on whether stochastic matrices will enable us to derive specific survival probabilities from arbitrary parameter combinations. It is interesting to note, however, that the Lotka-Volterra equations have (since their formulation in 1931) been further elaborated to consider diffusion as a factor affecting both predator and prey. Diffusion forces the smoothly varying solutions of the Lotka-Volterra equations into more complicated shapes. A historical note from Lew revealed that Alfred J. Lotka was an American mathematician who, a decade earlier, had formulated much the same equation as Volterra did.

Boyd exploited a phase diagram to analyze shark/fish population dynamics. At each time t plot the current numbers x of fish and y of sharks as the coordinates of a single point. As time advances and populations cycle, the point describes an erratic orbit about a fixed eye, or center. Boyd used the technique to study the effect of ocean dimensions on survival. He writes that "for the more rectangular worlds, the orbits lost their eyes, the trajectories became more jittery, and eventually became random walks." Square oceans are evidently preferable. Boyd, incidentally, has volunteered to organize a user group devoted to Wa-Tor. Readers may write to him for membership in the group as well as for a subscription to its newsletter, *Running Wa-Tor* (*see* List of Suppliers).

Among the innovations introduced by readers were a shark life-force, mutations, dual fish populations, and plankton. I neglected to mention in "Sharks and Fish on the Planet Wa-Tor" that the fish of Wa-Tor graze on omnipresent and omniabundant oceanic plankton. Lemon made this feature explicit by placing plankton at every point not occupied by a shark or fish. Plankton breed into otherwise empty spots and have the same relation to fish that fish have to sharks. Eternal populations exist here as well.

Couda's sharks gain or lose points of life-force depending on how well they eat. They can thus survive much longer without food than the primitive sharks of the standard Wa-Tor can. Couda sent plots (as did many of the other Wa-Tor programmers) that are remarkably similar to the Hudson's Bay Company data.

Connett uses two species of fish. One is the standard Wa-Tor variety; the other always breeds into any empty point to the south or east. Because of its mobile tendency, the second species often outlasts the first. Rudy Iwasko of Sacramento, Calif., proposed that sharks and fish be given characteristics of size, speed, and agility. These were to be under genetic control. Berggren wrote his system, called EVOLVE, two years ago. It resembles WATOR except that it lets the animals evolve according to environmental pressures. In this way, Berggren reasoned, populations would arrive at an equilibrium favoring long-term survival.

No one succeeded in solving the toroidal pursuit problem. I shall now reveal one half of the solution so as not to deny readers the pleasure of finding the other half. Remember that at each turn the fish moves and then the two sharks move. As in Wa-Tor, standing still is not allowed. Imagine four rays emanating from the lone fish. Each ray follows a diagonal and twists around the torus, sooner or later rejoining itself. Once both sharks occupy a pair of opposite rays, it does not matter which way the fish moves; one shark pursues at a constant distance and the other shark closes in. The fish is doomed. I leave it to readers to discover how sharks hunt the rays, so to speak.

The Evolution of Flibs

Imagine an abstract sea inhabited by abstract organisms called finite living blobs, or flibs. Each flib is equipped with the simplest decision-making apparatus possible. This is the biological equivalent of what computer scientists call a finite automaton. Each flib also contains a single chromosome consisting of a string of symbols that encodes the automaton. The flibs inhabit a primordial, digital soup in constant flux. These changes must be predicted accurately by the flib if it is to survive.

In the primordial soup I recently set simmering in my computer, flibs that predicted poorly died out. The best predictors left progeny that sometimes improved on ancestral performance. Eventually a line of perfect predictors evolved.

Flibs and their evolutionary tendencies illustrate nicely a form of programming known as the genetic algorithm. Pioneered by John H. Holland of the University of Michigan in the 1960s, the technique is sometimes able to solve difficult problems by evolving a sequence of approximate solutions. New solutions are produced by mating the best of the old solutions with one another. Before long a new solution that is superior to its parents appears and joins the list of preferred breeders. Genetic algorithms have been applied with some success to pattern recognition, classifier systems, pipeline operation, symbolic layout, and a small number of other problems. In my computer soup the technique yielded superior flibs. Was this success due to the general efficacy of the genetic-algorithm method or to the simplicity of the predictive task facing the flibs? The question is hard to answer. It can be pondered and the underlying phenomenon can be reproduced by any interested reader who has a computer within reach.

A finite automaton has a finite number of states; an input signal causes it to change automatically from one state to another. The kind of automaton used in a flib also generates signals. Incoming and outgoing signals are represented within the automaton by symbols. When a signal is received, the automaton changes state and emits a second signal.

A state-transition table is useful for representing the process. For example, a finite automaton that is capable of assuming three states, A, B, and C, and that can handle afferent and efferent 0s and 1s fits nicely into a 3-by-4 table. For each state the automaton might find itself in, and for each symbol it might receive, there are two entries. The first entry gives the corresponding output symbol; the second entry gives the state that the automaton next assumes:

	0		1	
A	1	B	1	C
B	0	C	0	B
C	1	A	0	A

The automaton represented by this table might well find itself in state C at some time. If the automaton receives a 1, the table tells us the automaton will next generate a 0 and enter state A.

Another representation, easier for humans to read, is the state-transition diagram, in which circles represent states and arrows represent transitions. If an automaton goes from one state to another when it receives a specific symbol, an arrow should be drawn from one state circle to another. The arrow should be labeled both with the input symbol that caused the transition and with the resulting output symbol (*see* Figure 85).

A finite automaton always begins its operations in a specific state, called the initial state. At each tick of an imaginary clock a new symbol

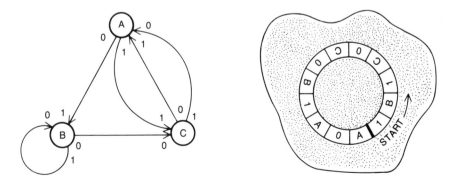

Figure 85   A state-transition diagram (*left*) and a corresponding flib with its chromosome (*right*).

arrives, a new symbol leaves, and a new state is entered. The automata used in my flibs all send and receive the same two symbols, 0 and 1.

How is one to interpret the behavior of a flib if so little is known about the creature's biology? Therein lies the joy of abstraction. The symbols received by the automaton are merely sensory messages from the environment. In corresponding fashion, an output symbol can be viewed as a response by the organism to the environment's most recent condition.

The concept of a flib is so flexible that input and output can represent a great variety of specific biological phenomena. For example, an input signal could represent a chemical or temperature gradient. The corresponding output symbol could be a command to an effector that controls cilia, or a spore-forming mechanism. A task of great importance to a creature wishing to evolve to some minimally acceptable level (say that of a university professor) is to predict the environment. To a flib the environment is a seemingly unending sequence of 0s and 1s. Insofar as symbols received indicate significant events, there is clearly some advantage in the ability of a flib to predict the next symbol, particularly if under some more specific interpretation of flib functioning the flib's survival were enhanced.

Most flibs are rather poor at predicting their environment in this sense. For example, the flib described by the state-transition table given above responds to the environmental sequence

$$0111000010110\ldots$$

with the outputs

$$1000011001000\ldots$$

At each stage of its operation the flib's output is its prediction of the next symbol to arrive from the environment. To find the number of correct predictions shift the output sequence one symbol to the right and compare it bit by bit with the input sequence. Count the number of matching symbols. In this case the flib predicted correctly only six of the 12 incoming symbols, a score that is no better than might result from random guessing.

One can easily demand too much from a finite automaton. Indeed, it is unfair to ask a flib to predict any nonperiodic environment. Readers might like to ponder this point for a moment. Why must a perfectly predicted sequence of input symbols consist of the same basic string endlessly repeated? For example, the 3-state flib that failed the prediction test just set for it succeeds brilliantly on the following environmental sequence:

01001101001101010011 . . .

Here the environment marches to the beat of a simple repetition, 010011.

There are several dozen 3-state flibs, but only a few of them can predict this sequence perfectly. Among flibs that have more than three states perfect predictors for a given environmental sequence are rare and become more so as the number of states increases. Predictability depends heavily on the period of the sequence: no n-state flib will ever be able to predict the sequence that results from continued repetition if the basic string of symbols is too long. There is evidently a relation between the number of states a flib can have and the largest period in a sequence that it predicts perfectly. Readers might enjoy discovering the relation for themselves. What is the longest period an n-state flib can predict?

A flib is more than a finite automaton trying to predict its environment; it has a chromosome. Flibs periodically breed (by some unknown method). An examination of the chromosome in its relation to a flib's finite automaton shows how the inherited genes determine the behavior of the offspring. Start with the state-transition table and strip away the rows, one at a time, from top to bottom. Join the rows together end to end and then join the beginning of the string to its end. The result is a circular chromosome as in the illustration on the right in Figure 85.

Before the final joining operation, the chromosome of our 3-state exemplar appears as a string of 12 genes:

1B1C0C0B1A0A

Strictly speaking, the symbols in this string are alleles. An allele is a specific form of a gene that appears at a given locus. As such, a gene can be specified either by its name or by its locus. Thus the seventh symbol from the left controls a flib's output symbol when it is in state B and a 1 is received from the environment. The locus here is 7.

I recently set up a primordial soup containing 10 4-state flibs in my personal computer. Before 1000 of the time units I call chronons had passed none of the original flibs was alive. All had been replaced by superior predictors. The display screen showed the highest and lowest scores attained in the current population. The lowest score fluctuated a good deal; the highest score crept slowly upward (*see* Figure 86). Just when I was beginning to give up hope that a perfect predictor would evolve, one suddenly appeared, whereupon the highest score jumped to 100.

All of this raises the question of just how flibs evolve in my computer soup. Periodically a cosmic ray zips through the broth and strikes a

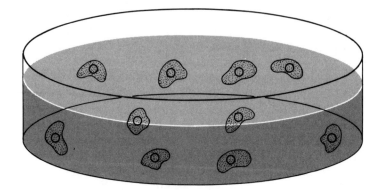

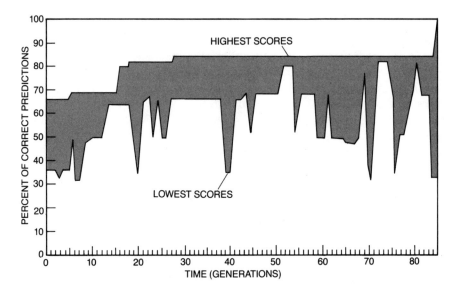

Figure 86 A soup of 10 flibs (*top*) evolves a perfect predictor (*bottom*).

random chromosome at a random locus; the result is that a specific gene is changed from one allele to another. For example, in the following 4-state flib chromosome the gene at locus 3 controls the output symbol for the transition from state *A*, when the creature receives a 1:

$$0D1C0D0B1A0C1B1A$$

A cosmic ray striking this gene changes the chromosome slightly:

$$0D0C0D0B1A0C1B1A$$

Mating is the other source of variation in the flib gene pool. During the mating season the highest-scoring flib shuffles genes with a randomly selected flib. The offspring bears a composite chromosome. One part comes from the superior parent, the other from the winner of the mating lottery. The composition resembles a phenomenon called crossover that takes place in real chromosomes. In flib chromosomes crossover can be illustrated by combining the first (unaltered) chromosome listed above with another:

$$1A1B0D1A0C1D1B0C$$
$$\uparrow \qquad \uparrow$$

Arrows indicate randomly selected crossover points. The offspring's chromosome is identical with that of the second parent as far as the first crossover point. Between points it is identical with the first parent's chromosome. After the second point it is again identical with the chromosome of the second parent (*see* Figure 87):

$$1A1C0D0B0C1D1B0C$$

Before actually writing and testing the primordial program, I was somewhat skeptical of the value of crossover breeding. I was surprised to find, however, that if the first parent is a reasonably good predictor, the offspring tends to be as well.

Readers may judge the issue themselves by writing a program called AUTOSOUP. Listed, the program does not extend much beyond a single

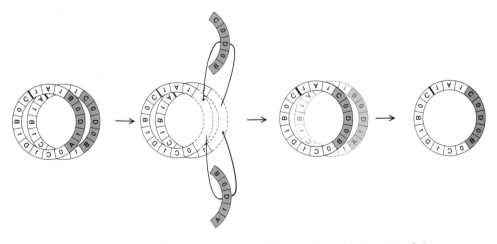

Figure 87   Crossover of two flib chromosomes, and the resulting chromosome of the offspring (*right*).

page. It consists of four modules embedded in a loop. A limit that defines the top score should be set. As long as the top score is less than the limit the program should continue to run through the four modules.

In the first module the 10 flibs are scored on a sequence of 100 environmental symbols. The second module identifies the flibs with the highest and lowest scores that result. In the third module the top-scoring flib is bred with a randomly selected mate. The offspring of this union replaces the bottom-scoring flib. In the fourth and last module a cosmic ray arrives, strikes a random flib, and causes a mutation. Just before the program invokes the third (breeding) module a random number is selected. If the number falls below a certain threshold, the program will skip around the breeding module and execute the mutation module immediately. The threshold can be set to any level. Certain settings, however, are better than others; if the breeding module is executed too often, the small population quickly becomes dominated by the genes of the top-scoring flib. The gene pool loses diversity and evolution slows to a painful crawl if not to a downright standstill. Evolution slows down, in any event, as the scores get higher. The top-scoring flib remains on the scene for a lengthening period because it becomes increasingly unlikely that flibs superior to it will evolve.

Four arrays are useful in AUTOSOUP. They are called *chrom*, *state*, *score*, and *e*. *Chrom* is a two-dimensional array of 10 flibs and 16 genes. *Chrom(i,j)* refers to the *j*th gene of the *i*th flib. *State* and *score* contain the current state and score of the 10 flibs. The fourth array, *e*, contains the basic string used to generate environmental symbols. This array is received from the keyboard at the beginning of the program.

Flibs are evaluated by means of a double loop. The outer loop generates 100 environmental symbols and the inner loop increases the score of each flib if it correctly predicts the next symbol. One can test 4-state flibs adequately on environments of period 6, a challenge of intermediate difficulty. Perfect predictors may require a day's run to evolve in a period-8 environment, whereas period-4 environments are almost no challenge at all. Two tricks are useful in this module. The first trick retrieves the next environmental symbol from the outer-loop index *i* by computing *i* modulo 6; the result is the remainder of *i* on division by 6. The number can be used to index the array *e*. As *i* runs from 1 to 100 the computed index runs through the array repeatedly, producing the proper sequence of environmental symbols. Given the index of the current symbol, the next symbol is easy to compute and look up. This symbol is compared with the prediction made by each flib in turn.

The second trick enables the program to find the flib's next state quickly and determine its output merely by scanning the chromosome. Instead of representing the four states by *A*, *B*, *C*, and *D*, the numbers 0, 1, 2, and 3 are used as entries in the array *state*. If the environmental symbol is called *symb*, the output of the *i*th flib can be found by first using a simple formula:

$$l = 4 \times state(i) + 2 \times symb$$

Then *chrom(i,l)* should be identified. The locus *l* on the *i*th flib's chromosome yields its output when the creature is in state *i* and is receiving input *symb*. The next state occupies the locus *l* + 1.

The module that determines the top and bottom flibs uses an exercise common in elementary programming courses: given an array of *n* numbers, write a program that finds the largest number. The solution involves setting a variable called *top* to 0 and then scanning the array within a simple loop. Each entry is then compared with *top*. If it is larger than *top*, *top* should be replaced by that entry. The index should be saved as well. The same procedure can be inverted and used to find the bottom score. This time a variable, *bot*, should be set at 100 and replaced by entries that are smaller.

The third module breeds the top-scoring flib with a randomly selected member of the population. The only difficulty in writing this segment arises in the selection of the two crossover points. I think it is easiest to select two random integers c_1 and c_2 from the range 1 through 16. If c_1 is greater than c_2, their values should be exchanged. With just a little finesse readers will discover how three loops that range from 1 to c_1, c_1 to c_2, and c_2 to 16 supply the machinery to move elements of *chrom* on the breeding rows into the destination row, which is occupied by the doomed flib with the lowest score.

In the fourth module a random flib index and a random *locus* should be selected. The parity of *locus* determines whether a state gene or an output gene is to mutate. If the value is 0, then 1 modulo 2 should be added to the number already stored there. This flips the bit, so to speak. If the *locus* value modulo 2 is 1, then 1 modulo 4 should be added to the array entry. This changes the state stored there.

Have I cheated? Surely a systematic change of state from 0 to 1 to 2 to 3 and back again is hardly a random effect. My answer is that it is random enough: the number of states is small enough so that one cannot expect the final outcome of the program to be much different from the outcome when more randomly selected states prevail. Indeed, I also cheated in a mild way by choosing c_1 and c_2 so carelessly: the method guarantees an advantage for certain substrings in relation to others. Again, I think differences between AUTOSOUP and a statistically corrected crossover selection procedure would be slight. Either way there is so much juggling of genes and cracking of chromosomes that the top flib is hard put to recognize its own grandchildren.

The only parts of AUTOSOUP as yet unspecified are its beginning and its end. The flibs initially occupying the soup should be selected randomly. For each gene in each flib an integer should be selected from the appropriate range and assigned to that gene. Finally, when a flib first exceeds the limit set in the outer loop, AUTOSOUP should print it.

Readers embarking on this genetic adventure are warned that there is much exploring to do. Perhaps some explorers will become addicted. Questions to be answered concern the presence of evolution and its speed. When an environment period is too long for a 4-state perfect predictor to evolve, how fit do the flibs get? How do changes in the length of the period affect the amount of time it takes a perfect predictor to evolve? Nothing in the AUTOSOUP description prevents extending the program to 5- and 6-state flibs. One can even alter the program to explore nonperiodic environments or ones that occasionally change their basic string.

Automaton soup was inspired by a book that appeared in the early 1960s. Titled *Artificial Intelligence through Simulated Evolution*, the book describes a series of experiments in the evolution of automata by Lawrence J. Fogel, Alvin J. Owens, and Michael J. Walsh (*see* Bibliography). Automata were asked to predict periodic sequences and were allowed to evolve much the same way as our flibs. No breeding or crossover was allowed in this austere study, however.

It was Holland who suggested that I add the crossover facility to the automaton soup. As noted above, Holland is the acknowledged father of the genetic algorithm. Practitioners of the discipline, growing steadily in number, met at their first large-scale, funded conference, held at Carnegie-Mellon University. They discussed a wide range of theories and applications. A problem explored in several papers serves as an interesting introduction to the subject of genetic programming.

Called the traveling salesman problem, it poses the following challenge: Given a map of n cities connected by a network of roads, find the shortest tour of the n cities. Such a tour can then be used by a salesman or saleswoman to minimize travel expenses. In spite of my inclusion of salespeople of both sexes, the foregoing description has a 1940s ring to it. But more modern methods of travel and actual costs are easily incorporated without changing the mathematical skeleton implicit in the statement.

It is entirely possible that a tour of minimum length can be made to evolve just as perfect flib predictors evolved from lesser flibs. Each tour should be encoded in a chromosome. The shortest tours should be bred in the hope of obtaining yet shorter offspring. Crossover yields the chromosomes of the progeny.

It is a beguiling task to choose a good representation for a tour. For example, if one simply uses a list of the cities in the order visited, the offspring may not even be a tour. To get around this difficulty the authors of one paper, John Grefenstette, Rajeev Gopal, Brian Rosmaita, and Dirk Van Gucht of Vanderbilt University, propose an ingenious chromosome. The representation for a five-city tour such as *a, c, e, d, b* turns out to be 12321. To obtain such a numerical string reference is made to some standard order for the cities, say *a, b, c, d, e*. Given a tour such as *a, c, e, d, b*, systematically remove cities from the standard list in the order of the given tour: remove *a*, then *c, e*, and so on. As each city is removed from the special list, note its position just before removal: *a* is first, *c* is second, *e* is third, *d* is second, and, finally, *b* is first. Hence the chromosome 12321 emerges. Interestingly, when two such chromosomes are crossed over, the result is always a tour (*see* Figure 88). With such a representation tours can now be bred, so to speak, for fitness.

Most practitioners of the art of genetic algorithms readily admit that the traveling salesman problem is one of their greatest challenges. Although experiments with the representation just described were not

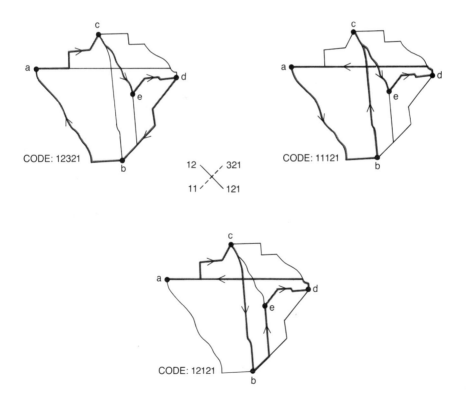

Figure 88   Two parent salesman tours (*top*), and an offspring (*bottom*) resulting from genetic crossover.

very encouraging, there are other genetic algorithms that perform better on the problem.

Still, no genetic algorithm has ever been able to conquer the traveling salesman problem in any well-accepted sense. This is undoubtedly owing to the difficulty of the problem itself. Because it is what theorists call *NP*-complete, it may be doomed to eternal insolubility in the practical sense.

Addendum

"The Evolution of Flibs" featured flibs: finite living blobs that attempt to predict changes in their environment. In the primordial computer soup, during each generation the best predictor crosses chromosomes with a randomly selected flib. Increasingly accurate predictors evolve until a perfect one emerges.

A flib is essentially a finite automaton. That is, it has a finite number of states, and for each signal it receives (a 0 to a 1) it sends a signal and enters a new state. The signal sent by a flib during each cycle of operation is its prediction of the next signal to be received from the environment.

Some readers gave their flibs impossible prediction tasks. No flib will ever evolve that can predict a sequence of random bits. Nor will flibs ever develop to predict primes. It is perfectly reasonable to ask a flib to predict a repeating binary sequence. For example, there is a 4-state flib that will predict the repeating eight-symbol sequence 01100010. Even a repeating sequence, however, can tax the predictive abilities of a flib if its basic string is too long in relation to the number of states in the flib. As it happens, no 4-state flib will ever predict the repeating sequence 010010111. Why not?

The simplest answer to the question involves a process I call creeping induction. Imagine a 1-state flib. It might predict the endless repetition of the basic string 01. For each of the two possible signals the flib receives there is one response: if a 0 is received, the flib sends a 1 and then reenters the same state. If it receives a 1, it sends a 0. A basic string of three symbols, say 011, is beyond the ability of a 1-state flib to predict because the automaton simply does not have an adequate stock of responses. A 2-state flib, on the other hand, has four possible responses, two for each state. Thus it can predict a repeating string of up to four symbols but not one of five symbols; when the fifth symbol is reached, the flib must repeat an earlier response. The argument is clear. An n-state flib may predict a basic string that is at most $2n$ symbols long but not a string $2n + 1$ symbols long. There is some pleasant distraction to be had in devising a basic string eight symbols long and then constructing by hand the 4-state flib that will predict it. The perfect predictor thereby obtained is essentially unique. It is possible to measure the success of one's AUTOSOUP program by comparing the perfect predictor that evolves from it with the flib already constructed.

Several readers found ways to make AUTOSOUP run faster. For example, there is not much point in testing the current batch of flibs on a sequence of 100 environmental symbols if the basic string is only six symbols long. One repetition of the string will produce 12 environmental symbols, which should be enough for most purposes.

Philip Kaaret of Princeton University has pointed out that the program can also be shortened if two flibs rather than the entire population are scored on each execution of the main loop. After all, only two flibs (at most) have changed: the lowest-scoring flib has been replaced by a new hybrid, and one other flib has perhaps been struck by a cosmic ray.

The speedups obtained by shortening the environmental test sequence and by eliminating the test altogether for old flibs are roughly equivalent. Now there will be time to evolve n-state flibs that can predict repeated basic strings as many as $2n$ symbols long.

From his letter it appears that Ed Coudal of Park Ridge, Ill., was loath to send his lowest-scoring flib directly to the choir celestial. Instead he bred it with the highest-scoring flib at each cycle. By following this scheme Coudal could in fewer than 40 generations derive flibs capable of predicting a six-symbol basic string.

The Extinction of Trilobites and Survival of Smiths

In southern Ontario and western New York State are some of the finest and most fossiliferous exposures of middle Devonian rocks in the world. One of them lies near my home. There, in a quarry that teems with ancient life, I once met the compound gaze of a trilobite staring at me from a bed of shale. In the delicate process of removing it I heard a shuffling and whirled to discover a bearded man peering over my shoulder. "A marvelous specimen of *Phacops rana*," he announced. "Too bad they're all extinct." He was a professor of paleontology, and his name was Smith. "Why," I wondered aloud, "did the trilobites become extinct?" Professor Smith gazed into space and then answered my question with another one: "Why is the name Smith so common?"

The real answers to both questions would trace a complex and irreversible interplay of genetic and environmental factors. Approximate answers, however, emerge from two computer programs that simulate the evolution of trilobites and names in similar ways. One program tries to mimic the great extinctions of the Paleozoic era. It was originally devised by David M. Raup, a well-known paleontologist at the University of Chicago, and it randomly traces the development of a phylogenetic tree: with each tick of the geologic clock the end of each branch of the tree grows, branches, or dies with a certain probability. The random evolutionary pattern generated by the program bears a surprising resemblance to the fossil record, and both show mass extinctions.

The second program imitates the proliferation and extinction of English family names from 1350 to the present. The program is the brainchild of Christopher M. Sturges and Brian C. Haggett, who are both employees of the British Ministry of Defence. Sturges and Haggett trace genealogies in their spare time, and they were puzzled by the gradual disappearance of many names from the available records. Could such a disappearance be a chance event? The two sought to find out by writing a simulation program. They discovered that as many as three-fourths of the family names common in 1350 would disappear by chance alone in the next 636 years.

Any reader who wants to travel in a probabilistic time machine can write a simplified version of each program that nonetheless captures the essential features of the original. In the first program you will traverse hundreds of millions of years as you watch genera or entire phyla of unknown and unnamed creatures diversify or die out. In the second program mere hundreds of years will pass, but the interest is more human. Which family names will triumph, the Smiths or the Smedleys?

The program I call PALEOTREE begins with a single primordial creature. In order to preserve the paleontological flavor of the simulation it seems appropriate to give the creature a scientific name: *Paleoplasmus radiculus*. Readers are free to abuse Latin with equal abandon. For a given, arbitrary time PALEOTREE represents the total population of *P. radiculus* as a single node, or point, on a tree. Every population of creatures belonging to the same biological category as *P. radiculus* and descended from it is also shown as a node; the program makes no attempt to count the number of living specimens in the biological category that are represented by the node at any given time.

In an instant millions of years are allowed to pass, and the program inspects the evolutionary results. Perhaps the old population of creatures retains its biological integrity for another few million years. If it does, the original node gives rise to a new one, connected by a line to its progenitor. Perhaps instead the original population is successful and diversifies into a new biological category. That outcome can be represented as a Y-shaped branch at the original node. One branch of the Y leads to a new node representing the continuation of the original biological category, and the second branch leads to a new node representing the beginning of a new category. The final possibility is that the original population becomes extinct. In that case the original node simply terminates and no branches lead away from it.

PALEOTREE randomly determines the fate of each node it generates in the tree: is the population to continue unchanged, is it to give rise to a new biological category, or is it to become extinct? Taken at face value, however, the three possibilities do not really reflect the rich structure of biological evolution. As I have described the program so far, all the creatures descended from a common ancestor are monophyletic; in other words, they are related closely enough to be put in the same broad biological category, and so they belong to the same tree. Nevertheless, evolutionary development occasionally leads to a new broad category or to a mass extinction when entire categories die out. Taxonomists recog-

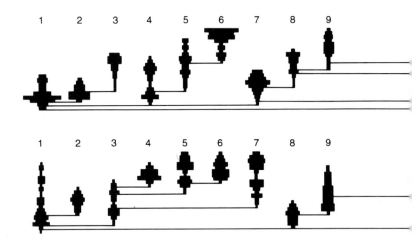

nize many such categories, from varieties and subspecies to phyla and kingdoms. For the sake of simplicity PALEOTREE recognizes only two categories, the species and the genus; any other interpretation of the two categories would do as well.

In PALEOTREE a genus can give rise to an entire new genus. The mechanism is simple: a new species branches away from the old genus to found a new genus. What is really just another branch in the evolutionary tree is viewed as a tree in its own right. Of course, a tree (or genus) can also become extinct: all its species die out. The number of species that make up a genus at a given time is called its diversity, which measures not only its genetic richness but also the likelihood that it will survive. There is a pretty method for graphing the results of an experiment with PALEOTREE: each genus is represented by a symmetrical stack of horizontal bars that resembles a spindle. Each bar represents a new epoch, and the length of the bar at a given level of the stack gives the diversity of the genus at the corresponding epoch. The resulting stack reminds me of a bizarre home-lighting display (*see* Figure 89).

It is easy and instructive to generate a tree and its associated spindle by hand. Make a dot on a piece of paper and roll a pair of dice. If the sum of the numbers showing on the dice is 2, 3, or 4, the species immediately becomes extinct. *P. radiculus* is stillborn and no branches emerge from the dot. If the sum is 9 or 10, the species diversifies. Two short lines branch upward from the dot, and a dot is made at the end of each line. If the sum showing on the dice is any other number, the species does not change. A single line sprouts upward and terminates in another dot. For each epoch the experiment is repeated for each species that is not yet extinct. The procedure gives rise to a tree, and the number of dots at any given level of the tree can then be plotted as the length of a bar in a spindle diagram (*see* Figure 90).

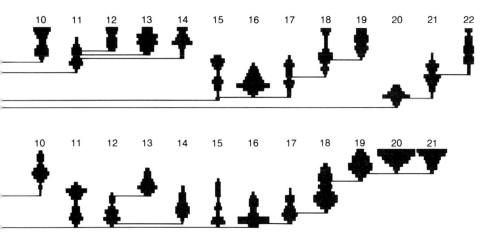

Figure 89 Evolutionary development, branching, and speciation of biological genera, simulated by David M. Raup's version of the computer program PALEOTREE.

When the dice are rolled, the probability that a species will become extinct in the next epoch is 1/6, or .167, the probability that it will diversify is 7/36, or .194, and the probability that it will remain unchanged is 23/36, or .639. These probabilities approximate the ones assumed in PALEOTREE, and they give rise to similar trees. Since the probabilities of extinction are somewhat smaller than those of diversification, one might expect some trees to go on forever. Do they? I should be happy to hear from readers willing to stay up all night to find out.

In order to draw a spindle diagram it is not necessary to maintain a tree for each genus. PALEOTREE merely counts the number of species that make up a genus at each epoch, and it keeps a record of the branching between the genera. Both functions can be handled by a double array called *history*. The columns represent genera and the rows represent epochs. Thus *history* (i,j) is the number of species present at time i in the jth genus. When PALEOTREE has simulated evolution for the desired number of epochs, one can print the array *history* and use its entries to draw the spindle diagrams by hand. Readers with some experience in graphics programming might try adding a program that draws the spindles automatically, but a detailed description of that exercise would require a column in its own right.

To run PALEOTREE in its simplest form one must type the number of epochs, or "generations," at the beginning of the program. The number is preserved by the program under the name *numgen*, and it limits the value of the index i for the array *history*. The value of i increases in unit increments from 1 to *numgen* as the program executes its outer loop. A second loop inside the first one is indexed by the value of j in the array

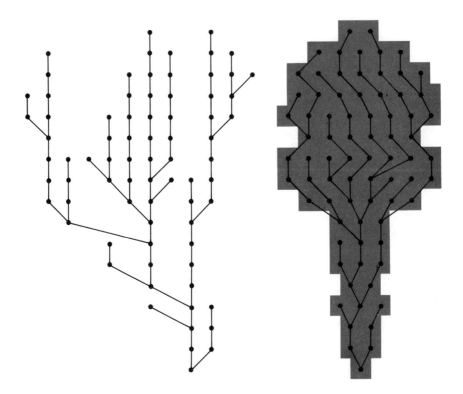

Figure 90   Speciation within a genus, determined by the roll of a pair of dice.

history; each value of *j* corresponds to a genus. A variable called *max* is also defined in order to calculate the limit of the index *j*. Because only one genus is present at the beginning of a run, *max* is initially set equal to 1. As the outer loop is repeatedly executed the number of genera waxes and wanes. For each new epoch *max* is set equal to the number of genera in the previous epoch. A variable called *lmax* is then set equal to the value of *max* at the beginning of the *j* loop, and *j* runs from 1 to *lmax*.

Within the second loop PALEOTREE looks up the number of species currently included in the *j*th genus, and it stores the number in a temporary variable called *temp*. The program then enters its third and innermost loop, which determines the fate of each species in the *j*th genus. The index *k* of the inner loop can be regarded as a counter for the species. It runs from 1 to *temp*, and the value of *temp* is also transferred to the entry *history*(*i* + 1,*j*) in the array, which is destined to give the number of species in the *j*th genus in the next epoch *i* + 1.

For each species, or in other words for each value of *k*, a random number between 0 and 1 is selected by means of the random-number instruction of one's programming language. If the random number is less than .15, the kth species becomes extinct and *history(i + 1,j)* is decreased by one unit. If the random number is greater than .8, the kth species produces an evolutionary offshoot and *history(i + 1,j)* is increased by one unit. The procedure ensures that species become extinct with probability .15 and that they give rise to new species with probability .2.

The program written by Raup, on which PALEOTREE is based, determined new genera by a form of retrospective analysis that is a bit too complicated to describe here. Raup has noted, however, that reasonably similar results can be obtained more simply: assume each species gives rise to a new genus with the rather slender probability .02. The assumption must be incorporated into the innermost loop. If the random number governing the fate of the kth species is greater than .98, PALEOTREE turns aside for a moment to create a new genus instead of a new species.

Several housekeeping details are important in this part of the program. First *max* is increased by 1 and the *i*th entry in the new column of the array *history*, namely *history(i,max)*, is set equal to the index *j* of the genus that gave rise to it. In this way the array can store information at the beginning of the newly created genus about the identity of the genus that gave rise to it. The reader (or a plotting program) can thereby determine the origin of each genus. In epoch *i + 1*, its first stage of real evolution, the newly created genus includes just one species. Accordingly the entry *history (i + 1,max)* is set equal to 1, and evolution continues normally thereafter.

Given the probabilities set up in the program, some genera almost inevitably become extinct. In that case the column of *history* corresponding to a newly extinct genus becomes a 0 and *max* must be decreased by 1. In some programming languages this circumstance can lead to difficulties. Instead of effectively ignoring such a column in the array, the innermost loop may execute once or twice in spite of the fact that *temp* is 0. Some languages may assume such a loop is running decrementally, from 1 to 0, and so the genus may have one or two chances for a miraculous rebirth. To avoid the situation one must insert a test into the beginning of the innermost loop: if *temp* is 0, the rest of the loop must be skipped.

As usual, readers may want to tinker with the programs suggested in this department. For example, how is diversity affected if the probability of extinction within a genus is increased from .15 to .2? Will equal probabilities for branching and extinction cause all life to die out? It will be interesting to hear from readers who encounter mass extinctions or slender survivals.

It should surprise no one that the second program is quite similar to PALEOTREE in structure and function. Remember that it mimics the extinction and survival of family names. Indeed, it can be obtained from PALEOTREE by removing the procedure that creates new genera. I call it NEOTREE.

In NEOTREE an array called *history* also keeps track of events as time goes on. When the program starts, however, *history* holds 1000 entries instead of only one. The entries represent 1000 English surnames prevalent in the year 1350. It would be foolhardy (but not without a certain antiquarian charm) to incorporate 1000 real names into the program. Instead each column of *history* represents a single family whose name unfortunately must be the numerical index of the column. The initial entry in each of the 1000 columns is 1, which represents one English nuclear family: a mother, a father, and a number of children. Actually the program keeps track only of the males, the family members who bear the surname to the next generation.

It would be highly unrealistic to imitate the program PALEOTREE and limit a given line of descent to two new families in each generation. Hence in NEOTREE each family is allowed to generate from zero to six new families. The innermost loop of NEOTREE operates on family names in the same way as the innermost loop of PALEOTREE operates on genera. When NEOTREE considers the *j*th name, for example, the variable *temp* is set equal to the number of families currently bearing the *j*th name. Each family is considered in turn by the innermost loop. A random number then determines the number of marrying males a family will produce.

Sturges and Haggett employ a table derived from a statistical analysis of genealogical records to determine the probabilities for the seven possible fates of family names (*see* Figure 91). For example, the statistical probability is .317 that a family will produce no males destined to marry. The probability is .364 that it will produce one such male, and so on.

The random numbers generated by the program are readily converted into a table of possible outcomes reflecting the probabilities that a family will give rise to various numbers of marrying males. For example, if the random number lies between 0 and .317, the family will have no marrying males. The family (if not the name itself) will become "ex-

NUMBER OF MALES WHO MARRY	0	1	2	3	4	5	6
PROBABILITY	.317	.364	.209	.080	.023	.005	.001

Figure 91   Statistical summary of English marrying males since 1350.

tinct." If the random number lies in the range between .317 and .681 (the sum of .317 and .364), the family will give rise to one marrying male. In other words, the random number will lie in the second range approximately 364 times out of 1000, and that proportion matches the probability obtained from the statistical analysis. The rest of the table is constructed in a similar way.

Once NEOTREE has determined the fate of a given family for a new generation it acts exactly like PALEOTREE. At the beginning of the ith generation the number of families with surname j is stored in the variable *temp*. The index k of the innermost loop then runs from 1 to *temp* and *temp* is stored in *history*$(i + 1, j)$, just as it is in PALEOTREE. For each family with name j that produces no males who marry, *history*$(i + 1, j)$ is decreased by one unit, thereby reflecting the fact that one less family will bear the name j in the next generation. For each family with name j that produces one marrying male *history*$(i + 1, j)$ is left unchanged. For each family with name j that produces two marrying males the value of *history*$(i + 1, j)$ is increased by one unit, and so on.

In a sense NEOTREE and PALEOTREE lead to opposite results. In NEOTREE, for example, count each generation as 28 years; the period from 1350 to 1986 thus requires 22 or 23 generations of computation. What proportion of family names vanish in that time? Sturges and Haggett found that the number of family names steadily diminishes and that nearly three-fourths of the names disappear over the 636-year period. Perhaps some readers will have the tenacity to run NEOTREE long enough to predict the year the original 1000 names will be reduced to one!

The results of PALEOTREE have been quite different: as one would expect, and in spite of extinctions of the genera, life becomes gradually more diverse. As time passes the net number of genera tends to increase. One would expect some of them to become so filled with species that they would be virtually immune to chance extinction before the universe collapses. Nevertheless, in Raup's initial version of the program there were also an unusually large number of extinctions, and that result was puzzling.

PALEOTREE was developed in the 1970s, when a number of scientists were drawing attention to the apparent evidence for mass extinctions in the fossil record. If the evidence could be believed, such mass extinctions could have been caused by geologic or astrophysical catastrophes. Working with Stephen Jay Gould of Harvard University and others, Raup proposed that a fast simulation program such as PALEOTREE could serve as a null hypothesis: if it generated mass extinctions similar to the ones observed, there would be less urgency to explain them as catastrophic effects.

In fairness to Raup I must point out that before he wrote the program he had no reason to doubt the existence of mass extinctions. He expected to find little or no correlation between the results of his program and the broad fluctuations in the fossil record. Actually, however, he found the correlation to be quite high. Some phylogenetic lines generated by the program branched and broadened, whereas others petered out, just as they do in the fossil record. There were even occasions when several lines became extinct at the same time. What need was there to invoke an ice age or the collision of an asteroid if chance alone could explain the record of abrupt disappearances in nature?

Steven M. Stanley of Johns Hopkins University made a telling criticism of Raup's interpretation of his results soon after they were published. Stanley pointed out that the number of species the program allowed in a genus was too small to be realistic. The smaller the number of species in a genus is, the more likely it is that probabilistic fluctuations will lead to the genus's extinction. In a real genus the number of species is generally high enough to withstand such a fluctuation. Hence in spite of the mass extinctions that arose in Raup's simulation, the ones in the fossil record might not be a statistical artifact. Raup immediately recognized the validity of Stanley's criticism and now supports the view that mass extinctions were probably not the result of random change.

One reason for the low species diversity found in Raup's results was that the program initially declared rather small arrays; the arrays artificially limited each genus to at most 40 species. As Raup puts it, "We didn't realize at the time how important size would be." His program did not lump more than one species into a single array entry as PALEOTREE does because he wanted to be able to reconstruct the entire evolutionary tree for each species and then inspect the process of random speciation closely.

Another reason for the low species diversity is that both Raup's program and PALEOTREE begin with a single species and build up from it. Such a model might best approximate the evolution of very early life, when the diversity of species was low. Readers who wish to see Stanley's criticism in action should initially supply *history* with 100 genera, each having 100 species. Are mass extinctions still encountered? I shall report unusual events, whether for trilobites or for Smiths.

Addendum

NEOTREE, a program that mimics the extinction of family names, caught the fancy of more readers than did PALEOTREE, a program that models the evolution of genera and species.

Many readers were content to follow the evolution of a single genus without a computer, merely by tossing a pair of dice: a total of 2, 3, or 4 on the dice would make a species extinct, a 9 or a 10 would give birth to a new species, and any other total would cause no change. The probabilities corresponding to these outcomes are respectively 6/36, 7/36, and 23/36. In my own experiments I had noticed the branching trees that trace the evolution often die out. But how many of the survivors, I wondered, would go on living forever? I. Jack Good of Virginia Polytechnic Institute and State University in Blacksburg, Va., pointed out that the single root of the equation $1/36(6 + 23x + 7x^2)$ lying between 0 and 1, namely the root 6/7, is the probability that such a tree is finite. Hence a seventh of my trees are destined for immortality. Robert M. Solovay of the University of California at Berkeley reached the same conclusion by an elementary argument. Meanwhile in Park Ridge, Ill., Edgar F. Coudal repeatedly ran the program needed to trace the complete evolution of a tree. Thinking that all the trees were destined for finitude, Coudal began generating them one evening in order to determine their average size. He writes that occasionally a tree would fill his screen, and an out-of-bounds condition built into the program would terminate the run. Not suspecting that infinity was the culprit, his thoughts turned to the consequences of the screen limit for theoretical paleontology: "Wouldn't [David M.] Raup [of the University of Chicago] be interested to find that . . . Nemesis cycles are really only coincidental out-of-bounds errors in the eternal CPU?"

Readers who tried NEOTREE all report the same results from the experiment with 1000 family names. Given typical male birth patterns, the number of names decreased by three-fourths in just over 20 generations. For example, James W. Cox of Ottawa, Ont., found that half of the family names disappear in only three generations and two-thirds of them are extinct in 10 generations. There is a kind of stability thereafter. Matthew M. Cammen of Painted Post, N.Y., explains it this way: "After, say, 50 generations most of the names have over 100 living males who marry." Will the number of family names never shrink to one? Craig J. Albert of New York, N.Y., is skeptical. Experience with NEOTREE suggests that one must be "extraordinarily tenacious" in waiting for the event. The answer, as always, depends on the model adopted. For an abstract model in which the population grows continually perhaps 200 names will go on forever. No computer, however, can house more than a finite number of human tokens. When the limit is reached, the number of names will start to decline. After the year googolplex A.D. ($10^{10^{100}}$) either Smith or Chan will be lost forever.

WORLD SEVEN

Core Wars

Core War is the game in which programs do their level best to kill each other inside the arena afforded by a computer's memory. Three excursions take the reader from the game's first description in May, 1984, to a Core War tournament held in Boston in September, 1986. Core War programs are the recreational counterpart of nasty pieces of software that go by names like worms, viruses, trojan horses, and so on. In such cases the infected computer may lose its software. When asked by reporters whether I think there might be a core war of sorts going on at this very moment, between malicious programs invading or defending sensitive military computers, I feel bound to reply that I really cannot say with any authority that such things are not happening.

In the meantime the battle programs in the game called Core War get meaner every year.

Core War

Two computer programs in their native habitat—the memory chips of a digital computer—stalk each other from address to address. Sometimes they go scouting for the enemy; sometimes they lay down a barrage of numeric bombs; sometimes they copy themselves out of danger or stop to repair damage. This is the game I call Core War. It is unlike almost all other computer games in that people do not play at all! The contending programs are written by people, of course, but once a battle is under way the creator of a program can do nothing but watch helplessly as the product of hours spent in design and implementation either lives or dies on the screen. The outcome depends entirely on which program is hit first in a vulnerable area.

The term Core War originates in an outmoded memory technology. In the 1950s and 1960s the memory system of a computer was built out of thousands of ferromagnetic cores, or rings, strung on a meshwork of fine wires. Each core could retain the value of one bit, or binary digit, the fundamental unit of information. Nowadays memory elements are fabricated on semiconductor chips, but the active part of the memory system, where a program is kept while it is being executed, is still sometimes referred to as core memory, or simply core.

Battle programs in Core War are written in a specialized language I have named Redcode, closely related to the class of programming languages called assembly languages. Most computer programs today are written in a high-level language such as Pascal, Fortran, or BASIC; in these languages a single statement can specify an entire sequence of machine instructions. Moreover, the statements are easy for the programmer to read and to understand. For a program to be executed, however, it must first be translated into "machine language," where each instruction is represented by a long string of binary digits. Writing a program in this form is tedious at best.

Assembly languages occupy an intermediate position between high-level languages and machine code. In an assembly-language program each statement generally corresponds to a single instruction and hence to a particular string of binary digits. Rather than writing the binary numbers, however, the programmer represents them by short words or abbreviations called mnemonics (because they are easier to remember than numbers). The translation into machine code is done by a program called an assembler.

Comparatively little programming is done in assembly languages because the resulting programs are longer and harder to understand or modify than their high-level counterparts. There are some tasks, however, for which an assembly language is ideal. When a program must occupy as little space as possible or be made to run as fast as possible, it is generally written in assembly language. Furthermore, some things can be done in an assembly language that are all but impossible in a high-level language. For example, an assembly-language program can be made to modify its own instructions or to move itself to a new position in memory.

Core War was inspired by a story I heard some years ago about a mischievous programmer at a large corporate research laboratory I shall designate X. The programmer wrote an assembly-language program called CREEPER that would duplicate itself every time it was run. It could also spread from one computer to another in the network of the X corporation. The program had no function other than to perpetuate itself. Before long there were so many copies of CREEPER that more useful programs and data were being crowded out. The growing infestation was not brought under control until someone thought of fighting fire with fire. A second self-duplicating program called REAPER was written. Its purpose was to destroy copies of CREEPER until it could find no more and then to destroy itself. REAPER did its job, and things were soon back to normal at the X lab.

In spite of fairly obvious holes in the story, I believed it, perhaps because I wanted to. It took some time to track down the real events that lay behind this item of folklore. (I shall give an account of them below and in the Addendum.) For now it is sufficient to note that my desire to believe rested squarely on the intriguing idea of two programs doing battle in the dark and noiseless corridors of core.

In 1983 I decided that even if the story turned out not to be true, something like it could be made to happen. I set up an initial version of Core War and, assisted by David Jones, a student in my department at the University of Western Ontario, got it working. Since then we have developed the game to a fairly interesting level.

Core War has four main components: a memory array of 8000 addresses, the assembly language Redcode, an executive program called

MARS (an acronym for Memory Array Redcode Simulator), and the set of contending battle programs. Two battle programs are entered into the memory array at randomly chosen positions; neither program knows where the other one is. MARS executes the programs in a simple version of time-sharing, a technique for allocating the resources of a computer among numerous users. The two programs take turns: a single instruction of the first program is executed, then a single instruction of the second, and so on.

What a battle program does during the execution cycles allotted to it is entirely up to the programmer. The aim, of course, is to destroy the other program by ruining its instructions. A defensive strategy is also possible: a program might undertake to repair any damage it has received or to move out of the way when it comes under attack. The battle ends when MARS comes to an instruction in one of the programs that cannot be executed. The program with the faulty instruction—which presumably is a casualty of war—is declared the loser.

Much can be learned about a battle program merely by analyzing its actions mentally or with pencil and paper. To put the program to the test of experience, however, one needs access to a computer and a version of MARS. The programs could be made to operate on a personal computer. Indeed, documents describing such MARS systems are available for those who would like to set up a Core War battlefield of their own (*see* List of Suppliers).

Before describing Redcode and introducing some simple battle programs, I should say more about the memory array. Although I have noted that it consists of 8000 addresses, there is nothing magical about this number; a smaller array would work quite well. The memory array differs from most computer memories in its circular configuration: it is a sequence of addresses numbered from 0 to 7999 but it thereupon rejoins itself, so that address 8000 is equivalent to address 0. MARS always reduces an address greater than 7999 by taking the remainder after division by 8000. Thus if a battle program orders a hit at address 9378, MARS interprets the address as 1378.

Redcode is a simplified, special-purpose assembly-style language. It has instructions to move the contents of one address in memory to another address, to alter the contents arithmetically, and to transfer control forward or backward within a program. Whereas the output of a real assembler consists of binary codes, the mnemonic form of a Redcode instruction is translated by MARS into a large decimal integer, which is then stored in the memory array; each address in the array can hold one such integer. It is also MARS that interprets the integers as instructions and carries out the indicated operations.

A list of the elementary Redcode instructions is given in the table on page 280. With each instruction the programmer is required to supply at

The instruction set of Redcode, an assembly language for Core War

INSTRUCTION	MNEMONIC	CODE	ARGUMENTS		EXPLANATION
Move	MOV	1	A	B	Move contents of address *A* to address *B*.
Add	ADD	2	A	B	Add contents of address *A* to address *B*.
Subtract	SUB	3	A	B	Subtract contents of address *A* from address *B*.
Jump	JMP	4	A		Transfer control to address *A*.
Jump if zero	JMZ	5	A	B	Transfer control to address *A* if contents of address *B* are zero.
Jump if greater	JMG	6	A	B	Transfer control to address *A* if contents of address *B* are greater than zero.
Decrement: jump if zero	DJZ	7	A	B	Subtract 1 from contents of address *B* and transfer control to address *A* if contents of address *B* are then zero.
Compare	CMP	8	A	B	Compare contents of addresses *A* and *B*; if they are unequal, skip the next instruction.
Data statement	DAT	0		B	A nonexecutable statement; *B* is the data value.

least one argument, or value, and most of the instructions take two arguments. For example, in the instruction JMP −7 the mnemonic JMP (for "jump") is followed by the single argument −7. The instruction tells MARS to transfer control to the memory address seven places before the current one, that is, seven places before the JMP −7 instruction itself. If the instruction happened to be at address 3715, execution of the program would jump back to address 3708.

This method of calculating a position in memory is called relative addressing, and it is the only method employed in Redcode. There is no way for a battle program to know its own absolute position in the memory array.

The instruction MOV 3 100 tells MARS to go forward three addresses, copy what it finds there, and deliver it 100 addresses beyond the MOV instruction, overwriting whatever was there. The arguments in this instruction are given in "direct" mode, meaning they are to be interpreted as addresses to be acted on directly. Two other modes are allowed. Preceding an argument with an @ sign makes it "indirect." In the instruction MOV @3 100 the integer to be delivered to relative address 100 is not the one found at relative address 3 but rather the one found at the address specified by the contents of relative address 3 (*see* top table on page 281). A # sign makes an argument "immediate," so that it is treated

The three-step mechanism of indirect relative addressing

412	412	412
413 DAT 22	418 − 5 413 DAT 22	413 DAT 22
414	414	414
415 [MOV @3 100]	415 [MOV @3 100]	415 [MOV @3 100]
416	416	416
417	417	417
415 + 3 418 DAT −5	418 DAT −5	418 DAT −5
419	419	419
420	420	420
•	•	•
•	•	•
•	•	•
514	514	514
515	515	415 + 100 515 DAT 22
516	516	516
GET ADDRESS OF SOURCE	GET DATA TO BE COPIED	COPY DATA TO DESTINATION

not as an address but as an integer. The instruction MOV #3 100 causes the integer 3 to be moved to relative address 100.

Most of the other instructions need no further explanation, but the data statement (DAT) requires some comment. It can serve as a work space to hold information a program may need to refer to. Strictly

The encoding of Redcode instructions as decimal integers

MNEMONIC	ARGUMENT A	ARGUMENT B	OPERATION CODE	MODE DIGIT: ARGUMENT A	MODE DIGIT: ARGUMENT B	ARGUMENT A	ARGUMENT B
DAT		−1	0	0	0	0000	7999
ADD	#5	−1	2	0	1	0005	7999
MOV	#0	@−2	1	0	2	0000	7998
JMP	−2		4	1	0	7998	0000

ADDRESSING MODES:	IMMEDIATE	#	0
	DIRECT		1
	INDIRECT	@	2

speaking, however, it is not an instruction; indeed, any memory location with a zero in its first decimal position can be regarded as a DAT statement and as such is not executable. If MARS should be asked to execute such an "instruction," it will not be able to and will declare that program the loser.

The decimal integer that encodes a Redcode instruction has several fields, or functional areas (*see* bottom table on page 281). The first digit represents the mnemonic itself, and two more digits identify the addressing mode (direct, indirect, or immediate). In addition four digits are set aside for each argument. Negative arguments are stored in complement form: −1 would be represented as 7999, since in the circular memory array adding 7999 has the same effect as subtracting 1.

The instructions making up a simple battle program called DWARF are listed in the table on page 282. DWARF is a very stupid but very dangerous program that works its way through the memory array bombarding every fifth address with a zero. Zero is the integer signifying a nonexecutable data statement, and so a zero dropped into an enemy program can bring it to a halt.

Assume that DWARF occupies absolute addresses 1 through 4. Address 1 initially contains DAT −1, but execution begins with the next instruction, ADD #5 −1. The effect of the instruction is to add 5 to the contents of the preceding address, namely the DAT −1 statement, thereby transforming it into DAT 4. Next DWARF executes the instruction

DWARF, a battle program, lays down a barrage of "zero bombs"

ADDRESS	CYCLE 1			CYCLE 2			CYCLE 9		
0									
1	DAT		−1	DAT		4	DAT		14
2	ADD	#5	−1	ADD	#5	−1	ADD	#5	−1
3	MOV	#0	@−2	MOV	#0	@−2	MOV	#0	@−2
4	JMP		−2	JMP		−2	JMP		−2
5				—		0	—		0
6									
7									
8									
9							—		0
10									
11									
12									
13									
14							—		0
15									
16									
17									

at absolute address 3, MOV #0 @−2. Here the integer to be moved is 0, specified as an immediate value. The target address is calculated indirectly in the following way. First MARS counts back two addresses from address 3, arriving at address 1. It then examines the data value there, namely 4, and interprets it as an address relative to the current position; in other words, it counts four places forward from address 1 and hence deposits a 0 at address 5.

The final instruction in DWARF, JMP −2, creates an endless loop. It directs execution back to absolute address 2, which again increments the DAT statement by 5, making its new value DAT 9. In the next execution cycle a 0 is therefore delivered to absolute address 10. Subsequent 0 bombs will fall on address 15, 20, 25, and so on. The program itself is immobile but its artillery threatens the entire array. Eventually DWARF works its way around to addresses 7990, 7995, and then 8000. As far as MARS is concerned, 8000 is equal to 0, and so DWARF has narrowly avoided committing suicide. Its next missile again lands on address 5.

It is sobering to realize that no stationary battle program that has more than four instructions can avoid taking a hit from DWARF. The opposing program has only three options: to move about and thereby elude the bombardment, to absorb hits and repair the damage, or to get DWARF first. To succeed through the last strategy the program may have to be lucky: it can have no idea where DWARF is in the memory array, and on the average it has about 1600 execution cycles before a hit is received. If the second program is also a DWARF, each program wins 30 percent of the time; in 40 percent of the contests neither program scores a fatal hit.

Before taking up the other two strategies, I should like to introduce a curious one-line battle program we call IMP. Here it is:

MOV 0 1

IMP is the simplest example of a Redcode program that is able to relocate itself in the memory array. It copies the contents of relative address 0 (namely MOV 0 1) to relative address 1, the next address. As the program is executed it moves through the array at a speed of one address per cycle, leaving behind a trail of MOV 0 1 instructions.

What happens if we pit IMP against DWARF? The barrage of 0s laid down by DWARF moves through the memory array faster than IMP moves, but it does not necessarily follow that DWARF has the advantage. The question is: Will DWARF hit IMP even if the barrage does catch up?

If IMP reaches DWARF first, IMP will in all probability plow right through DWARF's code. When DWARF's JMP −2 instruction transfers execution back two steps, the instruction found there will be IMP's MOV 0 1. As a result DWARF will be subverted and become a second IMP end-

IMP vs. DWARF: Who wins?

7978	MOV	0	1	
7979	MOV	0	1	
7980	—	0		
7981	MOV	0	1	
7982	MOV	0	1	
7983	MOV	0	1	
7984	MOV	0	1	
7985	—	0		
7986	MOV	0	1	
7987	MOV	0	1	
7988	MOV	0	1	
7989	MOV	0	1	
7990	—	0		
7991	MOV	0	1	
7992	MOV	0	1	
7993	MOV	0	1	
7994	MOV	0	1	} IMP
7995				
7996				
7997				
7998				
7999				
0				
1	DAT		7994	
2	ADD	# 5	− 1	DWARF
3	MOV	# 0	@ − 2	
4	JMP	− 2	0	
5	—	0		
6				
7				
8				
9				
10	—	0		
11				

lessly chasing the first one around the array. Under the rules of Core War the battle is a draw (*see* the table on page 284). (Note that this is the outcome to be expected "in all probability." Readers are invited to analyze other possibilities and perhaps discover the bizarre result of one of them.)

Both IMP and DWARF represent a class of programs that can be characterized as small and aggressive but not intelligent. At the next level are programs that are larger and somewhat less aggressive but smart enough to deal with programs in the lower class. The smarter programs have the ability to dodge an attack by copying themselves out of trouble. Each such program includes a segment of code somewhat like the one named GEMINI, shown in the table on page 285. GEMINI is not intended to be a complete battle program. Its only function is to make a copy of itself 100 addresses beyond its present position and then transfer execution to the new copy.

GEMINI, a program that copies itself to a new position in the memory array

DAT		0	/pointer to source address
DAT		99	/pointer to destination address
┌─►MOV	@ −2	@ −1	/copy source to destination
CMP	−3	#9	/if all 10 lines have been copied . . .
JMP	4		/. . . then leave the loop;
ADD	#1	−5	/otherwise, increment the source address . . .
ADD	#1	−5	/. . . and the destination address . . .
└─JMP	−5		/. . . and return to the loop
MOV	#99	93	/restore the starting destination address
JMP	93		/jump to the new copy

(The left-most column is labeled vertically: LOOP)

The GEMINI program has three main parts. Two data statements at the beginning serve as pointers: they indicate the next instruction to be copied and its destination. A loop in the middle of the program does the actual copying, moving each instruction in turn to an address 100 places beyond its current position. On each transit through the loop both pointers are incremented by 1, thereby designating a new source and destination address. A compare instruction (CMP) within the loop tests the value of the first data statement; when it has been incremented nine times, the entire program has been copied, and so an exit from the loop is taken. One final adjustment remains to be made. The destination address is the second statement in the program and it has an initial value of DAT 99; by the time it is copied, however, it has already been incremented once, so that in the new version of the program it reads DAT 100. This transcription error is corrected (by the instruction MOV #99 93) and then execution is transferred to the new copy.

By modifying GEMINI it is possible to create an entire class of battle programs. One of these, JUGGERNAUT, copies itself 10 locations ahead instead of 100. Like IMP, it tries to roll through all its opposition. It wins far more often than IMP, however, and leads to fewer draws, because an overwritten program is less likely to be able to execute fragments of JUGGERNAUT's code. BIGFOOT, another program employing the GEMINI mechanism, makes the interval between copies of a large prime number. BIGFOOT is hard to catch and has the same devastating effect on enemy code as JUGGERNAUT does.

Neither BIGFOOT nor JUGGERNAUT is very intelligent. So far we have written only two battle programs that qualify for the second level of sophistication. They are too long to reproduce here. One of them, which we call RAIDAR, maintains two "pickets" surrounding the program itself (see Figure 92). Each picket consists of 100 consecutive addresses filled with 1s and is separated from the program by a buffer zone of 100 empty addresses. RAIDAR divides its time between systematically attacking dis-

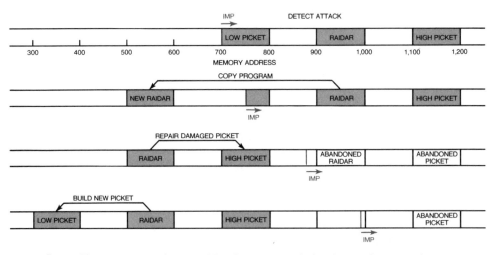

Figure 92   RAIDAR, a sophisticated battle program, eludes the simpler IMP in the memory array of Core War.

tant areas of the memory array and checking its picket addresses. If one of the pickets is found to be altered, RAIDAR interprets the change as evidence of an attack by DWARF, IMP, or some other unintelligent program. RAIDAR then copies itself to the other side of the damaged picket, restores it, constructs a new picket on its unprotected side, and resumes normal operation.

In addition to copying itself a battle program can be given the ability to repair itself. Jones has written a self-repairing program that can survive some attacks, although not all of them. Called SCANNER, it maintains two copies of itself but ordinarily executes only one of them. The copy that is currently running periodically scans the other copy to see if any of its instructions have been altered by an attack. Changes are detected by comparing the two copies, always assuming that the executing copy is correct. If any bad instructions are found, they are replaced and control is transferred to the other copy, which then begins to scan the first one.

So far SCANNER remains a purely defensive program. It is able to survive attacks by DWARF, IMP, JUGGERNAUT, and similar slow-moving aggressors—at least if the attack comes from the right direction. Jones is currently working on a self-repair program that keeps three copies of itself.

I am curious to see whether readers can design other kinds of self-repairing programs. For example, one might think about maintaining two or more copies of a program even though only one copy is ever executed. The program might include a repair section that would refer to an extra copy when restoring damaged instructions. The repair section could even repair itself, but it might still be vulnerable to damage at some positions. One measure of vulnerability assumes that a single instruction has been hit; on the average, how many such instructions, if they are hit, ultimately cause the program to die? By this measure, what is the least vulnerable self-repairing program that can be written?

Only if reasonably robust programs can be developed will Core War reach the level of an exciting game, where the emphasis is shifted from defense to offense. Battle programs will then have to seek out and identify enemy code and mount an intensive attack wherever it is found.

I may have given the impression that Redcode and the entire MARS system are fixed. They are not. In spare moments we have been experimenting with new ideas and are certainly open to suggestions. Indeed, we have been experimenting so much with new programs and new features that some battles remain to be fought in our own system.

One idea we have been playing with is to include an extra instruction that would make self-repair or self-protection a little easier. The instruction PCT A would protect the instruction at address A from alteration until it is next executed. How much could the vulnerability of a program be reduced by exploiting an instruction of this kind?

In the guidelines offered above we describe not only the rules of Core War but also how to set up a memory array and write a MARS system in various high-level languages. We also suggest how to display the results of a Core War battle. For now the following rules define the game with enough precision to enable pencil-and-paper players to begin designing battle programs.

1. The two battle programs are loaded into the memory array at random positions but initially are no closer than 1000 addresses.
2. MARS alternates in executing one instruction from each program until it reaches an instruction that cannot be executed. The program with the erroneous instruction loses.
3. Programs can be attacked with any available weapon. A "bomb" can be a 0 or any other integer, including a valid Redcode instruction.
4. A time limit is put on each contest, determined by the speed of the computer. If the limit is reached and both programs are still running, the contest is a draw.

The story of CREEPER and REAPER seems to be based on a compounding of two actual programs. One program was a computer game called DARWIN, invented by Victor A. Vyssotsky of AT&T Bell Laboratories. The other was called WORM and was written by John F. Shoch of the Xerox

Palo Alto Research Center. Both programs are some years old, allowing ample time for rumors to blossom. (DARWIN was described in *Software: Practice and Experience*. A vague description of what appears to be the same game is also given in the 1978 edition of *Computer Lib*.)

In DARWIN each player submits a number of assembly-language programs called organisms, which inhabit core memory along with the organisms of other players. The organisms created by one player (and thus belonging to the same "species") attempt to kill those of other species and occupy their space. The winner of the game is the player whose organisms are most abundant when time is called. Douglas B. McIlroy, also of AT&T Bell Laboratories, invented an unkillable organism, although it won only "a few games." It was immortal but apparently not very aggressive.

WORM was an experimental program designed to make the fullest use possible of minicomputers linked in a network at Xerox. WORM was loaded into quiescent machines by a supervisory program. Its purpose was to take control of the machine and, in coordination with WORMS inhabiting other quiescent machines, run large applications programs in the resulting multiprocessor system. WORM was designed so that anyone who wanted to use one of the occupied machines could readily reclaim it without interfering with the larger job.

One can see elements of both DARWIN and WORM in the story of CREEPER and REAPER. In Core War, REAPER has become reality.

Addendum

Responses to "Core War" on its initial publication in "Computer Recreations" (SCIENTIFIC AMERICAN, May, 1984), ranged from simple requests for supplementary guidance on the game to descriptions of complete Core War systems already in operation. In between were numerous anecdotes about CREEPER-like programs inhabiting real systems (including worms in Apples), discussions of programs as genes, and speculations about defensive and offensive strategy. Only a few important developments can be mentioned here; others will be discussed in "Core War Encore."

What happens when an IMP runs into a DWARF? One possibility was explained earlier: DWARF transfers control to IMP's code and becomes a second IMP endlessly chasing the first one. Another possible outcome has the opposite effect. Suppose DWARF has just jumped back to its first instruction when IMP copies itself over DWARF's data location. The situation is then as follows:

$$
\begin{array}{llll}
\text{IMP} \rightarrow & \text{MOV} & 0 & 1 \\
\text{DWARF} \rightarrow & \text{ADD} & \#5 & -1
\end{array}
$$

$$\text{MOV} \quad \#0 \quad @-2$$
$$\text{JMP} \quad -2$$

Since it is DWARF's turn to execute, it adds 5 to IMP's code, turning it into MOV 0 6. Then IMP executes, copying itself six spaces ahead, well clear of DWARF, which then bombs its next address (specified by the numerical code corresponding to MOV 0 6). On IMP's next turn something curious happens: it executes the first line of DWARF's program, so that for a time the game is played by a "double dwarf" pointlessly shooting up the core array while the object of its attack inhabits its own body and does exactly the same thing!

David Menconi of Milpitas, Calif., a game designer at Atari, Inc., has suggested making this very phenomenon a regular feature of Core War by allowing each battle program to execute in two places at once. Thus even if a program loses one "self," a second self might be able to repair the damage. Edsel Worrell of Bethesda, Md., suggests the somewhat more general scheme of n selves, all executing the same program at different addresses.

Robert Peraino of George Mason University wrote a Core War system for the Apple II+ computer, compensating for the machine's small word size by using a two-dimensional array of 2000 by two bytes. Bill Dornfield of AMF, Inc., wrote a complete Core War system in extended BASIC on a Hewlett-Packard 9816/26 desktop computer.

The most impressive system to date was constructed by three graduate students: Gordon J. Goetsch and Michael L. Mauldin of Carnegie-Mellon University, and Paul G. Milazzo of Rice University. Mauldin demonstrated the program on a VAX computer in my department at the University of Western Ontario. In an impressive screen display the entire core array is shown, with the position of each contending program marked by a capital letter and the areas affected by the program marked by the corresponding lowercase letter.

Mauldin has invented a battle program called MORTAR that operates like DWARF except that its bombs are directed according to the sequence of Fibonacci numbers (1, 1, 2, 3, 5, and so on, each number being the sum of its two predecessors). Oddly enough, DWARF beats MORTAR 60 percent of the time, but MORTAR invariably kills a three-part self-repairing program called VOTER. On the other hand, VOTER survives attacks by DWARF and regularly defeats it.

Goetsch, Mauldin, and Milazzo have analyzed MORTAR and conclude that if a battle program is longer than 10 instructions, it must be self-repairing in order to defeat MORTAR. No program longer than 141 instructions, however, can repair itself fast enough to survive an attack by MORTAR.

Core War Encore

When I originally wrote "Core War," it had not occurred to me how serious a topic I was raising. My descriptions of machine-language programs, moving about in memory and trying to destroy each other, struck a resonant chord. According to many readers, whose stories I shall tell, there are abundant examples of worms, viruses, and other software creatures living in every conceivable computing environment. Some of the possibilities are so horrifying that I hesitate to set them down at all.

The French spy thriller *Softwar: La Guerre Douce* (English translation published by Holt, Rinehart & Winston) provides a geopolitical fantasy of this type. Authors Thierry Breton and Denis Beneich spin a chilling yarn about the purchase by the Soviet Union of an American supercomputer. Instead of blocking the sale, American authorities, displaying studied reluctance, agree to the transaction. The computer has been secretly programmed with a "software bomb." Ostensibly bought to help with weather forecasting over the vast territory of the Soviet Union, the machine, or rather its software, contains a hidden trigger; as soon as the U.S. National Weather Service reports a certain temperature at St. Thomas in the Virgin Islands, the program proceeds to subvert and destroy every piece of software it can find in the Soviet network. To the extent that such scenarios represent real possibilities, I am tempted to say, "If we must have war, by all means let it be soft." On the other hand, the possibility of an accident due to the intimate connection between military software and weapons-control systems gives me pause.

Inspired by a June 1959 SCIENTIFIC AMERICAN article on self-reproducing mechanisms by L. S. Penrose, Frederick G. Stahl of Chesterfield, Mo., created a miniature linear universe in which humble creatures lived, moved, and (after a fashion) had their being. Stahl writes:

"Like Core War, I set aside a closed linear segment of main memory in which a creature was simulated by modified machine language. The machine was an IBM Type 650 with drum memory. The creature was programmed to crawl through its universe eating food (nonzero words) and creating a duplicate of itself when enough food was accumulated. Like Core War, I had an executive program which kept track of who was alive and allocated execution time among the living creatures. I called it the LEFT HAND OF GOD." Stahl goes on to discuss his program's ability to reproduce. He also describes an interesting mutation mechanism: a program being copied might experience a small number of random changes in its code. However, Stahl reports, "I abandoned this line of work after one production run in which a sterile mutant ate and killed the only fertile creature in the universe. It was apparent that extraordinarily large memories and long computer runs would be needed to achieve interesting results."

A similar story concerns a game called ANIMAL in which a program tries to determine what animal a human is thinking of by playing a form of Twenty Questions. David D. Clark of the Massachusetts Institute of Technology Laboratory for Computer Science writes that the employees of a certain company devotedly played ANIMAL. While it resembles neither a battle program nor even Stahl's simple creatures, ANIMAL achieved the ability to reproduce itself in the corridors of core through the efforts of a programmer to enhance a key feature of the game: when the program guesses incorrectly what animal the human has in mind, it asks the human to suggest a question it might ask to improve its future performance. This feature, Clark continues, led the programmer to invent a certain trick for making sure that everyone always had the same version of ANIMAL.

"On a very early computer system, which lacked any shared directory structure, but also lacked any protection tools, a programmer invented a very novel way of making the game available to several users. A version of the game existed in one user's directory. Whenever he played the game, the program made a copy of itself into another directory. If that directory had previously contained a copy of the game, then the old version was overwritten, which made the behavior of the game change unexpectedly to the player. If that directory had previously had no version of ANIMAL, the game had been offered to yet another user."

Clark recalls that ANIMAL was such a popular game that eventually every directory in the company system contained a copy. "Furthermore, as employees of the company were transferred to other divisions . . . they took ANIMAL as well, and thus it spread from machine to machine within the company." The situation would never have become serious had it not been for the fact that all those copies of this otherwise innocuous game began to clog the disk memory. Only when someone devised a more "virulent" version of the game was the situation brought under control. When the new version of ANIMAL was played, it copied itself into other directories not once but twice. Given enough time, it was thought, this program would eventually overwrite all the old versions of ANIMAL. After a year had passed, a certain date triggered each copy of the new ANIMAL program. "Instead of replicating itself twice whenever it was invoked, it now played one final game, wished the user 'goodbye' and then deleted itself. And thus ANIMAL was purged from the system."

Ruth Lewart of Holmdel, N.J., once created a monster (of sorts) without even writing a program. Working on her company's time-sharing system, she was preparing a demonstration version of a teaching program when she decided to make a backup copy on another time-sharing system. When the original system began to seem sluggish, she "switched to the backup system, which was very responsive—for all of 3 minutes, by which time there was no response and utter chaos on the screen of my graphics terminal. It was not possible for any user to log on or to log off from the system. The conclusion was inescapable—my program was somehow at fault! Despite my panic, I suddenly realized that I had specified an ampersand as the terminal's field separator character. But the ampersand was also the character used by the computer system to spawn a background process! The first time the computer read from the screen, it must have intercepted the ampersands meant for the terminal, and spawned a number of processes, which in turn each spawned more processes, ad infinitum." A frantic long-distance call informed a system administrator of the source of the disease and the mainframe computer was then shut down and restarted. Needless to say, Lewart changed the ampersand to a less dangerous character. Her program "has been humming happily ever since."

Even though Core War programs are not spawned in this manner, additional copies can enhance their survival. Several readers suggested three copies of a program be made so that the copy currently executing could use the other two copies to determine whether any of its instructions were wrong. The executing program could even replace a faulty instruction with a viable one. A similar idea lies behind SCAVENGER, a program designed to protect mass-storage files from error when backup copies are made on magnetic tape. Arthur Hudson, who lives in Newton, Mass. (and works for yet another unnamed company), writes: "Anyone who used much magnetic tape found himself beset by an alien force called the Law of Joint Probability." Hudson goes on to cite various errors connected with the handling of tapes and shows that, although each kind of error has a relatively small chance of happening, the probability of at least one of them occurring is uncomfortably large. He continues:

"Fear not, SCAVENGER is with you: If you place a mass-storage file in its care, it will copy the file on three magnetic tapes without bothering you with housekeeping details. Even if the computer crashes logically (as it did several times per day), the run backlog usually will not be destroyed; when the computer comes back up, whatever SCAVENGER worms are in the backlog will run in their turn. Each tape is written by a separate run schedule from a master runstream."

Owners of Apple computers should beware a mean little program called APPLE WORM, created by Jim Hauser and William R. Buckley of California Polytechnic State University at San Luis Obispo. Written for the Apple II in 6502 assembly language, this species of worm replicates itself on a merry little journey through the host Apple. Initially one loads a special BASIC program (*see* Figure 93) that in turn loads the worm into low memory (the part with low addresses). The BASIC program, on the other hand, occupies high memory.

"Because the WORM is loaded into one of the graphics areas of the machine, you can watch the WORM as it begins its headlong (actually, taillong) dash into high memory.... After the WORM leaves the graphics window ... you can wait until the WORM erases all of high memory (including the BASIC program) and crashes into the system ROMS."

Hauser and Buckley plan to publish a collection of worms in the not too distant future. They have designed a Worm Operating System and have even written a video game with Worm as one of its main characters.

Another software threat has been propounded by Roberto Cerruti and Marco Morocutti of Brescia, Italy. Inspired by the translation of the column on Core War in the Italian edition of SCIENTIFIC AMERICAN, *Le Scienze,* the two sought a way of infecting the Apple II computer, not with a worm but with a virus. Reports Cerruti:

```
1    IF PEEK (104) = 134 GOTO 10
2    POKE 104, 134: POKE 134 * 256,0
3    PRINT CHR$(4) "RUN APPLE WORM"
10   HOME: POKE - 16302,0: POKE - 16304,0: POKE 1023,160
20   FOR I = 0 TO 94: READ D: POKE 1024 + I, D: NEXT I
30   POKE - 16368,0
40   IF PEEK ( - 16384) < 128 GOTO 40
50   CALL 1024
100  DATA 160,255,200,185,255,3,153,127,4,192,95,208,245,
     160,18,190,76,4,24,189,128,4,105,128,157,128,4,189,129,
     4,105,0,157,129,4,192,13,208,18,238,23,4,173,23,4
200  DATA 141,151,4,206,31,4,173,31,4,141,159,4,136,208,211,
     173,167,4,72,173,176,4,141,167,4,104,141,176,4,76,128,
     4,7,20,25,28,33,46,55,61,65,68,72,75,4,16,40,43,49,52
```

Figure 93   A worm that inhabits Apples.

"Marco thought to write a program capable of passing from one computer to the other, like a virus, and 'infecting' in this way other Apples. But we were not able to conceive it until I realized that the program had to 'infect' floppy disks, and use the computers only like a media from a disk to the other. So our virus began to take shape.

"As you know every Apple diskette contains a copy of the Disk Operating System, which is bootstrapped by the computer at power on. The virus was an alteration in this DOS, which at every write operation checked his presence on the disk and, if not, would modify in the same way the DOS on the disk, thus copying itself on every diskette put in the drive after the first power up. We thought that installing such a DOS on some disks used in the biggest computer shop in our city, Brescia, would cause an epidemic to spread in the city.

"But was it a real epidemic, of such unharming viruses? No, our virus should be malignant! So we decided that after 16 self-reproduction cycles, counted on the disk itself, the program should decide to re-initialize the disk immediately after bootstrap. Now the awful evil of our idea was clear, and we decided neither to carry it out, nor to speak to anybody about our idea."

That was kind of Cerruti and Morocutti. In a personal computer the disk operating system is the ultimate arbiter of the fate of programs, data and all else. In the scheme just described the infected disk operating system erases the disk whence it came and can therefore never be loaded again except from a new disk. The diseased DOS could even cause an irritating message to be displayed periodically:

IS YOUR DISK
SLIPPING?
It's time you got
DOS DOCTOR
available on disk at a
computer store near you

The viral infection just described has already happened on a small scale. Richard Skrenta, Jr., a high school student in Pittsburgh, wrote such a program. Instead of wiping disks or displaying advertisements, this form of infection caused subtle errors to appear throughout the operating system.

"All of this seems pretty juvenile now," writes Skrenta, but "Oh woe to me! I have never been able to get rid of my electronic plague. It infested all of my disks, and all of my friends' disks. It even managed to get onto my math teacher's graphing disks." Skrenta devised a program to destroy the virus, but it was never as effective as the virus itself had been.

There is a good problem implicit here and I would be both unimaginative and irresponsible for not posing it: in one page or less describe DOS DOCTOR, a program on disk that somehow stamps out such electronic epidemics. Many disks used by a personal computer contain copies of its DOS. When started up, the computer obtains its copy of the DOS from the disk. This DOS will still be in charge when other disks, also containing copies of the DOS, are run. If it is infected, the DOS currently in charge may alter the other copies of the DOS or even replace them with copies of itself. But how to counteract such virulence?

In the initial version of Core War the main challenge was to enable battle program A to protect itself from stray hits generated by battle program B. If such protection could be more or less guaranteed, then evolution of the game was to proceed to the next level, where programs would have been forced to seek each other out and develop concentrated attacks.

In an effort to guarantee such protection, I suggested the instruction

PCT *A*

where *A* is the relative address (either direct or indirect) of an instruction that is to be protected. A single attempt to change the contents of that address would be prevented by MARS, the game's supervisory system. The next attempt, however, would succeed. It seemed to me that by employing a simple loop, any battle program could protect all its own instructions from stray bombs long enough to be able to launch an undistracted probe for the other program. The table below displays such a self-protecting program in schematic form. The protection loop consists of six instructions, four of them executed at each cycle through the loop. Thus a battle program of *n* instructions (including the loop) would require nearly $4 \times n$ executions to have complete protection from a single hit. This salutary shielding is hardly proof against a dwarf program that hurls two shots at each location.

This loop protects combatants from stray bombs

DAT		0	/pointer to address being protected
ADD	# 1	− 1	/increment protection address
PCT	@ −2		/protect the address
CMP	# 102	−3	/if all 102 instructions protected . . .
JMP	2		/ . . . then leave loop
JMP	−4		/otherwise re-enter it.
		⋮	
	BODY OF MAIN BATTLE PROGRAM		
		⋮	

There is another use of this instruction, unforeseen earlier. Stephen Peters of Timaru, New Zealand, and Mark A. Durham of Winston-Salem, N.C., independently thought of using PCT offensively. A program called TRAP-DWARF lays down a barrage of 0s in the usual way but then protects each deposit against overwriting. This means that an unwary enemy program may fall into one of these traps in the course of writing itself into a new area. The instruction meant for the location occupied by a protected 0 would of course have no effect on that location. Later, when the new program's execution reaches that address, it dies because 0 is not an executable instruction. PCT may be worthy of inclusion in some future version of Core War but I shall shelve it for now in the interest of simplicity, the game designer's touchstone.

Other reader ideas varied from the two-dimensional Core array suggested by Robert Norton of Madison, Wis., to the range-limitation rule suggested by William J. Mitchell of the mathematics department at Pennsylvania State University. Norton's idea is largely self-explanatory but Mitchell's suggestion requires some elaboration. Allow each battle program to alter the contents of any location up to a distance of some fixed number of addresses. Such a rule automatically keeps DWARF from doing any damage outside this neighborhood. The rule has many other effects as well, including a strong emphasis on movement. How else can a battle program get within range of an opponent? The rule has much merit and I hope that some of the many readers with a Core War system of their own will give it the further exploration it deserves.

Norton also suggests that each side in a Core War battle be allowed more than one execution. The same idea occurred to many other readers. Indeed, I have decided to adopt the suggestion. Core War now assumes a previously lacking wide-open character.

The change is made by adding the following instruction, called a split, to the official Core War list (*see* table on page 297).

SPL *A*

When execution reaches this point, it splits into two parts, namely the instruction following SPL and the one *A* addresses away. Because this immediately allows each Core War player to have several programs running at once, it is necessary to define how MARS will allocate such executions. Two possibilities exist.

To illustrate them suppose one player has programs A_1, A_2, and A_3, whereas the other player has programs B_1 and B_2. One alternative is to have all the first player's programs run, followed by those of the second player. The order of execution would thus be A_1, A_2, A_3, and then B_1 and B_2. The cycle would repeat indefinitely. The second alternative is to have the programs of the two players alternate. In this case the sequence

The list of instructions for Core War programs

INSTRUCTION	MNEMONIC	CODE	ARGUMENTS		EXPLANATION
Move	MOV	1	A	B	Move contents of address *A* to address *B*.
Add	ADD	2	A	B	Add contents of address *A* to address *B*.
Subtract	SUB	3	A	B	Subtract contents of address *A* from address *B*.
Jump	JMP	4	A		Transfer control to address *A*.
Jump if zero	JMZ	5	A	B	Transfer control to address *A* if contents of address *B* are zero.
Jump if greater	JMG	6	A	B	Transfer control to address *A* if contents of *B* are greater than zero.
Decrement: jump if zero	DJZ	7	A	B	Subtract 1 from contents of address *B* and transfer control to address *A* if contents of address *B* are then zero.
Compare	CMP	8	A	B	Compare contents of addresses *A* and *B*; if they are unequal, skip the next instruction.
Split	SPL	9	A		Split execution into next instruction and the instruction at *A*.
Data statement	DAT	0		B	A nonexecutable statement; *B* is the data value.

would be A_1, B_1, A_2, B_2, A_3, B_1, and so on. The two schemes are quite different in effect. The first scheme puts great emphasis on unlimited proliferation and seems thereby to limit the role of intelligence in the game. The second scheme, however, implies that the more programs either player has running, the less often each will be executed. A law of diminishing returns seems appropriate in this context and I have therefore adopted the second scheme. The purpose of the game, in any event, is to bring all enemy programs to a halt.

The new instruction is rife with creative possibilities. As an illustration of the humblest issue possible, there is a battle program called IMP GUN:

> SPL 2
> JMP −1
> MOV 0 1

Consider what happens when execution first arrives at the top of this program. The instruction SPL 2 means there will be two executions allotted to this program later: both JMP −1 and MOV 0 1 will be performed. The first instruction causes the program to recycle and the second sets an IMP in motion. The IMP will move down, of course, since the target of the MOV command will always be the next address, as indicated by the (positive) 1. The IMP is thus spawned on each program cycle and an endless stream of IMPs run pattering through Core bent on the destruction or subversion of hostile programs. At first glance it may seem that no defense is possible against such an army of IMPs, but in fact one is. Enter IMP PIT, an even simpler program set in motion by an SPL command in some larger assembly of instructions wishing to protect its upper flank:

$$MOV \#0 \quad -1$$
$$JMP \quad -1$$

At each execution, IMP PIT places a 0 just above itself in the hope of zapping an oncoming IMP. Here the execution-allocation rule is critical. If IMP GUN belongs to A and IMP PIT belongs to B, then A needs n turns to execute n IMPs; only one IMP can arrive at the location just above the IMP PIT. Other things being equal, B has to execute IMP PIT only once to terminate an arriving IMP.

In the expanded Core War game, one imagines each side generating and deploying small armies of programs individually shaped to detect, attack, protect, and even repair. Many subtleties such as the one suggested by John McLean of Washington, D.C., await further investigation. McLean imagines a specialized trap program that places JMP commands at various addresses throughout the Core array in the hope of landing a JMP command inside an enemy program. Each JMP so placed would transfer execution of the enemy program to the trap program, causing it to go over to the enemy, so to speak.

One major problem in need of resolution emerges from the melee of battle programs. What is to prevent a battle program for one side from attacking its colleagues? A recognition system appears to be necessary.

Among the many readers who constructed Core War systems three deserve special mention: Chan Godfrey of Wilton, Conn., Graeme R. McRae of Monmouth Junction, N.J., and Mike Rosing of Littleton, Colo., have taken special care in defining and documenting their projects.

Addendum

A Core War network has been formed. The director is Mark Clarkson; readers who would like to be on the network mailing list or who would like to volunteer for special functions should get in touch with Clarkson at the address given in the List of Suppliers.

The possibility of a DOS DOCTOR program on disk that interdicts viral infections of personal computers may be more remote than I thought. Norman Ramsey of Ithaca, N.Y., concludes that DOS DOCTOR can function diagnostically but not therapeutically. Ramsey designed a program that relied on "a second viral DOS, which writes itself on diskettes exactly as does the diseased DOS but does not cause disease." The benign virus thwarts infection by preemptively occupying memory space. His program, Ramsey adds, had some amusing bells and whistles. "It could even display a message at boot time, 'Fear not—DOS DOCTOR is with you,' to indicate to the user that his DOS is safe." Unfortunately Ramsey went on to invent a virus smart enough to evade its remedial analog.

The doctor-cum-virus idea also occurred to Joe Dellinger, a biophysicist at Stanford University. Strangely enough, his intention was to create not a doctor but merely an innocuous virus that could pass unnoticed from disk to disk. Dellinger was inspired by the analogy between programs and living creatures. Both might have parasites. In particular, a disk operating system could carry a virus whose continued reproductive success would hinge in part on its never being noticed. A key feature of Dellinger's virus is to infect only the DOS on 48K slave disks: master disks thus always contain a clean DOS. Taking up almost "no room" on infected disks, this undetectable virus checks the host DOS each time it is copied onto a new disk. Its vested interest in the continued health of its host causes it to make certain that the copying is accurate. Dellinger reports that he shared the program for the benign virus with friends. Two of them, he fears, were careless, so that the strain may have spread beyond California. How can you tell whether your DOS has Dellinger's virus? He says there may be a half-second swishing noise when the virus copies itself.

Software viruses may not be as virulent as I implied earlier. Kenneth L. Kashmarek of Eldridge, Iowa, points out that a virus cannot spread to a disk carrying an operating system different from the host disk's. Kashmarek write-protects his disks, a precaution that will certainly halt the spread of any virus—unless, of course, the write-protect software has already been circumvented. He also asks whether it is right to discuss in public media viruses and other computer diseases. I do not doubt that compromised software is a serious subject. I think that computer epidemics of the kind I have been describing loom in the near future. In my opinion, "forewarned is forearmed." It is my hope that public discussion will spur research into antidotes.

Meanwhile the source of the rumor that sparked the invention of Core War has finally been revealed. In "Core War" I told the story of CREEPER and REAPER. In "Core War Encore" I described ANIMAL, a game program similar to the Core War software that replicated itself in the computers of all players who used the same time-sharing system. The author of this program, John Walker of Sausalito, Calif., has stepped forward to claim responsibility for the most successful version. Actually ANIMAL is only part of the story. Inside the game program was another piece of software called PERVADE that was responsible for reproducing the program. Written in January, 1975, PERVADE was a subroutine able, when called, to create "an independent process that, while the host program was going about its business, would examine the directories accessible to its caller. If a directory did not contain a copy of the program, or contained an older version, PERVADE would copy the version being executed into that directory. PERVADE was very fastidious and took great care not to destroy, for example, an unrelated user program with the same name."

The First Core War
Tournament

Core War—the game in which specialized programs do their level best to destroy one another—was in the spotlight in September, 1986 at the first international Core War tournament held at the Computer Museum in Boston, Mass. Of 31 programs entered, three emerged as most robust. The ultimate victor was a program called MICE. Its author, Chip Wendell of Rochester, N.Y., received a handsome trophy that incorporated a core-memory board from an early CDC 6600 computer.

Written by human beings, the Core War programs are on their own as they spar in the arena of a computer's memory. The section of memory reserved for the struggle is called the core, after an obsolete form of memory constructed from miniature ferromagnetic rings known as core elements. The game has generated so much enthusiasm that it has sparked the formation of the International Core Wars Society. The game was recently modified by the society; the new version lays out the format that players will follow for now.

The basis of Core War—and the ammunition of the recent tournament—is a battle program written in a special, low-level language called Redcode. A set of 10 simple instructions enables a program to move information from one memory location to another, to add and subtract information, to alter the order in which its instructions are executed, and even to have several instructions executing simultaneously (*see* the table on page 302).

The simplest Redcode program consists of just one MOV instruction: MOV 0 1. The program, which is called IMP, causes the contents at relative address 0 (namely the MOV instruction itself) to be transferred to relative address 1, just one address ahead of itself. Redcode instructions are normally executed consecutively. This means that after the

A summary of Redcode, an assembly language for Core War

INSTRUCTION	MNEMONIC	ARGUMENTS		EXPLANATION
Data statement	DAT		B	A nonexecutable statement; B is the data value.
Move	MOV	A	B	Move contents of address A to address B.
Add	ADD	A	B	Add contents of address A to address B.
Subtract	SUB	A	B	Subtract contents of address A from address B.
Jump	JMP	A		Transfer control to address A.
Jump if zero	JMZ	A	B	Transfer control to address A if contents of address B are zero.
Jump if not zero	JMN	A	B	Transfer control to address A if contents of address B are not zero.
Decrement: jump if not zero	DJN	A	B	Subtract 1 from contents of address B and transfer control to address A if contents of address B are not zero.
Compare	CMP	A	B	Compare contents of addresses A and B; if they are equal, skip the next instruction.
Split	SPL	A		Split execution into next instruction and the instruction at A.

MOV 0 1 instruction is executed the computer will try to execute an instruction at the next address. There is, of course, now an instruction occupying that address: the MOV 0 1 command just copied there. As a consequence IMP patters from address to address through the core, mindlessly destructive. It leaves a trail of MOV 0 1 instructions behind it.

To avoid being overrun a Core War program must at the very least contain an IMP-STOMPER. The safeguard consists of two instructions executed cyclically:

$$\text{MOV } \#0 \; -1$$
$$\text{JMP } -1$$

The first command moves the integer 0, symbolized by #0, to the relative address −1; in other words, every time the MOV command is executed the location just above it (the only direction from which IMPs can attack) is filled with a 0. The second instruction is the JMP command. When it is executed, it transfers the stream of execution, or flow of control, to the address at relative location −1, namely the address just above the JMP. Each execution cycle of the program causes a 0 to be slammed down on any IMP that may have arrived just above the IMP-STOMPER. Consequently the IMP is erased.

As a program runs, it can have more than one stream of execution. If execution encounters the command SPL A in a Redcode program, it splits into two streams. One stream goes to the instruction that immediately follows SPL A and the other jumps to the instruction at relative address A. Unfortunately the MARS system cannot execute both instructions simultaneously; it executes one of the instructions on the next turn after that. What might be thought an incredible advantage is somewhat adumbrated; the more concurrent streams of execution a program has, the slower each stream proceeds. This is only fair, however. In the case of multiple streams of execution a battle program is declared the winner when all its opponent's streams have died out. At such a point MARS, which would still expect to find an executable instruction, can find only the computational equivalent of shell holes and bomb craters.

To illustrate the SPL command, here are the first five instructions of my own entry in the Core War tournament. It is called COMMANDO for reasons that will soon become clear.

$$MOV \ \#0 \ -1$$
$$JMP \ -1$$
$$SPL \ -2$$
$$MOV \ 10 \ 113$$
$$SPL \ 112$$
$$\cdot$$
$$\cdot$$
$$\cdot$$

Readers will recognize an IMP-STOMPER in the first two instructions. Execution of the actual program begins at the third instruction, SPL -2. On COMMANDO's next two turns the first and fourth instructions will be executed. On the two turns after those, the second and fifth instructions will be executed. Each stream proceeds independently of the other and at half the speed, so to speak. In the code above, COMMANDO sets the IMP-STOMPER running on its own. Then it moves another IMP (patiently waiting 10 addresses beyond the second MOV instruction) to a distant location (113 addresses beyond). The second IMP is activated by the second SPL command.

COMMANDO's remaining instructions copy the entire program into a new segment of the core, 100 addresses beyond its present location. The new copy, like a commando just parachuted into enemy territory, is activated by a JMP command in the original program. The old copy of COMMANDO, except for the IMP-STOMPER, ceases to run. Then the entire cycle of copying begins again.

How would COMMANDO fare against its competitors? The tournament was organized to provide for as many engagements as possible between the 31 entries. A complete round robin, in which every program fought all others in turn, would have required 465 battles, more than time would allow. Consequently the entries were divided arbitrarily into two nearly equal groups, division I and division II. A round robin was then held within each division.

Imagine the strange mixture of emotions I felt when COMMANDO emerged as the winner of division II. On one hand I was proud that my cybernetic child had done so well. At the same time I was somewhat mortified at the prospect of winning the tournament overall. Since I had consented to serve as a commentator for the finals, my objectivity (and credibility) would undoubtedly be strained.

The top four programs from each division were then entered in a new round robin. Three programs emerged victorious from the fray, CHANG1 by Morrison J. Chang of Floral Park, N.Y., and two entries by Chip Wendell, MIDGET and MICE. My COMMANDO fell by the wayside, mortally wounded. The final win by MICE came oddly; MIDGET and MICE both fought CHANG1 to a draw, but MICE captured the deciding point by beating MIDGET.

The contest between each pair of finalists consisted of four consecutive battles. The time limit on each engagement was 15,000 instructions per side, or approximately two minutes of real time. In each case the two battle programs were placed in random, nonoverlapping positions in the core and allowed to have a go at it. As it happened, each battle between a given pair of programs always had the same result. In the case of MICE versus CHANG1 the result was four draws.

It is fascinating to watch a Core War in progress. The display used at the tournament shows the core as a succession of cellular strips (*see* Figure 94). Each cell represents a single address in the core, and the last cell in the bottom row is contiguous with the first cell in the top row, in keeping with the circular structure of the core. The program that has the first move initially occupies address 0 and subsequently fills consecutive core locations. Its color is white. The opposition occupies a randomly selected segment of locations not overlapping those assigned to the first program. The color given to the second program is gray. The color of a cell in the display is determined by the last program to alter the address it represents. In this way one has an engaging overview of the action.

Against a black screen MICE and CHANG1 crept about, launched IMPs, hurled bombs, and reproduced (parthenogenetically). One of the contests was typical: CHANG1 began as a strip of white cells in the upper left-hand corner of the screen and the birth of MICE was heralded by a gray

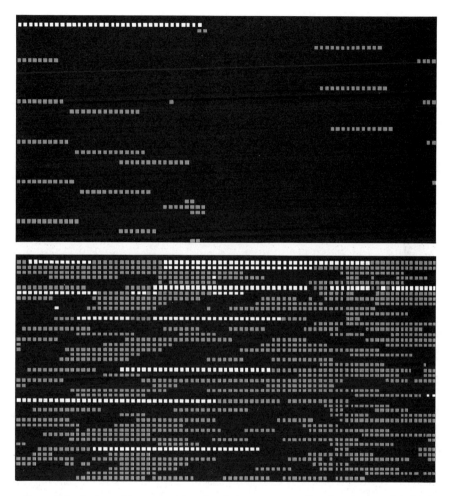

Figure 94   Early and late stages in a battle between MICE (*gray*) and CHANG I (*white*).

strip that appeared less than halfway down the screen. Immediately MICE began to proliferate rapidly.

One of the shortest self-replicating programs I know, MICE has just eight instructions, two of which create a new copy of the program some 833 addresses beyond its present location in the core (*see* table on page 306). The two instructions demonstrate a few additional features of the Redcode language:

loop MOV @*ptr* <5
DJN *loop ptr*

Contenders for the Core War championship

	CHANG 1				MICE			
	MOV	# 0	− 1	ptr	DAT	# 0		
	JMP	− 1		start	MOV	# 12	ptr	
	DAT		+9	loop	MOV	@ptr	<5	
start	SPL	− 2			DJN	loop	ptr	
	SPL	4			SPL	@3		
	ADD	# − 16	− 3		ADD	# 653	2	
	MOV	# 0	@ − 4		JMZ	− 5	− 6	
	JMP	− 4			DAT	833		
	SPL	2						
	JMP	− 1						
	MOV	0	1					

The word *loop*, which is simply a label that stands for an address, makes Core War programs easier to write. The DJN (short for decrement and jump on nonzero values) command causes execution to jump to the instruction labeled *loop* if the value stored at another address (labeled *ptr*) is not yet 0. The @ sign indicates a system of reference known as indirection; when the MOV command is executed, it does not move the contents of the location labeled *ptr* but instead moves the contents of the contents, so to speak. The number stored at *ptr* is the address of the datum to be moved. In this case the datum is one of MICE's instructions.

The number stored at *ptr* continually changes owing to the decrementing function of the DJN command. The number starts at the last program address and steadily decrements to 0, at which point the copying loop is finished. In a similar manner the address at which the instructions are to be stored is also given by indirection. The relative address 5 initially holds the number 833 and the first instruction moved by MICE lands 832 addresses beyond the MOV command; as indicated by the < sign, the target address is decremented and MOV is executed. MICE copies itself tail first.

An SPL (split) command immediately following the loop transfers execution to the new copy of MICE. But following this successful birth the parent program begins anew. There is no limit to how many progeny a single program of this type may produce. And each new program does the same thing. MICE, indeed!

So it was that in a typical contest with CHANG1, MICE bred with incredible rapidity. Soon the screen was full of little gray strips. In the meantime CHANG1 had activated a kind of IMP factory at its downstream end. The factory was achieved with only three instructions:

SPL 2
JMP −1
MOV 0 1

When execution arrives at the SPL command, it splits into two branches. One of them transfers execution to MOV 0 1. The other executes the JMP −1 instruction, which begins the process anew. In the meantime one IMP has already left the assembly line on a mousing mission. One problem with profligate IMP production is that a large number of independent streams of execution slows down every process executed; 1000 IMPs move 1000 times slower and more painfully than a single IMP. In any event, the fateful horde emerged slowly at the top of the display screen as an ever lengthening solid white strip. Would they be able to subvert MICE?

While the IMPs were reproducing, some of the MICE copies were killed by data bombs from CHANG1. A data bomb usualy consists of a 0 that is launched by a MOV command into what one hopes is enemy territory. The key instruction in Chang's program is MOV #0 @ −4. The 0 is moved to an address contained in a location that is four instructions above the MOV command. The location is continually incremented by 16 to ensure a well-spaced barrage.

As some MICE were dying in this manner, the IMPs began to exert their destructive influence. But each copy of the original MICE program carries with it a suicide option; it continually checks on whether its first instruction (which is a data statement consisting of 0 alone) is still 0. If it is not, MICE allows execution to proceed to a (nonexecutable) data statement and dies quietly rather than lose its soul to a tiny fiend.

If some copies of MICE were being killed by data bombs and others were executing their own execution, so to speak, to avoid capture, how did MICE survive? The answer surely lies in its profligate spawning of new copies. Many of these, after all, landed on enemy IMPs. Indeed, before time was called one copy of MICE had landed on CHANG1's home program and destroyed it. CHANG1, however, had created enough IMPs to tide it over until the closing buzzer sounded. The battle was a draw.

The art of Core War programming is surely still in its infancy. Progress will be incremental and cumulative. Some intrepid programmer will discover infallible remedies against IMPs and another will discover simple means of self-repair. Readers wanting to keep abreast of the latest developments may subscribe to *The Core War Newsletter* by writing to William R. Buckley (*see* List of Suppliers). Readers who want to write battle programs should probably join the International Core Wars Society. Mark Clarkson currently directs the society and would welcome new members. One does not have to join the society, however, to order the all-important "Core War Standards" document from Clarkson. It precisely describes the syntax and semantics of Redcode programs; one cannot be a Core Warrior without it (*see* List of Suppliers).

Battle programs of the future will perhaps be longer than today's winners but orders of magnitude more robust. They will gather intelligence, lay false trails, and strike at their opponents suddenly and with determination. Such trends may already be in evidence by the time this book goes to press. In the meantime readers have ample opportunity to express their cleverness and cunning in Redcode language.

The original Core War Tournament owes much of its success to Mark and Beth Clarkson as well as to Gwen Bell, president of the Computer Museum, and Oliver Strimpel, its associate director and curator. It seems worthwhile to conclude with a brief note on the museum itself.

The Computer Museum in Boston is apparently the only museum in the world devoted entirely to computers. Housed in a renovated (and now chic) warehouse on the Boston waterfront, it features old vacuum-tube monsters, PCs for personal play, walls adorned with stunning graphics, a complete NORAD SAGE computer system, and a host of exhibits that entertain and educate. Readers visiting a certain famous old ship in the Boston harbor can have their computational cup of tea right next door.

Bibliography

WORLD ONE

The Mandelbrot Set

Hoffman, Dean, and Lee Mohler. *Mathematical Recreations for the Programmable Calculator*. Hasbrouck Heights, N.J.: Hayden Book Co., 1982.

Mandelbrot, Benoit B. *The Fractal Geometry of Nature*. New York: W. H. Freeman and Company, 1983.

Robert, Francois. *Discrete Iterations*. Translated by Jon Rokne. New York: Springer-Verlag, 1986.

Wallpaper for the Mind

Gardner, Martin. "Mathematical Games." SCIENTIFIC AMERICAN, February, 1971, 112–117.

Hayes, Brian. "Computer Recreations." SCIENTIFIC AMERICAN, October, 1971, 22–36.

WORLD TWO

Analog Gadgets

Garey, Michael R., and David S. Johnson. *Computers and Intractability: A Guide to the Theory of N-P Completeness*. San Francisco: W. H. Freeman and Company, 1983.

Isenberg, Cyril. *The Science of Soap Films and Soap Bubbles*. Teito Ltd., 5 Elton Road, Clevedon, Avon, England, 1978.

Gadgets Revisited

Gardner, Martin. *Aha! Gotcha: Paradoxes to Puzzle and Delight*. New York: W. H. Freeman and Company, 1982.

Hoffman, Dale T. "Smart Soap Bubbles Can Do Calculus." *The Mathematics Teacher*, May, 1979, 377–385.

Vergis, Anastasios, Kenneth Steiglitz, and Bradley Dickenson. "The Complexity of Analog Computation." *Technical Report No. 337*, Department of Electrical Engineering and Computer Science, Princeton University, February, 1985.

Golomb Rulers

Bloom, Gary S., and Solomon W. Golomb. "Applications of Numbered Undirected Graphs." *Proceedings of the IEEE* 65, no. 4 (April, 1977): 562–570.

Carter, W. E., D. S. Robertson, J. E. Pettey, B. D. Tapley, B. E. Shultz, R. J. Eanes, and Miao Lufeng. "Variations in the Rotation of the Earth." *Science*, June, 1984, 957–961.

Gardner, Martin. *Wheels, Life and Other Mathematical Amusements*. New York: W. H. Freeman and Company, 1983.

Moffet, Alan T. "Minimum-Redundancy Linear Arrays." *IEEE Transactions on Antennas and Propagation* AP-16, no. 2 (February, 1963): 562–570.

Hypercubes

Abbott, Edwin A. *Flatland: A Romance of Many Dimensions*. New York: New American Library, 1984.

Manning, Henry P., ed. *The Fourth Dimension Simply Explained: A Collection of Essays Selected from Those Submitted in the Scientific American's Prize Competition*. Mineola, N.Y.: Dover Publications, 1960.

Weeks, Jeffrey R. *The Shape of Space: How to Visualize Surfaces and Three-Dimensional Manifolds*. New York: Marcel Dekker, 1985.

WORLD THREE

Conversations with RACTER

Krutch, John. *Experiments in Artificial Intelligence for Small Computers*. Indianapolis: Howard W. Sams and Co., 1982.

RACTER, with an introduction by William Chamberlain. *The Policeman's Beard Is Half-Constructed*. New York: Warner Books, 1984.

Winograd, Terry. *Understanding Natural Language*. New York: Academic Press, 1972.

Facebender

Brennan, Susan E. "Caricature Generator: The Dynamic Exaggeration of Faces by Computer." *Leonardo* 18, no. 3 (1985): 170–178.

McDermott, Jeanne. "Face to Face: It's the Expression that Bears the Message." *Smithsonian*, March, 1986, 112–123.

Perceptron Misperceptions

Minsky, Marvin, and Seymour Papert. *Perceptrons: An Introduction to Computational Geometry.* Cambridge, Mass.: The MIT Press, 1969.

Rosenblatt, Frank. *Principles of Neurodynamics: Perceptrons and the Theory of Brain Mechanisms.* Hasbrouck Heights, N.J.: Spartan Books, 1962.

A Checkers Program that Never Loses?

Hopper, Millard. *Win at Checkers.* Mineola, N.Y.: Dover Publications, 1956.

Krutch, John. *Experiments in Artificial Intelligence for Small Computers.* Indianapolis: Howard W. Sams and Co., 1982.

Levy, David. *Computer Gamesmanship: The Complete Guide to Creating and Structuring Games Programs.* London: Century Publishing, 1983.

Wiswell, Tom. *The Science of Checkers and Draughts.* San Diego, Calif.: A. S. Barnes and Co., 1973.

Automated Magic

Gardner, Martin. *Mathematics, Magic and Mystery.* Mineola, N.Y.: Dover Publications, 1956.

Lorayne, Harry. *The Magic Book: The Complete Beginner's Guide to Anytime, Anywhere, Sleight-of-Hand Magic.* New York: Putnam Publishing, 1977.

Sherwood, John C. *The Conjurer's Calculator (Magic with a Pocket Computer).* Mickey Hades International, Box 476, Calgary, Alberta, Canada, 1976.

WORLD FOUR

One-Dimensional Computers

Berlekamp, Elwyn R., John H. Conway, and Richard K. Guy. *Winning Ways for Your Mathematical Plays.* Orlando, Fla.: Academic Press, 1982.

Dewdney, A. K. *The Planiverse.* New York: Poseiden Press, 1982.

Wolfram, Stephen. "Computer Software in Science and Mathematics." SCIENTIFIC AMERICAN, September, 1984, 188–203.

Three-Dimensional Life

Anthony, Piers. *Ox.* New York: Avon, 1976.

Artwick, Bruce A. *Microcomputer Displays, Graphics, and Animation.* Englewood Cliffs, N.J.: Prentice-Hall, 1984.

Berlekamp, Elwyn R., John H. Conway, and Richard K. Guy. *Winning Ways for Your Mathematical Plays,* Vol. 2: *Games in Particular.* Orlando, Fla.: Academic Press, 1982.

Graetz, J. M. "The Origin of Spacewar." *Creative Computing* 7, no. 8 (August, 1981): 56–67.

Busy Beavers

Hopcroft, John E. "Turing Machines." SCIENTIFIC AMERICAN, May, 1984, 86–98.
Minsky, Marvin L. *Computation: Finite and Infinite Machines.* Englewood Cliffs, N.J.: Prentice-Hall, 1967.

WORLD FIVE

The Towers of Hanoi and the Chinese Rings

Afriat, Sydney S. *The Ring of Linked Rings.* London: Gerald Duckworth and Co., 1982.
Ball, W. W. Rouse. *Mathematical Recreations and Essays.* Revised by H. S. M. Coxeter. Toronto: University of Toronto Press, 1974.
Buneman, Peter, and Leon Levy. "The Towers of Hanoi Problem." *Information Processing Letters* 10, nos. 4 and 5 (July, 1980): 243–244.
Gardner, Martin. "Mathematical Games." SCIENTIFIC AMERICAN, August, 1972, 106–109.

Anagrams and Pangrams

Gardner, Martin. "Mathematical Games." SCIENTIFIC AMERICAN, February, 1977, 121–126.
Hofstadter, Douglas R. "Metamagical Themas." SCIENTIFIC AMERICAN, January, 1983, 14–22.

WORLD SIX

Five Easy Pieces

Deo, Narsingh. *System Simulation with Digital Computer.* Englewood Cliffs, N.J.: Prentice-Hall, 1983.
Knuth, Donald E., ed. *The Art of Computer Programming,* Vol. 2: *Seminumerical Algorithms,* 2d ed. Reading, Mass.: Addison-Wesley Publishing Co., 1981.
Mims, Forrest M., III. "The Computer Scientist: Random Numbers." *Computers and Electronics,* November, 1984.

A Cosmic Ballet

Aarseth, Sverre J. "Direct N-Body Calculations." In *Dynamics of Star Clusters,* edited by Jeremy Goodman and Piet Hut. Norwell, Mass.: D. Reidel Publishing Co., 1985.
Chaitin, Gregory J. "An APL2 Gallery of Mathematical Physics—A Course Outline." IBM Research, P. O. Box 218, Yorktown Heights, N.Y., 10598, 1985.
Freedman, Daniel Z., and Peter van Nieuwenhuizen. "The Hidden Dimensions of Spacetime." SCIENTIFIC AMERICAN, March, 1985.

Lightman, Alan P., and Stephen L. W. McMillan. "A Unified N-Body and Statistical Treatment of Stellar Dynamics." In *Dynamics of Star Clusters*, edited by Jeremy Goodman and Piet Hut. Norwell, Mass.: D. Reidel Publishing Co., 1985.

Sharks and Fish on the Planet Wa-Tor

Roberts, Nancy, David F. Anderson, Ralph M. Deal, Michael S. Garet, and William A. Schaffer. *Introduction to Computer Simulation: The Dynamics Approach.* Reading, Mass.: Addison-Wesley Publishing Co., 1980.

Standish, Thomas A. *Data Structure Techniques.* Reading, Mass.: Addison-Wesley Publishing Co., 1980.

The Evolution of Flibs

Fogel, Lawrence J., Alvin J. Owens, and Michael J. Walsh. *Artificial Intelligence Through Simulated Evolution.* New York: John Wiley and Sons, 1966.

Grefenstette, John, Rajeev Gopal, Brian Rosmaita, and Dirk van Gucht. *Proceedings of an International Conference on Genetic Algorithms and Their Applications.* Edited by John J. Grefenstette. The Robotics Institute, Carnegie-Mellon University, 1985.

Holland, John H. *Adaptation in Natural and Artificial Systems.* Ann Arbor, Mich.: University of Michigan Press, 1975.

The Extinction of Trilobites and Survival of Smiths

Raup, David M. "Probabilistic Models in Evolutionary Paleobiology." In *Paleontology and Paleoenvironments: Readings from* American Scientist, edited by Brian J. Skinner. Los Altos, Calif.: William Kaufmann, Inc., 1981.

Raup, David M., Steven J. Gould, Thomas J. M. Schopf, and Daniel S. Simberloff. "Stochastic Models of Phylogeny and the Evolution of Diversity." *The Journal of Geology* 81, no. 5 (September, 1973): 525–542.

WORLD SEVEN

Core War

Kane, Gerry, and Doug Hawkins Legenthal. *68000 Assembly Language Programming.* Berkeley, Calif.: Osborne–McGraw-Hill, 1981.

Null, Aleph. "Darwin." *Software: Practice & Experience* 2, no. 1 (January–March, 1972): 93–96.

Core War Encore

Breton, Thierry, and Denis Beneich. *Softwar: A Novel.* Translated by Mark Howson. New York: Henry Holt and Co., 1986.

Elmer-DeWitt, Philip. "War Games." *Time*, October, 1984, 109.

List of Suppliers

The following individuals, institutions, and corporations will supply items mentioned in *The Armchair Universe*. Prices and availability must be determined by contacting the supplier. The list is organized alphabetically by topic.

Anagrams and Pangrams

Anagram Algorithm
James A. Woods
NASA Ames Research Center
Moffett Field, Calif. 94035

Pangram Document
Lee Sallows
Buurmansweg, 30
6525 RW Nijmegen
The Netherlands

Cellular Automata

Images
Stephen Wolfram
Center for Complex Systems Research
508 South 6th Street
Urbana, Ill. 61801

Booklets
The Game of Three-Dimensional Life
Carter Bays
Department of Computer Science
University of South Carolina
Columbia, S. C. 29208

Glider Gun Guidelines
Stephen Wolfram
Center for Complex Systems Research
508 South 6th Street
Urbana, Ill. 61801

Software

The Game of Three-Dimensional Life
Carter Bays
Department of Computer Science
University of South Carolina
Columbia, S. C. 29208
(three-dimensional Life)

James R. Jackson
Graduate School of Management
University of California
Los Angeles, Calif. 90024
(Life and related games)

Neil J. Rubinking
300 Page Street
San Francisco, Calif. 94102
(totalistic cellular automata)

Six Worlds
Turing Omnibus, Inc.
P.O. Box 1456
London, Ontario
Canada N6A 5M2
(totalistic cellular automata)

Checkers

Organization

William B. Grandjean
American Checkers Federation
3475 Belmont Avenue
Baton Rouge, La. 70808

Cluster

Booklets

An APL2 Gallery of Mathematical Physics
Gregory J. Chaitin
IBM Thomas J. Watson Research Center
P.O. Box 218
Yorktown Heights, N. Y. 10598

Software

Brian Davis
3711 Greenock Blvd.
Ann Arbor, Mich. 48103
(CLUSTER-like program)

Six Worlds
Turing Omnibus, Inc.
P.O. Box 1456
London, Ontario
Canada N6A 5M2
(CLUSTER)

Core War

Newsletter

The Core War Newsletter
William R. Buckley, Editor
5712 Kern Drive
Huntington Beach, Calif. 92649

Organization

International Core War Society
Mark Clarkson
8619 Wassall Street
Wichita, Kans. 67210

Software

William R. Buckley
5712 Kern Drive
Huntington Beach, Calif. 92649
(Core War for IBM PCs)

Mark A. Durham
8282 Cambridge Street # 507
Houston, Tex. 77054
(Core War for Amiga)

Hypercubes

Software

Six Worlds
Turing Omnibus, Inc.
P.O. Box 1456
London, Ontario
Canada N6A 5M2
(HYPERCUBE)

Film	*The Hypercube: Projections and Slicing* International Film Bureau, Inc. 332 South Michigan Avenue Chicago, Ill. 60604

Mandelbrot Set

Images	Heinz Otto Peitgen, MAP ART Forschungsgruppe Komplexe Dynamik Universitat Bremen 2800 Bremen 33 West Germany ART MATRIX P. O. Box 880 Ithaca, N. Y. 14851
Newsletter	*Amygdala* Rollo Silver, Editor Box 111 San Cristobal, N. Mex. 87564
Software	Rollo Silver Box 111 San Cristobal, N. Mex. 87564 (List of additional suppliers) *Six Worlds* Turing Omnibus, Inc. P.O. Box 1456 London, Ontario Canada N6A 5M2 (MANDELZOOM)

Puzzles

Bill's Baffling Burr	Bill Cutler Puzzles 405 Balsaam Lane Palatine, Ill. 60067
Coffin's Cornucopia	Stewart T. Coffin 79 Old Sudbury Road Lincoln, Mass. 01773

Engel's Enigma   Douglas A. Engel
                                  General Symmetrics, Inc.
                                  2935 W. Chenango Circle
                                  Englewood, Colo. 80110

PANEX   Tricks Limited
                                  71 Shinozakicho
                                  7 Chome, Edogawa-ku
                                  Tokyo 133, Japan

Booklets   *The Conjurer's Calculator* and
                                  The Circuited Sorcerer
                                  Mickey Hades International
                                  Box 2242
                                  Seattle, Wash. 98111

RACTER

Software   John D. Owens
                                  INRAC, Inc.
                                  12 Schubert Street
                                  Staten Island, N. Y. 10305
                                  (RACTER and Inrac)

Wallpaper for the Mind

Software   Tony Smith
                                  P.O. Box 256
                                  38 Ardoch Street
                                  Essendon, Victoria 3040
                                  Australia
                                  (PATTERN BREEDER)

                                  Six Worlds
                                  Turing Omnibus, Inc.
                                  P.O. Box 1456
                                  London, Ontario
                                  Canada N6A 5M2
                                  (WALLPAPER)

Wa-Tor

Newsletter   *Running Wa-Tor*
                               Milton Boyd, Editor
                               P.O. Box 267
                               Amherst, N. H. 03031

Software   *Six Worlds*
                               Turing Omnibus, Inc.
                               P.O. Box 1456
                               London, Ontario
                               Canada N6A 5M2
                               (WATOR)

Illustration Credits

Figure 1
Copyright © 1985 Art Matrix.

Figure 3
Courtesy of David Wiseman, University of Western Ontario.

Figure 4
Courtesy of Barry Martin, Aston University.

Figure 5
Courtesy of Tony D. Smith.

Figure 21
Courtesy of Dr. Thomas Banchoff, Dr. David Laidlaw, Dr. David Margolis, Brown University.

Figure 26
Courtesy of Dr. Susan E. Brennan, Hewlett-Packard Labs.

Figure 28
Courtesy of Dr. Susan E. Brennan, Hewlett-Packard Labs.

Figure 29
Courtesy of Dr. Susan E. Brennan, Hewlett-Packard Labs.

Figure 30
Courtesy of Dr. Susan E. Brennan, Hewlett-Packard Labs.

Figure 32
Courtesy of Pat Maculuso, Applied Data Science.

Figure 44
Courtesy of James K. Park, Massachusetts Institute of Technology.

Figure 45
Courtesy of James K. Park, Massachusetts Institute of Technology.

Figure 48
Courtesy of Dr. Carter Bays, Dr. Philip Moore, University of South Carolina.

Figure 49
Courtesy of Dr. Carter Bays, Dr. Philip Moore, University of South Carolina.

Figure 50
Courtesy of Dr. Carter Bays, Dr. Philip Moore, University of South Carolina.

Figure 51
Courtesy of Dr. Carter Bays, Dr. Philip Moore, University of South Carolina.
Figure 68
Courtesy of Lee Sallows, Catholic University of Nijmegen.
Figure 94
Courtesy of Oliver Strumpel, The Computer Museum, Boston.

Color Plate 1
Courtesy of Heinz-Otto Peitgen, The University of Bremen, West Germany.
Color Plate 2
Courtesy of Heinz-Otto Peitgen, The University of Bremen, West Germany.
Color Plate 3
Courtesy of James D. Scott.
Color Plate 4
Courtesy of Dr. Barry Martin, Aston University.
Color Plate 5
By Hüseyin Koçak, David Laidlaw, with the assistance of Thomas Banchoff, Fred Bishopp, and David Margolis.
Color Plate 6
Courtesy of Stephen Wolfram, The Center For Complex Systems Research.
Color Plate 7
Courtesy of Dr. Carter Bays, Dr. Philip Moore, University of South Carolina.

Index